A tribute of affection:
from a Sabbath School class
to their teacher.
Miss Rhoda Curtis.

Mary E. Fairchild
Sarah A. Curtis
Sarah Ward
Mary Heath
Mary Buck
Eliza Blodget.

Jared B. Flagg D.C. Hinman.

"Jesus, I give my <u>all</u> to Thee."

See Page 128

Mary E. Van Lennep

MEMOIR

OF

MRS. MARY E. VAN LENNEP,

ONLY DAUGHTER OF THE REV. JOEL HAWES, D. D.

AND

WIFE OF THE REV. HENRY J. VAN LENNEP,

Missionary in Turkey.

BY HER MOTHER.

SIXTH EDITION.

HARTFORD:
WM. JAS. HAMERSLEY.
1850.

STEREOTYPED BY
RICHARD H. HOBBS,
HARTFORD, CONN.

PRINTED BY
CASE, TIFFANY AND CO.,
HARTFORD, CONN.

PREFACE.

"That life is long that answers life's great end."

To few, perhaps, whose period of action was so limited, could the above sentiment be better applied, than to the subject of this memoir.

Her life, though short, was filled up with acts of beneficence and love; and although many of those acts, like fragrance borne upon the breath of morning, and then scattered by the winds of heaven, can never again be gathered; yet something remains in the memory of those who best knew her, and something more in her writings; and it is hoped that from these two sources a little volume may be made, which will be both interesting and profitable to the young.

In regard to the following memoir, it is proper to remark, that it was not attempted under the impression that the subject of it possessed extraordinary powers or attainments. Such qualifications, however desirable in themselves, or coveted by others, are not deemed indispensable to a life of usefulness.

A friend remarked, "I know of no character more worthy of being presented as a model for the young, than Mary's; and for this reason, among many others, that it exhibits no unattainable excellence. It was not by any extraordinary gifts of nature that she won all hearts, and adorned her Christian profession more than any other young person I ever knew,—it was the complete subjection into which she had brought her every wish and purpose, to the one object of promoting the happiness of others, and their spiritual welfare, that made her daily life such a steady light, and gave to her manners that indescribable sweetness, so that none saw her but to love her. I think, however, there was in Mary's disposition, a very *uncommon* share of affectionateness and simplicity, but of course I cannot judge as well as those who knew her in childhood, whether those traits were as striking then as in after years; though it seems to me that no self-cultivation, nor even the grace of God, could have supplied them, had they not always existed in an unusual degree. But on this account I should think her character would be a difficult one to delineate with distinctness."

The traits to which this friend of Mary alludes, the writer of this never expects to portray so that those who did not know her, could see them as exhibited in her life. The beautiful symmetry of her character, embodying as it did every social virtue, and every Christian grace, must have been seen, to be fully known and appreciated.

There is one circumstance, which, more than any other, prompts the wish to try to sketch something which shall do her justice. She was early called away from the field of her labors; and as she was eminently qualified and disposed to do good, it does seem to be no more than a suitable tribute to the promise she gave of future usefulness, to attempt to extend her influence beyond the brief period of her life.

Another reason for writing this memoir, is found in the melancholy satisfaction of recalling the incidents of a life, which, while its few, fleeting years were passing, was the source of so much happiness to the mourning survivors.

As this little work was not entered upon under the impression that the subject of it possessed extraordinary powers, so neither was it attempted under the impression that she was exempt from the faults and imperfections incident to our fallen state. Should a perfect character be held up to view as always having been such, it would immediately be felt by all, not to be just, nor true to nature. Mary had faults, but by the grace of God, she was able to correct them; and on this account her character seems a suitable one to present as an encouragement to those, who, conscious of their own imperfections, are attempting to reach some standard of excellence, which appears almost, if not altogether, unattainable.

It is hoped that this little volume will come to the aid of some such, as a star to guide their trembling steps, on their first entering the straight and narrow way; and it is believed that if her character could be truly presented, it would serve to allure others also into that path, which, to her, was as the "rising light, shining more and more unto the perfect day."

NOTE.—Unfeignedly grateful for the kind manner in which the Memoir has been received by an indulgent public, the author has carefully revised the work for a second edition, and has inserted a few items of additional matter, in the hope that it might make the volume somewhat more complete.

CONTENTS.

CHAPTER I

REMINISCENCES OF CHILDHOOD

Mary Elizabeth Hawes, second daughter of the Rev. Dr. Hawes, of Hartford, Connecticut, was born the 16th of April, 1821. The incidents of her childhood, if not remarkable, were yet such as to subject her to a somewhat severe moral discipline. By the time she was four years and four months old, a sister and brother had been removed from her by death, and, as she said, "she had been left alone *two times.*"

When Mary was five years old, she was sent to school. The following summer, the parent whose office it was more immediately to watch over and guide her unfolding faculties, observed with pain, that she was contracting a habit, which if not checked and overcome in childhood, would be a blight upon her otherwise lovely character, and greatly endanger, if not destroy, her happiness and usefulness in after life. It is a humiliating fact, that the propensity to deceive is one of the most common faults of childhood; but because it is thus common, it is not the less to be dreaded. Neither because it is a fault of childhood, should it be passed by under the mistaken impression that it will be felt and corrected in mature life. Mary's mother was fully sensible of the evil, and being desirous that the best means should be adopted for its correction, the father was applied to, for advice and assistance. Having reproved his little daughter for the fault, he concluded by announcing, that the next time any thing of the kind occurred, he should apply the punishment* recommended by the wise man, little thinking that it would ever be necessary to put the threat in execution. Ah, he little thought what ascendency an evil habit might acquire in a short time even, over the mind of a little child, or he would not have expected that the fear of punishment would of itself be sufficient, not only to deter from the fault, but also to form the opposite habit of truthfulness. It was not long before there was a repetition of the offence; not an aggravated one, but enough to show that even a beginning had not been made in its correction. "Why did you tell me of it?" exclaimed the agitated and grieved father, as he remembered his threat. But the word had gone forth, and the father's veracity must be maintained. Mary was sent to her room, and the bible was put into her hand, from which, portions had been selected for her to read and apply to her own case. As she was about being left to spend a long summer afternoon alone in her chamber, while her companions were abroad, enjoying the cool breezes in the fields and groves, she said in a tremulous voice, "I think I know what you and pa' are going to do with me; I think you are going to keep me on bread and water till I am penitent." The dear child, if penitence had been the only object aimed at, might then have been set at liberty. But something more must be gained—such an impression must be made upon her young mind, as should lead her to feel that she must make some effort herself to correct the fault, and she must not be left to suppose that saying "I am sorry," and even feeling so too, would of itself be sufficient. When her piece of bread and cup of milk were carried to

* See Proverbs, xix. 18.

her in the evening, she was in deep thought, and had evidently spent the afternoon in faithfully consulting the bible, with self reflection and prayer. In the morning, her father took her into his room, and having tenderly admonished her, he covered his face and inflicted upon her little hand enough of pain, to save himself from the charge of falsifying his word.

Mary spoke of this scene with gratitude in after life, and particularly of the delicate manner in which the thing was done; and said she had "always loved her father for it:" and it is believed that the recollection of her father's face, covered with his handkerchief while inflicting punishment upon his cherished and only daughter, following as it did a season of retirement and reflection, assisted her more than any thing else in forming that character for truthfulness, of which hers was ever afterwards so beautiful an illustration.

Amongst the plans adopted for her improvement, was one which is now recollected with much satisfaction. This was the daily reading of the bible to her. The practice was commenced when she was very young, and was continued with more or less interruption, long after she was able to read it herself. At first, selections were made, suited to her tender age, and it was also sometimes necessary to "translate" the language, to make it intelligible to her. In this way, the Old Testament, commencing at Genesis, and ending with the building of the second temple, bad been read to her several times, before she was seven years old. A half hour after tea, is now recalled with pleasant associations, as having been spent in this way, often for months uninterruptedly, when her own interest in the exercise made it not only a useful, but also a very desirable season.

Of scripture biography she would never tire; and as her

mind unfolded, she could be easily interested in those beautiful specimens of Hebrew poetry, scattered along in the first books of the Old Testament; the song of Deborah,* for instance. The vivid sketches of Hebrew life and manners which this song contains, the beautiful country where the scene is laid, between Mt. Tabor and "Kishon, that ancient river,"—the relief, too, which the country experienced, when delivered from the oppression under which it had groaned for so many years—much of this she could enter into and comprehend.

Even at this early age, there were pleasing indications of the facility with which she could afterwards throw herself into the situation of others. For instance, when at the close of the song just alluded to, the mother of Sisera is described as calling through the lattice, "Why tarry the wheels of his chariot?" and then comforting herself that the delay was only the necessary result of victory—that having conquered his enemies he waited to divide the spoil—even then, she could comprehend something of the disappointment and anguish of that mother, when the terrible reverse should be made known.

But her sympathies were not all expended upon the stories and the poetry. The details of history were often listened to with as much interest as the more glowing and picturesque descriptions. A single instance shall suffice. She was listening one evening to a passage in the history of the Israelites, when, after having been recovered by severe judgments from their idolatrous practices, they were beginning again to relapse, unable longer to restrain her grief, she exclaimed, "O, mamma, I know what you are going to read about, the people are going to be wicked, and then God will have to punish them again."

On the approach of her eighth birth-day, it was feared

* Judges, chap. *v*.

that before another anniversary of the event occurred, Mary would be deprived of the watchful care of her mother, who was suffering from protracted illness. The probability that in her tender age, she would be thrown upon her own resources for improvement and happiness, made her mother anxious to turn her attention more to the sober realities of life. The usual preparations to make it a day of gladness, were therefore exchanged for others more suitable to the circumstances of the occasion. Many little articles for the exercise and improvement of her taste were procured, such as paints, pencils, drawings, &c.; but one thing was done, which doubtless gave a decided turn to her religious feelings, which had heretofore appeared only in an incipient state.

Her mother had long been anxious for some evidence that she was safe in the fold of the good Shepherd, and this anxiety increased, as the probability strengthened that she would early be left without a maternal guide. To aid her in her efforts to fix in the mind of her child a sense of the importance of "seeking first the kingdom of heaven," she requested a friend to call and converse with Mary, on her birth-day, on this important subject. After a short interview, in which he had endeavored to impress upon her mind the happiness it would afford her through life, to have God for her father, followed by a very affectionate appeal to yield her young heart to him, he made this remark to her parents, "I shall expect to hear soon that Mary is a Christian, for I never saw truth sink into the mind as it did into hers, without being followed by such a result."

Little is recollected of the following year, as her mother was brought near to death, and Mary was left very much under her own guidance, but her sweet docility, and tender watchful care of her little brother, come as gleams of sunshine to relieve the mind as it recalls those long and wearisome months of deprivation and suffering.

During this period, her studies were very much interrupted, in consequence of her accompanying her brother to an infant school, and also her care of him after he was removed to another, collateral to the one which she attended. Still she made some progress. Some occasional exercises at home, were of use in eliciting her mental powers, which although slow in their development, were yet not deficient in interesting qualities. A friend of the family was preparing a course of elementary books for children, and to test them, frequently read parts of them to Mary and her brother. The same friend had another little exercise, which he carried on with her in a somewhat playful manner. He directed her to shut her eyes and describe external objects; gradually leading her mind to an attention to its own processes. In this way she very early acquired a tolerably correct knowledge of the simplest elements of mental philosophy; and although her studies at school were of little use to her, yet at home she was making some progress in mental as well as in moral culture.

CHAPTER II.

RELIGIOUS DEVELOPMENT.

The spring of 1831, is remembered as an important era in her life. It was seen at this time that her mind was more than usually tender in reflecting on religious truths. Whenever such truths were presented, she felt that she had a personal interest in them. Many tender and deeply interesting seasons are here recalled, which gave intimation that she had begun to realize her state as a sinner, needing pardon and peace with God. The impotency of the pen in describing such scenes, almost forbids the attempt; but one shall be briefly noticed here, which may serve as a feeble specimen of many others. Mary was sitting with her brother one Sabbath evening, when he asked her to sing one of his infant school songs. Turning to her mother, she said in a voice trembling and half suppressed by deep emotion—"I wish Thomas would like to have me sing,

> "A fallen creature I was born,
> And from the birth I've stray'd;
> I must be wretched and forlorn,
> Without thy mercy's aid."

Here her feelings overcame her, and she covered her face and wept.

It was near the close of her tenth year, when the scarlet fever, which had been in the city for some time, entered the family, and prostrated the brother before alluded to. Mary was soon taken with the disease herself, and her mother being occupied with her two little sons who were ill at the same time, she was obliged to consign Mary to the care of others. Those who attended upon her, were surprised and gratified to see her so composed and peaceful, while she was very ill, and fully aware of the dangerous nature of the disease; and they soon learned from herself, that she had been endeavoring to prepare for the issue, should the disease prove fatal to her. But she was spared, and her brother was taken.

A little previous to the death of this brother, an incident occurred which drew out her strong powers of sympathy, and very strikingly illustrated her forgetfulness of self, when she saw others in affliction, and also her very felicitous manner of imparting consolation. The disease had assumed a very alarming form, and the little sufferer was rent with convulsions, which it required no ordinary share of fortitude only to witness. The poor father, unable longer to endure the sight, turned away from the bed, and sought his room. Mary followed him. He threw himself upon the sofa, exclaiming, "I can't bear it, I can't bear it;" and he seemed to be struggling with emotions too painful to be borne. He had already been bereaved of three children, and now a fourth was about to be taken, and in a very distressing manner. He again exclaimed, "The hand of God is upon me; I don't know but I am to be written childless." Mary drew her seat closer to his, and laying her hand gently on his knee to gain his attention, she looked up in his face and said, "Father, you told us that God always had a *good reason* for every thing he did. And has he not a good reason *now?* and is it not right for him to make my little brother suffer so?" Finding her arguments unavailing, as she supposed, to soothe him, because that now he wept more freely, she took down from the shelf a hymn-book, and opening it, said, "dear father, let me comfort you, let me read a hymn to you, shall I?" The father's heart was too full to speak, and she opened to that very appropriate hymn of Doddridge, commencing,

"Peace, 'tis the Lord Jehovah's hand"—

When she came to the verse,

"Fair garlands of immortal bliss
He weaves for every brow,
And shall rebellious passions rise
When he corrects us now?"

her countenance shone as if a beam from heaven had shed its light there, and her voice and manner were such as seemed better befitting an angel than a frail child. A relative of the family had followed Mary and her father to the study, and had been a silent, but almost unnoticed observer of the whole; so absorbed was the father in his grief, and Mary in her attempts to soothe him. She said the scene was more touching, on account of the state of Mary at the time, who having just risen from a sick bed, was still weak and pale. She seemed also to be overwhelmed with the consciousness of her little brother's sufferings, to whom she was tenderly attached, and to feel that she must not now lay her bursting heart upon her father's bosom, for he needed comfort and support himself. In the trying emergency, she looked away from human sympathy, and sought in God something which might meet the painful circumstances of the case; and she thus, meekly, though unintentionally, taught a lesson of submission to His perfect will.

Her father, in speaking of it afterwards, remarked, that

he "had never before been so dealt with;" that "she talked like an experienced Christian."

Her brother's death took place soon after this, and she passed through the trying scene with a considerateness unusual for one of her tender age; and the result showed that it had been to her a season of rich spiritual improvement.

About this time, there were many meetings in the place, where children were addressed on the subject of religion, in a manner suited to their years. Mary was unable to attend any of them, but God was evidently teaching her, although in a different manner, at home. She was told that several of her young companions, who attended these meetings, were becoming interested in religion. This information made her increasingly thoughtful and serious.

Her father was expecting soon to go abroad, and her mother being occupied in making the necessary preparations, a little brother was committed to the care of Mary, and for a short time she was fully occupied in attending upon him. Though she never neglected her little charge, but always contrived to make him happy, still it was evident that her thoughts were on other things.

A week or two had passed in this way, when one day she was seen to be more than usually tender and thoughtful. An invalid friend was in the family, and this, together with other things, so constantly occupied her mother's attention, that Mary was necessarily passed by, without even a word, or any other attempt to ascertain the cause of her deep solicitude. But God was not passing her by, as the result showed. Soon after tea, having requested permission to retire, she went to her room. It was late in the evening, when her mother, hearing a soft voice which seemed to proceed from her chamber, went up to see if she was needing any thing. On opening the door, she found Mary in the attitude of retiring, and singing forth her thoughts in a low, sweet voice. Her countenance was beaming as with heavenly light, and she exclaimed, with an expression wholly indescribable, "O, mamma, I am so happy, I have found God." Her mother stood in silence, her hand still upon the latch, having been arrested by the grateful surprise; when Mary, supposing that she waited for an explanation of her not having retired earlier, offered as a reason, that she "had been praying a long time, and that it made her so happy she could not leave off." She said, "While I was speaking, God seemed near. It seemed as if he heard me; and I felt that I was speaking to a dear friend, and that He was near as when I speak to dear father." "O, mamma, I am so happy! I can pray now!" "I have found God!" she again exclaimed; and her shining countenance bore testimony, that although she might not have seen God "face to face," yet that He had met her, and had blessed her.

Some weeks after her father left home, she was visited with dangerous illness. Of the many remarks she made during this season, indicative of pleasant and profitable reflection, a few have been preserved in writing. An affectionate and valued friend,* in writing to her father, says, "Mary, as you have probably heard, has been ill. While suffering from fever, I was permitted to watch with her, and was delighted to find her mind in such a frame as was most desirable. The first thing she said to me was, 'O, Miss Chester, I have been thinking of the Saviour a great deal to-day; of his sufferings on the cross.' While looking at some beautiful flowers, she spoke of her own garden, and said she could not keep it free from weeds, without assistance; adding, 'it is just like our hearts,' and contin-

* Her Sabbath-School Teacher, Miss M. J. Chester.

ued the comparison in a way to which I could not do justice."

After her recovery, it was thought not best to confine her to the school-room, but to keep her abroad in the open air. She cultivated her garden, gathered mosses, and collected pebbles and shells, to build a mimic hermitage. For this purpose she used to ramble through the fields and groves, accompanied by her little brother; and at such times, her heart would flow forth in sweet and joyous communings with nature and its great Author. There was for many months an indescribable expression of peacefulness and joyousness, beaming from her countenance; it seemed to proceed from a sweet sense of her acceptance with God.

Some years after this, when she was about leaving the home of her childhood, to go to her Eastern home, she spoke to her mother of this happy season in her youthful days. She said it was in her memory "like a long, bright, happy dream;" "it was unlike the rest of her life, it was so free from care, and so full of happiness and peace." And it may be added, that to one who witnessed it, it seemed like a continual hymn of praise to God.

There was one circumstance, which, even more than the happiness she enjoyed, showed that she was at this time under divine teaching, and that her heart had indeed been touched with the love of God. It was this. From the moment she found relief in prayer, or, as she said, "could pray," she set about attempting to persuade her young companions to pray, and others also, whom she could influence. It is not known, whether she was successful at this time in her efforts, except in one instance. A poor girl, who lived at service in the family of a relative, was an object of much interest to Mary, and she attempted as she had opportunity, to impress upon her mind a sense of the importance of prayer. After laboring long, and waiting patiently, her feeble efforts were at length crowned with success.

To avoid a wrong impression being made by the fact just related, an impression that Mary was obtrusive, in her efforts to promote the spiritual welfare of others, it should be said, that in all her attempts of this nature, there was so much of quietness and secrecy, that but for their results, they would never have come to the knowledge of any, except the individuals concerned. In the case just mentioned, her efforts were wholly unknown to any, excepting the poor girl and herself. But when there was reason to hope that the object of her interest had indeed become a child of God, she could no longer refrain from telling her mother: and she did this, not to relate her own agency in the case, but to find relief for the fullness of her joy. Her heart was overflowing with gratitude for the happiness which this poor girl now experienced in the duty of prayer, and which Mary regarded as evidence of her having become a child of God. She hoped, also, to impart something of her own joy to her mother.

It was somewhere about this time, perhaps earlier, that her powers of voice began to be developed. Before this, she had indeed been able to bear her part in the music of the family, and in the infant school, but now she had the instructions of a master. The scene is still fresh in the memory of the writer, when Mary and a group of young companions used to assemble to practice singing. An hour in the cool of the long summer mornings, was devoted to this exercise. While yet the air was fragrant with the breath of flowers, and the birds were pouring forth their glad notes, the teacher was training the young voices of his pupils to a soft-toned violin. The little pieces which were given them to practice, were full of pure sentiments.

They were the natural expressions of joyous and grateful hearts; and there was also much in them that was fitted to inspire and to cherish a taste for natural enjoyments.

Mary had a high relish for all the appropriate amusements of childhood. Among these, the rural party, and the song, were her favorites. Always happiest when contributing to make others happy—delighting rather to place the May crown on the head of a friend, than to wear it herself. At the little concerts in which she bore a part, her gratification rose to its height, when some young friend sung with more than ordinary sweetness. At such times she would listen with breathless attention, and then, when all was over, she would offer her congratulations with such affectionateness, as left no doubt of her sincerity.

From the time Mary was ten years old, she had a strong desire to make a profession of religion; but her father being absent, she waited patiently the first half year; and after his return, another half year passed, and still this wish remained ungratified. Ever docile and confiding towards her parents, and yielding to their slightest wishes in other matters, yet in the matter of a profession of religion, she felt that she had a right to know why she was deprived of the privilege.

One Sabbath, when her mother returned from a communion season, she found Mary sitting in her room, apparently in deep thought. As she entered, Mary addressed her thus: "Mamma, when our Saviour said, 'do this in remembrance of me,' did he not mean to include children?" She was told as she had before been, that her father thought her too young to take so important a step. With great seriousness of manner, she asked, "how old must I be, before I obey Christ?" She was told that her father thought twelve, a suitable age to make a profession of religion; when, bursting into tears, she exclaimed, "I shall have to wait another year, and I have waited a whole year now."

During the following summer, the cholera, which had ravaged many parts of the country, entered New England, and there were such indications of its approach to our principal cities, as to arouse the vigilance of health committees and others, to prepare to meet it. One day Mary addressed her mother on the subject in this way: "Mamma, if you should be sick, I should not be frightened; I should know just what to do." She was asked if she should be frightened if she herself were to be sick, and also, if she had done every thing she would wish if the disease should prove fatal to her. The momentary uneasiness occasioned by her answering in the negative, was removed by her saying, "I should like to make a profession of religion first." Thinking she might be making a merit of this, she was asked if she thought it would make her any better. "O no," was her prompt reply; "but I do want to leave my name for Christ." When she was twelve years old, this wish of her heart was gratified, and with several youthful companions, she took her place at the table of the Lord; and seldom, it is believed, is that ordinance approached in a more acceptable manner.

Mary, at this time, was highly favored in her instructions at Sabbath school. Her father has made this remark of her Sabbath school teacher. "Out of her own family, no human being exerted a greater, or more happy influence in the formation of her Christian character, than Mary Jane Chester, afterwards Mrs. Hovey." Ever alive to the best interests of her pupils, she could not pass by the occasion when one or more of them professed their faith in Christ, by uniting themselves with his visible church, without some more than ordinary expression of the deep interest she felt in their spiritual welfare. The hymn which she selected for her young pupil to learn on this occasion, doubtless had a very favorable bearing on her Christian character ever after. It was often quoted by Mary, and is in memory so identified with her Christian course, and withal so beautiful, that it is presumed its insertion here will not be unacceptable.

"Jesus, I my cross have taken,
  All to leave and follow Thee,
Naked, poor, despis'd, forsaken,
  Thou, from hence, my all shalt be:
Perish ev'ry fond ambition,
  All I've sought, or hop'd, or known;
Yet how rich is my condition,
  God and heaven are still my own.

Let the world despise and leave me:
  They have left my Saviour too;
Human hearts and looks deceive me,
  Thou art not, like them, untrue;
And whilst thou shalt smile upon me,
  God of wisdom, love and might,
Foes may hate, and friends may scorn me,
  Show thy face, and all is bright.

Go, then, earthly fame and treasure,
  Come disaster, scorn and pain,
In thy service pain is pleasure,
  With thy favor loss is gain.
I have called thee Abba, Father,
  I have set my heart on thee;
Storms may howl, and clouds may gather,
  All must work for good to me.

Man may trouble and distress me,
  'T will but drive me to thy breast:
Life with trials hard may press me,
  Heaven will bring me sweeter rest.

Oh! 'tis not in grief to harm me,
While thy love is left to me;
Oh! 't were not in joy to charm me,
Were that joy unmix'd with thee.

Soul, then know thy full salvation,
Rise o'er sin, and fear, and care:
Joy to find in ev'ry station
Something still to do or bear.
Think what spirit dwells within thee,
Think what Father's smiles are thine:
Think that Jesus died to save thee:
Child of heaven, canst thou repine?

Haste thee on from grace to glory,
Arm'd by faith and wing'd by prayer;
Heaven's eternal day 's before thee,
God's own hand shall guide thee there.
Soon shall close thy earthly mission,
Soon shall pass thy pilgrim days;
Hope shall change to glad fruition,
Faith to sight, and prayer to praise."

Although its full, rich meaning, could not all be taken into the mind of one so young, and also inexperienced in the painful vicissitudes of life, yet to this full salvation her eye was steadily directed, and to the attainment of this, all else was made subservient. From this period, her relations to the other world never were lost sight of.

She early manifested an interest in missions. An incident which occurred when she was a little child, will show the ease and readiness with which she could be interested in the missionary cause. Her mother said to her one day, "here is a field for you, Mary," at the same time pointing out to her something which she could do to aid in the good work. With great seriousness of manner she replied, "If I am ever fit to be a missionary, I mean to go to the Flat-head Indians;" and it was ascertained that she had been interested in an account of this benighted people, which she had seen sometime previous in one of the public prints; and that their efforts to obtain the knowledge of "the true way to worship the Great Spirit," had so wrought upon her sympathies, as to lead her to form the purpose of one day going to instruct them herself.

After she had made a profession of religion, she took a more decided stand, in aiding, not only the missionary cause, but also the many objects of benevolence which came within her sphere. When Dr. Parker left this country for China, which was sometime during this year, she so arranged it, that a young friend, the daughter of a missionary, should be present when he took leave of the family for the last time. With her friend, she accompanied him to the gate, and when he requested to be remembered, her heart responded, and she instantly formed her plan how to do it. While returning to the house she said, "we will sew for him, Sophia;" at the same time offering her hand to her friend as a pledge.

She immediately formed a society of very little girls, making it a condition they should earn the penny they brought, by doing something for their mothers at home, as most of them were too young to sew. Her benevolent and inventive mind suggested many expedients to interest the little group, during the hour appropriated to the meeting. Sometimes she spread on the table around which they were arranged, something to please the eye, such as pictures, and specimens of natural curiosities; sometimes she told them stories to interest them in missions, and other benevolent objects—again with a delicate touch, she would endeavor to ascertain whether there were any indications of tenderness on religious subjects. One little girl, the most healthful and robust among the number, after meeting a few times, was suddenly removed by death. It was noticed, that the last time she was present, when she presented her penny, it was with a moistened eye; and it was hoped that these little meetings were among the means of preparing her for her early removal.

Before entering on any plan of benevolent effort, Mary counted the cost, and took advice of her seniors. In the formation of the society just named, she saw each mother separately, before inviting the children to join it, and while their approval gave her strength, a feeling of responsibility to them, gave consistency and earnestness to her efforts.

The avails of the first and second year were sent, and a letter was received in reply. The distant missionary wrote, that the communication from this little band was like cold water to one perishing with thirst; that while those on whom he had depended to cheer him, by writing to him in his exile, had disappointed him, yet God had put it into the hearts of these little ones, to comfort and encourage him in his work. Many an eye was moist as the letter was read and commented on, and doubtless many a resolution to persevere was then renewed.

CHAPTER III.

SCHOOL DAYS, AND RESIDENCE IN NEW HAVEN.

Mary entered the Hartford Female Seminary sometime during her twelfth year, and remained a pupil in that institution until August, 1838, at which time she graduated. Little, out of the ordinary course of studies in term time, and visiting by way of relaxation in vacations, is recollected to have occurred, excepting that she had an additional source of enjoyment in the acquisition of a new friend. Marion D——, a native of the south, was received into the family in June, 1836, and was Mary's room mate and companion in study, until the time of her leaving school. As both were only daughters, these young friends became tenderly attached to each other, and each felt that she had found a sister. In all that contributed to make up the daily routine of life's duties, enjoyments and petty trials, they were one. Marion became settled in her Christian views and feelings, and made a profession of religion while in the family with Mary; thus adding a new tie to the many which already bound them together. The parting of these young friends was painful to both. Particularly was it so to Mary, as in her case there were none of those alleviating circumstances, which so filled the mind of her friend, as to make her almost forget the coming separation. Marion was cheered with the prospect of meeting kind parents, and a large circle of affectionate brothers, in the "sunny south," while Mary was to be left almost alone, with no young heart to send back its sisterly response to her own.

A little incident which attended the parting of these friends, may not be uninteresting here. It was a delightful morning in the month of August, while it was yet dark, excepting that the stars shone with an unusual brilliancy, when the stage-coach, which was to convey Marion away, drove up to the door. The two friends walked hand in hand to the gate, when Mary's eye caught the constellation of Orion in the eastern sky. Directing the eye of her friend to it, they both stood for a few moments silently looking up at this splendid constellation, then parted, never more to meet, till the arch of this lower heaven, in all its brightness, shall have passed away. As she returned to the house, she seemed bewildered that Orion should have appeared at that time, saying, "I thought it was only in winter that we saw it in this place." Her mother reminded her that she had never been out under the open sky in the month of August, at four o'clock in the morning. This recalled at once her bewildered thoughts, and she stood for a few moments in the portico, over which a grape vine, heavily laden with fruit, was twining its branches. The cool morning air, which gently stirred the leaves, and shed forth the fragrance of the ripening clusters, seemed to soothe her throbbing temples and aching heart. Sometime after her death, amongst her papers, were found the following lines, which the foregoing incident seems to have suggested.

"ON SEEING ORION, IN AUGUST,
A FEW HOURS BEFORE SUNRISE."

" I little deem'd that thou wert near,
King of the starry throng!
I thought when fields were brown and sere,
'T was then thou'd pass along:
And yet I see thy bands of light
Beaming from yon blue vault,
Brighter than gems of eastern mines,
With glittering diamonds fraught.

How oft when winter's icy hand
Hath bound each vale and hill,
I've seen thee make thy nightly course
In grandeur, proud and still;
And one I lov'd was with me then,
And oft with her I look'd
Up to the cold blue sky where thou
Thy mighty circuit took.

We watch'd thee with thy starry train,
And thought that thou must look
In silent mockery on our earth,
As 't were a thing of nought.
And now, while on the clus'tring vines
The fruit hangs heavily,
Thy girdle in the east doth shine
Before the rising day.

And hast thou come, proud Orion!
At this our parting hour,
To call back days of happiness
Which we may see no more?
With mingled awe and grief we stand
Beneath thy pale cold beams,
While scenes of pleasure long gone by,
Pass us in saddened trains.

Thou shin'st upon our parting hour,
And still as years roll by,
Thou wilt pursue thy onward course,
Bright monarch! in the sky—
And e'en like Him, who plac'd thee high
Within thine azure home,
Thou all unchanged wilt onward pass
Round the eternal throne."

Mary was in the habit of expressing her feelings in poetry, when her sensibilities were roused, especially when about to be separated from a friend—but she did nothing which might lead to the knowledge of her writing poetry, except to put her pieces into the hands of the individuals for whom they were designed.

As she needed some relaxation after her long confinement in school, and also to be diverted from her sense of loneliness when her young friend left her, it was thought best that she should spend the winter following these events, in New Haven. But another reason for sending her there was, the many sources of improvement which would be open to her in that place.

This was a very important period to her, and perhaps the most critical one in her whole life. It was once remarked by a father, that "it is a very difficult thing to emancipate a child gracefully, from parental authority." Something analogous to this, might be said to have been the state of Mary at this time. She was just beginning to think and act for herself—she was about to find her place in society; and the position she now took, would in all probability be the one which she would maintain through life.

It was in the month of October, 1838, that she was taken to New Haven by her father, and placed for the winter in the family of Dr. Fitch. At the close of her first day in this family, she writes, "Dear father gave me much excellent advice during our ride, which I intend to remember. Do please, mother, write me soon and often, and tell me how I must conduct. I hope soon to become accustomed to the regulations of the family, and think I shall find much time to read and to improve—and now if my heart will keep right, I see not but that I may have a very pleasant and quiet winter."

At the close of the first week, she writes again,—" Nov 1st. I prize every moment which is spent in Mrs. Fitch's society. She appears to have read and thought much, and by conversing with her only a short time, I learn what would be of great value to me, if I could only remember it. She seems an observer of human nature, so much so, that she has found out my weak points already."

Again to her father she writes,—"I am very happy in the society of my dear Mrs. Fitch. Her views of life are so rational, and her Christian principles are such as I wish every one could possess. Her views coincide with yours, and my dear mother's, and with so many kind guardians to point out to me the path of duty, I should be very much in fault, should I mistake it."

In this family she found much to gratify her taste, particularly her love of flowers and music. A few slight notices of hers, may help to fill out a picture of her life at this time. "I have removed my writing apparatus to the green-house, but it is rather too tempting a place, for I have half a mind to jump up and look at the flowers, there are so many beautiful ones here." In the morning she writes, "The sun, as it shines in through the plants in the green-house, does look beautifully;" and again at evening, "I have just risen to see how softly and brightly the moon shines in upon the flowers, making it look like some fairy land."

She had naturally a rich and sweet voice, but for the modulation of this, as well as for her exquisite touch of the piano, she was greatly indebted to the fine musical taste of Dr. Fitch.

In regard to the manner of spending her time, she writes, "My time glides away smoothly and quietly here, and I hope it is spent usefully. The young ladies have invited me to join their sewing society, and as Mrs. F. approves of it, I have consented to do so. After prayers and breakfast, I read every morning a chapter to Mrs. Fitch in the French Testament, which I find very improving, for she is an excellent scholar in that language. We sew during the morning, when generally some one reads. At half past eleven, we go to the laboratory, where the chemical lectures are delivered; and this takes up all the remainder of the time until the dinner hour, which is at one o'clock. We make our calls during the afternoon, and write or sew, and have music during the evening."

Of her reading she says,—"Mrs. Fitch is reading Shakspeare with me, and some of Milton's short poems. We have just finished Marshall's Life of Washington, and found it very interesting, though he told us not much about the life of his hero, excepting as it was connected with the revolution. We have thought it best to read Sparks', also, because it contains many of his private letters, and also a large number of interesting facts, of which Marshall makes no mention."

To the books already named, were added many others equally valuable—and her reading during the winter was rendered both interesting and profitable, as it was enriched by the criticisms of Mrs. Fitch, which were highly discriminating and useful.

Besides the Chemical, she attended the Philosophical Lectures, and a valuable course on Ancient History; and also some shorter courses, on other subjects. Of these lectures, she was in the habit of taking notes, and often spoke of them pleasantly in her letters home.

Of the Chemical Lectures, she writes, "They are very interesting. The experiments are beautiful. To-day, Prof. Silliman made a thermometer, and we were all much interested with the process. I sat breathless while he heated the thin glass ball to expand the quicksilver and exhaust the air. There was danger that the ball would break with the heat, but Mr. S. was peculiarly fortunate, and nothing occurred to hinder the result."

Mary ever cherished the most grateful recollections of this winter. It was to her among the bright visions of the past—such as she never expected to meet with again. But whenever she spoke of the advantages of this winter, she always named first, the benefit which she derived from intercourse with Mrs. Fitch. Of this lady, she wrote, "I cannot feel sufficiently grateful, that I am permitted to enjoy the society and friendship of one so highly gifted in intellect, and of such warm, devoted piety."

To a friend, the summer after her return home, she writes thus: "I passed, as you very well know, a delightful winter; and I now look back upon it as the most important six months in my whole life. I believe it has given the coloring to my whole existence. I cannot find words to express my gratitude to my dear Mrs. Fitch. If I am ever of any use in the world, or if my mind is in any degree directed to worthy objects, it will, next to the exertions of my own dear parents, be owing to that excellent lady. She is just the friend I need, and never in this world will she know how much good she has done."

Mary remembered this winter as an important one to her on another account. So many new trains of thought passed through her mind, presenting such new views, and awakening such new emotions, that it seemed to her as if a change had passed over her whole being. A few weeks before her return home, she writes thus to her father.

"April 5th, 1839.—I feel, that during this winter, my views and feelings on many, nay, on almost every subject, have changed. When I think of what I was last summer, of the manner in which I then thought and acted, I am almost disposed to doubt my own personal identity, so different am I now. Yet I can hardly tell you the exact things in which my views differ from what they once were, and if you were to see me now, I do not know that I should appear changed. I believe I have thought more this winter than I ever did before in my whole life. I have read more than ever before.* I have already begun to think what I shall do this summer, and I hope some plans I have with regard to reading, may be put into execution."

"You told me in one of your letters,—'have more of Cato,'—and I have thought of it very often, since. Decision of character is what I need very much, and I have found out lately, that the want of it has been the cause of much of my weakness. It has been very easy to mark out any course of study I have wished to pursue, and to begin it in a very fair manner; but my want of firmness has made it very difficult for me to continue, and so, many plans of usefulness have been given up, for no other reason, than for the want of decision to carry them on. I have suffered so much for the want of it, that I fancy I could make out a

* Mary might have added, that she had written more than ever before. Her letters to her correspondents, during the six months she spent in New Haven, covered several quires of paper, compactly written. These contained some useful matter; particularly, her own views on various subjects; and there is a vein of sprightliness running through them, which makes them interesting to those to whom they were addressed; but they are chiefly valuable, as they are a faithful transcript of her affectionate, confiding heart.

very good catalogue of the evils to which its absence gives rise. But I do not wish to weary you, dear father, with an account of my weaknesses, though it is some comfort to me to understand myself; and I hope I am not yet too old to amend. Do you know, papa, I shall be eighteen very soon? Just think of your daughter being so old! Oh, I cannot think of it. I should like to be seventeen for a long, long time to come."

Time always passed rapidly with Mary. A moment is never recollected to have hung heavily upon her hands. She placed her standard of character high in every respect, and this led her sometimes to undertake more than could be accomplished. During this winter she wrote thus to her mother—"I do feel that it is best to have a high standard, for then we shall rise higher, although we may not entirely succeed in reaching it." An incident on the morning when she was twelve years old, here occurs to the mind of the writer. On entering the room where her birth-day presents were spread out upon a table, after casting a look at these mementos of affection, she turned to her mother, and with much emotion exclaimed, "Oh mamma, I have now entered my teens, and I have not accomplished half what I intended to have done."

In the somewhat extensive and varied circle in which it was her lot in life to move, there were not wanting occasions which might enable her to test the real value of earthly pleasures. The syren cup, in its rounds, was not unfrequently passed into her hand, and if she sometimes sipped of its sweets, it was not so much to see how near she could approach the boundaries of evil, and remain unharmed, as from the difficulty of ascertaining the right course. It was ever a study with her, how she might recommend the religion which was precious to herself, to those amongst whom she moved, who were destitute of it. For this, she was ever ready to sacrifice every thing but principle. An incident in her seventeenth year, may perhaps serve as an illustration of this part of her character. Into the musical circles of which she was, for several winters, a very happy member, dancing had been introduced, and she had taken a part in it, as a thing of course. At length, something occurred which turned her attention to the propriety of professors of religion participating in such an amusement. Her example was appealed to by a young professor, who attended public balls, in justification of the thing. When asked by a friend whether he thought the practice consistent with his Christian profession, he replied that "Mary Hawes danced." True, there was a difference between the two cases, but this was merely circumstantial. The difference related to the time, the place, the company, and not to the thing itself,—in both cases it was dancing. On hearing this, Mary promptly discontinued the practice, and gave the whole subject a serious and very careful investigation, which resulted in the conviction that, however right it might be for others, it was wrong for her, and she ever after conscientiously refrained from participating in it.

In a letter to one of her Hartford friends, during her winter in New Haven, she said, referring to the "Musicals," "They were very pleasant. I look back to those Friday evenings last winter, with much pleasure, yet with *some pain*, for I did suffer in refusing to join in the dancing. Perhaps it seemed strange, and too rigid to you, that M. and myself refused the entreaties of the girls—but though it did pain us to do so, as it appeared unkind, yet we could not in conscience join with them. There was no harm in *the thing itself*, and I suppose that I could, without injury to myself, have engaged in the amusement, and enjoyed it highly. Yet there were other things to be con sidered, which fully convinced me that it would be wrong for me to do it, however right it might be for others."

At first, Mary continued to meet with these circles, and unite with them in the music, but refrained from the dancing; but finding this rather annoying to her young friends, with their consent she retired when the dancing commenced, having first contributed her share to the musical entertainment of the evening. At length circumstances convinced her that it was best to refrain from both. These musical circles afforded almost the only recreation in which she could unite with others, at the time of her retiring from them. They were also composed of friends whom she tenderly loved, and in the promotion of whose happiness, she found her own increased. Her love of music was also such as few possess, and the exquisite delicacy of her taste, rendered her performance a rich addition to the entertainment of the evening, and made her friends exceedingly reluctant to have her retire. In addition to this, an entry in her private journal shows, that it was at a time when she "pined to mingle more in society." It is not surprising, therefore, that it should have cost her somewhat of a severe struggle to give them up. Besides, in refraining from a participation in what appeared wrong to her, she would place herself in the attitude of a reprover; and how could she do this? Her gentle nature shrank from the trial, but she sought and obtained strength from a higher source than man, and a consciousness of doing right sustained her.

As years passed by, and she gained more light upon the subject, having time to test the effect produced on the character of those who were in the habit of indulging in the amusement, and also being able to obtain from others whom she highly respected, the testimony which they could give her from their own experience, she reviewed this early decision with comfort and satisfaction.

And if she were now asked whether she regretted this decision, what response would come back from the hills of light, where she is uniting in the anthems of heaven? Would it be regret at this slight sacrifice? Would it not rather be regret, that while she had the opportunity, she made so few and so feeble sacrifices for "Him who loved her, and gave himself for her."

The course pursued by Mary in relation to the subject above referred to, had an eminently happy effect on her Christian character and influence; and now that she is gone, it is remembered by her parents with the most grateful satisfaction, that she was enabled, by divine grace, to take a stand so honorable to religion, and so adapted to prepare her for her early removal.

CHAPTER IV.

EXTRACTS FROM HER CORRESPONDENCE.

When it was in contemplation to prepare a brief Memoir of Mary, a friend* who knew her well, and who highly appreciated her, made the following suggestions in regard to the best way of doing this. "I think that her writings will give a more vivid impression of her character, than any thing else. They all show the same conscientiousness, warm feelings, and quick perception of the good and beautiful, which were so strikingly manifested in her life."

Believing this to be true, and also having abundant material of the kind, the remainder of the volume will be composed of sketches furnished by her own pen, with occasionally a remark or two in addition, by way of connection or explanation.

This plan is also in accordance with an opinion which Mary herself entertained. In a letter to a friend during the winter she spent in New Haven, she says, "I think there is no way in which the character of a person is so fully disclosed, as in his letters. The leading traits generally appear in one way or another. I believe what little character I possess, appears in my letters. We are sometimes better able to express our ideas and feelings in writing, than in conversation; and I have found out more

* The one addressed C. C.

of the character of my friends at Hartford, by their letters, than I should by being in their society for years."

The amount of her writing was indeed considerable, for one who occupied so quiet a station; and the friend just alluded to, was doubtless correct in saying, that "she wrote three times as much as most young ladies, who do not accomplish half what she did in other things, and yet are by no means idle." It should be added, that she seldom devoted to writing, that portion of time which is ordinarily spent in the daily, active duties of life. She had a surprising facility in saving the fragments of time, and making them tell in something tangible afterwards; and much of her writing was done in those odd moments which are usually spent in recreation or rest, or rather by most young persons in doing nothing at all. She had also a very good facility in the use of the pen, thinking and writing with great accuracy, seldom omitting a word or even a letter, and never copying. Facility and dispatch were, however, in her case, wholly the result of practice. When in her childhood, she first began to embody her ideas in a school composition, it seemed as if she never would be able to do this, and four or six lines at most, was all that her small stock of thought could possibly furnish. And then she had rather more difficulty than is usual, in learning to hold her pen, being naturally inclined to use the wrong hand, and there was always something of weakness in the right one.

Her correspondents were numerous, but it was only comparatively a few with whom she kept up a constant intercourse through the medium of the pen, whenever she was separated from their society. With these she communicated without reserve, on whatever interested her at the time, in something of the style of animated conversation. But her letters must speak for themselves, with this exception, however, that what are inserted in this volume, are only extracts, and therefore none of them can appear with the beauty and sprightliness which they wear as a whole.

Although in all her letters there were sufficient indications that she was always under the influence of religious principle, and that she greatly desired her friends might sympathise with her in this, yet there were times when she made a more than ordinary effort to turn their attention to the subject of religion. It is hoped that it will not be out of place, to insert a few of the many letters she wrote for this purpose, in this little volume, that so she, "being dead," may yet continue to speak to others, in the same simple and touching eloquence with which she was ever wont to plead for the care of the soul. They will therefore be dispersed through the remaining pages, according to their dates.

TO S——, ONE OF HER EARLY FRIENDS.

HARTFORD, *July*, 1838.

"Two weeks more, and my name will cease to be enrolled among those who attend the Seminary, and I shall have passed those old walls, never again to return as a pupil. It is a pleasant and also a painful thought. The *last* of any thing is sad, but I am inclined to think the last term of school is particularly so. The parting look at the old familiar seats, where we have so often bowed at the feet of learning, the farewells spoken with companions of our study, and more than all, the adieus to our beloved teachers, are painful tasks, but they will come. I have been for many years at the Seminary, until I am familiar with every spot, and I can truly say, that I have spent hours of unmingled pleasure there, and I do not think I shall ever meet happiness purer, and less tainted with earth, in any other place. Mr. B. is so good, so excellent, I feel that I have but just begun to know his worth; he takes such a kind interest in all his pupils, and watches so over us with a father's care. I feel more at leaving him than any one else. Mrs. Y., too, I shall always remember with love and respect. She has shown me great kindness, during all the time I have been at school.

We have had a very interesting time since you left us. I hope we feel thankful to our Heavenly Father for his goodness in giving us such a precious revival. When you return here, I think you will find a change in some of those who were gay and thoughtless when you left.

Dear S., may I be permitted to urge upon your attention that subject which I know has in time past interested you, and which I would hope does so still. Have you, my dear friend, retained any thoughts on the subject of religion, or has it all passed from your mind? Is there any more convenient season for which you are waiting, ere you make your peace with our Father in Heaven? He is such a good Father, that we would persuade you to come and make trial for yourself. He is waiting to make you his child. Can you stay away any longer from such a kind friend? Perhaps you think that you have friends enough, and happiness enough; but without God for your friend, and religion for your happiness, you are, and must ever be, destitute of true enjoyment.

You have permitted me, in time past, to address you on this subject, and may I not hope that you will excuse me now? O, my dear friend, when I see so many whom I love, entering the path of life, I think of one who has ever been dear to me, and I pray that she, too, may come and walk in that path which leads to happiness, and everlasting life. May it not be so, soon, dear S?"

The one to whom the following is addressed, was a very dear friend of Mary's, and she seems to have preferred writing, as it allowed her to use greater plainness with one with whom she found it to be a very delicate and difficult thing to converse on the subject of personal religion.

"I have wished for a long time, dear ——, to speak with you on a subject which should be interesting to us both; but whenever I have attempted, it seemed as if a spell bound me which I could not break. I do not wish to preach a sermon, for that is not my office, but I do wish, as a Christian, to speak to my dearest friend. On every subject we converse freely, and our sympathies on other subjects are also one. Should not our 'aims, our hopes,' be one? We are now entering upon the active concerns of life, and already do we form our opinions on the various subjects which come up before us, and ought we not at this important period of our existence, to consider the subject of religion, and to make up our minds as to the influence which its truths shall have over us through life? Dear ——, I have longed to tell you to what I feared your dissatisfaction with yourself was owing. Is it not to a want of fixed, Christian principle to guide you? Without such a principle for our guide, how can we expect to thread the wildering mazes of this life? The principles and maxims of the world are radically wrong, and the bible is our only guide. This is the golden clew to conduct us out of this labyrinth of uncertainty. You have said that you wish to study this winter—and will it not be best to begin at the fountain head of all knowledge, so that all you learn may serve to raise you higher in the scale of being? Ah, of what use will it be to study the works of God, if we are at variance with His righteous laws! It will but serve to increase our misery, if we, who see his wisdom and glory in the creation around us, still keep on sinning against him.

My dear friend, let me entreat you to think of this subject. Do not put it away lightly. You are living for eternity. O, that this truth might impress itself so upon you, that you could not forget it; that its voice might sound in your ear, whether in the gay throng, or the silence of your own chamber, till you should be compelled to stop and inquire what you should do to prepare for the scenes before you."

TO THE SAME.

NEW HAVEN, 1838.

"Oh, how much there is yet to know! This vast universe lies before us, with its infinite mass of matter and mind, and then there is an eternity in which to exercise our powers. Oh, ——, how much we may accomplish! Just in the spring time of our existence, with souls which will forever rise in purity and blessedness; or will forever sink in degradation and woe. Our careless, childish days have passed, and now the serious business of living and acting in God's universe, is beginning to be felt by us.

May we, my dear friend, have *One* for our guide, who will lead us on in the paths of wisdom and virtue, until we shall arrive at that state, where the soul will once more be in its native glory."

TO S——.

"I am sure, dear S——, you must have misunderstood my father in thinking he said the life of a sinner was easier than the life of a Christian—for I asked him yesterday, and he said, '*Oh, no*, the yoke which the sinner bears, is a much harder yoke than Christ's.'

Think, my friend, what the sinner's yoke imposes—the pride, the vanity, the selfishness and envy which ever accompany it; the secret irritation which it ever produces. Do you say that the Christian has all these, too? He may have them, but he is ever becoming more and more free from them. Besides, it is not Christ's yoke which is hard, but the remains of the yoke of sin. It is this which makes the Christian's course hard.

There is another difference in the two yokes. The one of sin bears down the spirit; becomes heavier and heavier, till it sinks the soul at last in ruin—while the other becomes lighter and lighter, until in the end it ceases to be a yoke, and the service of Christ becomes perfect freedom.

Why, my dear friend, do you shrink from being a Christian, when you have a much more difficult road to pursue by remaining a sinner? There may be flowers in the way, but with every flower there is poison and a thorn. The Christian way is one of peace; and as the trials, one by one, drop off, the way appears more and more lovely, easy and happy. 'The peace of God which passeth all understanding shall keep your minds and hearts, through Jesus Christ.' And again, 'To be spiritually minded is life and peace.'

Oh, my friend, why will you not believe the testimony of God when He says these things? He knows what is most for our good—what will make us most happy. He knows that if we give up searching for happiness among things which will only yield disappointment, and will come and love his service, that we shall be doing the thing which will alone promote our true happiness. The bible not only shows this, but the testimony of every true Christian shows it also. 'My yoke is easy, and my burden is light,' says our Saviour, and all who have really tried, have found it so. Why will you not try for yourself?

I have not the time, my dear friend, to say the half I wish, and I hope you will excuse the liberty I take in writing, for though I prefer conversation, I fear I shall not be able to see you much next week. Oh, that when I do see you, it may be to find you feeling that Christ's yoke is a delightful one. You cannot know the inward, holy peace which a true Christian has, till you enjoy it yourself. But be assured it is no fiction.

I wish that you would either come and see me, or write to me.

Ever your affectionate friend,

M. E. H.

TO HER FRIEND AT THE SOUTH,

THE SUMMER AFTER HER RETURN FROM NEW HAVEN.

HARTFORD, *July* 13, 1839.

"My dear M.—I returned yesterday from a delightful visit to Farmington, where I have been spending a few days in the lovely family of Mr. N. I took your letter with me, intending to have a pleasant time in writing to you among the groves and hills of that sweet place; but as every hour was occupied, I was obliged to forego the pleasure. You never went to the house I believe, but I know you would like it. The rooms are airy, yet home-like, and there is every thing to gratify the taste in music, flowers, books, drawings, &c. There is a wild little glen, just at the foot of the garden, which has been left in its natural state. I took my book there one morning, and found it a very fit place to read of highland scenes, as they are pictured by Scott. A seat has been built on the edge of the ravine, inclosed by a wooden parapet; and while I sat there and looked down on the little brook, which murmured at the bottom of the glen, and saw the sun-light dancing through the thick trees, and playing among the shadows, it seemed like a spot for a fairy queen to hold her court.

It is a year, a whole year, since we graduated. Can you believe it? I can; for never did a year seem so long in some respects, although it seems short in others. Tell me, Marion, which were happiest, school days, or days out of school? Ask me, and I will tell you that this last year has been the happiest of my whole life. I only wished you, dear M., a little nearer. I feel as though I had just begun to live; I have such new feelings, such delightful themes for contemplation—and then, I am so happy in my friendships. I believe there never was any one who has so much to be thankful for. To be sure I have trials; and who has not? How can we expect to live in this world, without some things to trouble us? My greatest trials are from my own evil heart. There are times when every thing looks gloomy and perplexed, and when I fear I shall never know the truth;* shall never be able to find its hiding place, in this labyrinth of perplexity. But our heavenly guide, who says, 'ask and ye shall receive,' will not leave in darkness any sincere inquirer after truth; and He who has said, 'be ye perfect, as your Father in heaven is perfect,' will He not guide our feeble steps, as we are attempting to follow him, until, purified from sin, we shall one day stand forth in our Creator's image? While gazing on the beauties of nature, amid the hills and groves of the country, I thought, what a heaven our earth would be, were the moral world as beautiful as the material. Dear M., do you not think that the goodness of our Heavenly Father strikingly appears, in permitting those who forget him, to enjoy so much of beauty and happiness as there is in this fair earth?

You don't know how very important I feel, in having so much to attend to at home, that my place is missed

* This state of mind might have been owing, in part, if not entirely, to her having read several of the then new and popular writings of the day, such as Emerson's, for instance, and several translations from the German, which, while they dazzled, also bewildered.

when I am absent. It has really raised my self esteem, to know that I am needed any where, and especially to know, that in the family circle I may be of some use. There seems to me no pleasanter sphere of usefulness than that which the eldest daughter has. It is such a comfort to take the weight of family duties off from mother, and to soothe father when he comes wearied from the affairs which occupy his time—and then it is delightful to aid brother in his lessons, and to watch his mind as it begins to unfold. How careful I must be, lest by a word of mine, that mind be directed wrong!

Tell me, dear M., how you succeed in all your plans. As only daughters, we have common sympathies; and may aid each other in devising ways for increasing our influence, and making it of the right kind.

I am writing to you, dear M., in the still noontide, when every thing seems to have gone to rest—but I have preferred talking with you, to yielding to the drowsy influence around."

Her taste, as it developed itself in the love of the beautiful in nature, threw a charm over her whole life, and contributed to enrich her intercourse with friends. It made her an exceedingly desirable companion in a rural party. There, away from the world, with friends whom she loved, she delighted to revel amidst the beauties of the fair creation around her.

The following description from her pen, of a scene that occurred in such a party, of which she was one, will give some idea of the ease and readiness with which she could contribute her share to enliven such an excursion. Its date, also, places it here.

NEW HAVEN, *August*, 1839.

"Dear ———,

"Yesterday afternoon we had a delightful ride to Saltonstall Lake. Is it not enchanting? Who would think that such a little fairy region was inclosed by those hills? While taking our refreshments, we heard voices on the opposite shore, and could discern female figures gliding amongst the dark trees—gentlemen, too, one with a guitar. We thought ourselves fortunate in selecting a different side from them, as they might have considered us as intruders. Dr. and Mrs. F. were too tired to ascend the hill, so J. and I thought we would beau ourselves up. We did not go round by the path, but clinging hold of the boughs of pine, we almost swung from place to place, it being too steep to admit of a firm foothold. It became easier after we had reached the regular path, and escaped the tangled brushwood; and we sauntered on at our leisure, while I sang loud and carelessly, using the freedom that this mountain land gave,

'Through the wood, through the wood, follow and find me,
Search every hollow, each dingle and dell;
I leave not the print of a footstep behind me,
So they who would see me, must seek for me well.'

A voice came up from the water, and it repeated with beautiful emphasis, every word of the song. I stood petrified with amazement and fear. I little expected to have awakened the echoes of the lake. J. enjoyed my embarrassment, and Mrs. F., who walked on the shore, called to her to have me respond to the echo. But the music from the water commenced again,—'Shall we meet again, Mary?' and I answered, 'never, oh never.'

Each word was heard with perfect distinctness in the clear regions where we stood, although neither party could see the other. We were hidden from the lake by thick pine trees, yet every ripple of the waters, and dipping of the oar, sounded upon the still air. Mrs. F. could see the musical boatmen, and she said they rested on their oars, looking up intently as they sung to wake 'the mountain echo.'

Thus we went on singing and responding many beautiful songs:

'Near the lake where droop'd the willow,'

'My heart's in the highlands,' &c.,

and many others. At last we sang our farewells, and J. and myself descended to the shore. I should not have been willing to have carried on this little frolic of romance, if I had not recognized the voice, (for it was no other than W——, the brother of the poet,) and had I not been certain also, that my own was not recognized, for he had never heard me sing before. We separated with no other recognition than what our songs afforded, and returned to the city.

I feel tempted to describe our lovely ride home in the evening,—but words express *so feebly* what we feel in beholding scenes in nature. We rode slowly along round the shore of the bay, watching the sun as it set, and threw its rays on the water. The dark clouds, which hung portentously in the western horizon, were lighted with gorgeous hues, and the brilliant reflection strangely contrasted with the sombre colors beneath. The day had been warm, and the breeze which came in from the sound, was refreshing to us after our rambles. Far away to the south-east, we could discern a few light sails, while the city lay stretched out before us, with its guardian rocks, presenting their bold outline to the sky. It was a scene which might tempt a painter's skill."

TO M. D.

October 1st, 1839.

"My dear M.—I am at present *very happy*, in the society of a new friend, who speaks the language of love, joy, hope, and every other feeling of the heart. Now, who do you think it is? You are no yankee, so I will tell you that the day before yesterday, I received a beautiful piano. My friends all come to see it, and it returns their attentions with such effect, that they are delighted. For myself I can say, that I never heard a more perfect instrument. Mr. G., our organist, whose taste is considered equal to any one in this country, says that it is the finest he has touched since he came to America. Such a union of brilliancy, softness, sweetness and power, is rarely surpassed by any instrument."

To another friend, she speaks of her piano thus: "Dr. F. came to try my new piano, and I was delighted with the high opinion he entertains of my 'rose-wood companion.' He thinks it the finest he has ever seen, and has paid it or me, a compliment, which is very flattering. He has set some beautiful verses to music, and inscribed it to his friend Mary, an honor she feels quite unworthy of. The music is very sweet, just suited to the words. If you were only here I would sing them to you."

The piano of which she speaks, was presented to her by some highly respected and much loved friends of her father's, and was a gift worthy the donors. Many were the devices of her grateful heart, to make to them some suitable expression of her sense of the favor they had done her; but she at last concluded, that to make it subservient to her better qualification for usefulness in life, would be the best return she could make them, and would also be in accordance with the object for which it was given her.

TO M. D.

HARTFORD, *October* 16, 1839.

"Oh, if you were only here, and I could talk with you instead of writing. I am seated where I can look far away to the south, and as I gaze on the scene before me, I can almost imagine that I see the spires and elms of my own New Haven, skirting the horizon. How often have I sat at this window, and wished that my vision might extend to that lovelv city. 'Tis a year next Monday, since I went there for the winter—what a thrill comes over my spirit, every time I think of last winter! I love to dwell on each little incident—every hour, almost every moment, is as fresh to my memory as if it had passed only yesterday. The last year has been my happiest; and why the recollection of it is mingled with sadness, I can hardly tell—perhaps because 't is past, never to return. If I should go there ever again to spend any time, it would not be like the last winter; for some of my dearest friends have gone, some have died, and some changed.

* * * * * * *

I must tell you something of the affairs of our little circle. We have a sewing society, which meets every fortnight on Tuesday, and a musical, every intervening Tuesday. Then we hope also to have a reading society, and these occupations, together with the Institute lectures, which are quite fashionable now, will take up a considerable portion of our time during the winter. We have our little prayer meetings, as usual, on Thursday afternoon of each week, and every Sabbath evening there is an exercise in Doddridge at the Lecture room. I have quiet, pleasant times at home in reading, and now and then, star gazing.*

You see how particular I have been to tell you of our affairs, so that if you choose to remember us this winter, you may imagine how we are situated. For myself I must say, that I hope the coming winter will be spent in such a manner, that when I look back upon it from the distant ages of eternity, it may be with approbation.

* * * * * * *

Had I been told a year ago, that M. would allow six months to pass, without writing to her northern friends, I should have said that the person who could make such an assertion, was unworthy of my confidence. I know that strange things happen in this world, and I must be prepared for them, but unfaithful friends are what I know very little about from experience. Thus far I have never been deceived in a friend, and though I cannot suppose that I shall always be so favored, yet I should be very sorry to know that Marion was the first to break the spell, the magic spell of friendship. I will therefore have all leniency now; and not think that M. has given up her northern friends. I will wait yet longer, for I cannot bear to come to such a conclusion."

TO THE SAME.

Hartford, *January* 29, 1840.

"Your long looked for letter, my dear Marion, came, and was received with much satisfaction. It set every thing right, so far as doubt of your friendship was concerned; and while we cannot help feeling a little sad, that our dear M. D. is to be forever lost, we hope to find in Mrs.

* To these details should be added, that some portion of each day found her actively employed in household duties, and that she was often abroad on errands of benevolence, or engaged in the same at home.

S. E., a friend who will possess the same sweet, affectionate qualities.

So, then, you are to be a good minister's wife, and lady of the parish; and while you are attending to the various preparations for the approaching eventful day, and arranging all the wedding paraphernalia, we are quietly pursuing our course, very much in the same way as when you was one of our number. Perhaps if you were to see us, you might think we were somewhat changed. You left us when our characters, though formed in the main, were yet in a state to receive any new impression, and if you were now to return, you might find opinions, and feelings, and principles quite new-modeled. I am inclined to think that the same is true of you. Your letters show that you have somewhat altered in your views of things, though I hope your character in general, bears a near resemblance to the M. who was once the joy of our social circle.

* * * * * * *

My beloved Sunday school teacher, Mrs. Hovey, has left us for her home in heaven. It seems a sad dream—I do not yet realize it. But it is so. We shall go to her, but she will never return to us. For some weeks past the world has looked dark to me, but heaven has been bright, as it has opened its portals to receive our beloved friends to its mansions of rest.

I am thinking of going to New Haven for a few days; but it will be a sad visit—so many absent from our circle—some in the busy tumult of life, and some in 'the spirit land.' But 'passing away,' is written on every thing earthly. How sweet it is to look beyond this misty, gloomy world, where all things are shrouded in dim twilight, to the bright, pure Heaven, where 'the sunshine of glory eternally reigns.'

Am I wrong in writing to you thus, when you are in the

midst of so much happiness? I know, dear M., that to you the world must wear a beautiful countenance, and life appear to pass amid green vales and clear streams, and beneath blue and smiling skies. I pray that it may always be thus fair. I know it will be so, if your way is illumined by the Sun of Righteousness, and if, amid the storms which may ere long beat upon it, your spirit shall catch, and reflect, the rays of glorious brightness, which even through the gloom, come to us from the world of light and peace.

And now our paths in life are really to be different. Yours will be one, where many responsibilities will meet you; but of whatever nature these may be, I shall ever pray that you may have strength to meet them. May you have the light and peace of a Christian hope to shine, not only on your bridal day, and on each festal scene, but also to gild, with a quiet lustre, the sober duties of life which will follow; and, happy in your husband's love, may you pass through life usefully, until at length you shall arrive at that world, where only is known the full bliss of friendship.

We should love to be present with you on the 19th. If we all come as a band of spirits around your bridal train, will you not bid us welcome?

Did you receive a letter from me which was written in July? I was very happy at that time, and dreamed away many long summer days in bright anticipations and sweet remembrances. Now the dreamer is becoming a little more sober. How could she help it? when so many she loved have departed, either to distant lands of this same rolling orb, or to unknown regions in this vast universe, which can be reached only through death's gateway. What scenes are every hour transpiring in distant worlds, while we go wandering on in this little globe, so much occupied with what appear to us as 'vast designs,' that we scarcely look beyond to the universe around, from which we are separated by only a breath."

TO ——.

February 16, 1840.

"I have wanted, many times during this week, my dear ——, to renew our conversation on the topics which occupied us on Monday. It is a too deeply interesting subject, which concerns our eternal welfare, to give it only a passing attention. A winter's walk in a noisy city, is no place nor time to converse on such themes. I long for the time to come, when we can go and converse amid the woods and fields, and talk of that world which will be our home, when this has passed away. My dear friend, I do want you to think of your preparation for that world.

You say you 'do not feel.' That is one reason why you should *think*. How is it we become interested in any subject? Is it not by giving our attention to it? Dear ——, you are now confined by a sickness, which shuts you out from general society. Is it not therefore a favorable time to think of God, and of your duty to him; of the Saviour, and of all that he has suffered to redeem you from death; of all his Spirit is now doing, to win you to the love and service of God, and to raise you to heaven? Be persuaded to give it your whole attention. A passing thought will not do. Is a day too long? Would you think so if you were saved by it, and in some distant age, from the heights of purity and wisdom which you had attained, should look back on that one day spent in seriously pondering the question of your soul's salvation?"

Mary had a contemplative mind, slightly tinged with sadness, and yet she was never melancholy. She has noticed this trait, or habit of mind, in her private journal;

for, as she said, it seemed to constitute a part of her very being, and she watched its influence on her Christian character, with great carefulness. She says of herself, "I cannot hear a strain of music, or gaze on the quiet sky, without having an under current of sadness mingling with my deep enjoyment. From a child I have felt it. When quite young, I remember wondering why I felt half sad, half happy, on one sunny summer afternoon, when, upon a long green hillside where I was playing, the sunlight lay so still and beautiful. It was the commencement of a feeling which has since grown, so as to tinge my whole character. Every thing I most enjoy is most sad." She "mused on nature," with a Christian's, as well as "with a poet's eye." Some sketches from her pen, illustrative of this trait, will be placed here on account of the date they bear.

MUSINGS.

LAST DAY OF SPRING, 1840.

"Again are these exquisite, though soul-sickening days with us in all their oppressive loveliness. The soft winds stir among the green boughs, scattering the last blossoms of spring upon the verdant turf.. Above us, the skies smile in their ever varying beauty. The trees, robed in fresh foliage, hanging not heavily, as in sultry summer days, wave gracefully in the fragrant breeze, while the sunlight dancing in the shadows beneath them, sheds a softened radiance over leaf and flower; or rests in golden beauty on gentle slopes and meadows of living green. Beautiful warblers plume their bright wings, and soar far away into the vault of heaven, where soft clouds rest like a snowy veil above earth's loveliness. And I have come to my old familiar seat. How soft the light steals in through the half-closed shutters! With what a gentle sound do the ever varying tones of nature fall upon my ear! And yet my soul is not still. Oh, ye days of beauty, tell us why, in all your loveliness, ye do wake mournful chords within us? Tell us why each whisper of the breeze calls forth a gush of sadness from our burdened hearts, and as we bend in silent admiration, a something all too deep for utterance, presses on the soul with its heavy weight?

I was much interested this morning with a verse in "Mrs. Hemans' Voice of Music," embodying the thought that the sadness which even the most joyous melody awakens, is for the want of a perfectness, which can never be found on earth, and for which the soul seeks in vain. Or, as she beautifully expresses it,

> "A something which finds not its answer here,
> A chain to be clasped in a holier sphere."

It is this *something*, which stirs our spirits, as we wander amidst nature's lovely haunts. In the dark grove, where cool waters flow, on gentle knolls where we rest at even, and watch, as the beams of day are fading, till the gold melts away to the rose, and with a blushing beauty die upon the sky,—in such shaded spots, and silent hours, the spirit, even in its deep gladness, sighs that there is still a void within which nothing here can fill. But in that purer, brighter world which revelation opens to our view, the full tide of joy may ever swell and know no check. There, no sad remembrance shall mar our peace, no sorrow cast its leaden weight on our spirits, as we drink in the glorious beauty of this vast universe."

TO C. C.,

WITH LONGFELLOW'S PSALM OF LIFE, AND OTHER PIECES.

September, 1840.

"It may be, my dear C., that these lines, which to me have such fascination, are not of the kind which you like;

and yet I thought that the spiritual beauty which characterizes the whole, could not but fill and enrapture the soul, with you as with me. There is about the Psalm of Life, so much of inspiration, that one feels after reading it, ready 'to suffer and be strong,' in any path through this life.

What a mysterious thing it is *to exist*, to have a being in the universe. Sometimes the thought comes with overwhelming power, that I *am existing*, and shall *exist forever;* and that my smallest actions, slightest thoughts, have some connection with the world, the universe around. Dear C., may each thought, each act of ours, bring us nearer to that perfection for which we are aiming,—or as Longfellow says, may we

> 'Learn to act, that each to-morrow,
> Find us farther than to-day.' "

TO C. C.

HARTFORD, *Dec.* 15, 1840

"Many thoughts have been suggested to my mind by your note, dear C., which I have longed to sit down and give to you. Not that they are important, as mine, but because I know you will sympathize with me in all that concerns my preparation for the unknown and untried future. Dear C., I feel that for one I am too apt to forget it. How much must be done, before these natures of ours can become fit for the society of the pure and holy of heaven. It is thoughts like these, that make me feel I have been dreaming. How do all the beautiful creations of a poet's fancy, all the speculations of a philosopher, appear, when compared with the work which God has given us to do. Help me, my dear friend, to keep my eye steadily fixed upon this work. 'So teach us to number our days, that we may apply our hearts unto wisdom,' is a petition we need daily to offer. Let us pray for each other, that our characters may be formed after the true Christian model, and so we be prepared for our eternal home.

* * * * * * * *

What lovely evenings we have had lately. There is something in a winter's sunset, peculiarly tranquilizing. A holy calm seems to veil the earth, when the evening star looks down 'so still and saint-like.' If I could have only one hour in a day to myself, it should be just as the sun-light fades, and while the evening star lingers above the horizon. What lessons of peace and truth does it read us; how it seems to point away from this narrow earth, to regions of perfect holiness and love. Do not those gentle beams give promise of a purer life beyond the grave? It is not my style to weep often, but the solemn teachings of the evening star, have power 'in sudden gushes the tears to bring,' yet not such tears as music calls forth, 'which refresh not and still must fall.' But we must talk together again of music."

TO M.,

ON HEARING THAT SHE HAD RETURNED TO THE HOME OF HER YOUTH, IN WIDOWHOOD, ONLY SIX MONTHS AFTER SHE HAD LEFT IT.

HARTFORD, *Dec.* 19, 1840.

"We have often, my dear Marion, in days gone by, mingled our hearts together, both in joy and sorrow, and you know not now how earnestly I long to annihilate the distance between us, that I may express to you, what it is not possible to put on paper, the deep sympathy we all feel in the affliction which our Heavenly Father has seen fit to send you. How little we thought of the future! This life of ours would indeed be a mystery, were it not for the cheering light which revelation throws upon it; and our spirits would sink beneath the load of afflictions which weigh them down, were it not for the support which the gospel of Christ affords. There we can find rest for the aching heart.

Marion, the sad lessons of life have been early taught us, and we have found that 'the change which must come over the spirit of our dreams,' exists not merely in a poet's fancy. Yet, is it not well? Do we not need the lesson? If we might always have our friends with us here, and if our intercourse were not embittered by some trial, should we not make of them idols, and twine about them our heart's best affections?

I feel, my dear sister, that it is but poor sympathy I can give, and it is with fear I am writing, lest I touch the broken harp strings with too rude a hand. There is *One*, and I love to think that, to that *One*, my dear friend, in her days of happiness, was no stranger, who, while he wounds, can heal. Is it not strange that we should need affliction to draw our hearts to this, our best friend?

When I wrote to you, dear M., of the afflictions with which many families here have been visited, it seemed almost wrong for me to intrude such sad tales upon your bridal days. How little I thought that a few short months would have rendered you familiar with other than joyous scenes. Will you not write to me, and permit me to sympathize with you? 'We have been friends together,' and shall we not in sorrow as well as in joy, mingle our hearts? Speak to me of your comforts in this your affliction, that when I taste the cup of sorrow, which sooner or later must be tasted by all of us, I too may know how to be supported.

You have still a blessing in your dear precious parents. But I very well know that it is not in the power of any earthly friend to take the place of a lost one. And why should we wish this? Our lost friends, who sleep in

Jesus, will one day be all restored. They may, even now, be around our path, as guardian angels, blessing us by their silent presence, and shedding, though unseen, a sweet and heavenly influence around us. And will they not welcome us to heaven?

How little do the sufferings of this life appear, in comparison with the eternal weight of glory which will follow this short season of trial. That 'eternal weight of glory!' Our feeble, imperfect minds, cannot comprehend it. But God, our Father, will prepare us for it. Shall we not, therefore, submit cheerfully to the discipline of His hand and feel,.

'That by the light and shade, through which our pathway lies,
By the beauty and the grief alike, we're training for the skies.'

Your name is often mentioned here with affectionate interest. We remember the young, lively M., who left us so full of health and happiness. And you remember us in our school girl days, full of hopes and pleasures. Two years have not passed so lightly over us, but that the sober lines of life have checked ours in some degree. In the varied scenes of coming years, may we find our characters becoming moulded into the image of our blessed Saviour, and whether we pass through happiness or adversity, may we be advancing towards heaven.

Dear Marion, you have one more tie to endear that heavenly home to you; and the ties there will continue to strengthen, as one by one, those of earth become severed.

Sabbath evening. I have just returned, my dear M., from a service in our lecture room. I wish you could be with us again in these meetings. They remind me of the last winter you spent here, when so many whom we loved became Christians. It is delightful to see one and another of my friends choosing the path to heaven. Would that we might all, like a band of sisters, pursue it together! Our dear ———, lovely and beloved, and satisfied with the blessings which are showered around her way, has still to choose that happiness which alone is enduring. I know she is remembered in your prayers. Let us, dear M., pray continually for this dear friend, lest she perish, and the guilt be ours."

TO C. C.

HARTFORD, *Dec.* 31, 1840.

Ten o'clock. Two hours more, the old year's death knell.

"It were much more fitting for you, my dear C., to write me a new-year's letter, 'naitheless,' I will not let the evening pass without thanking you for your kind, refreshing note, which came to me on a weary morning, like a spring to one in a desert land.

I am in but a poor mood for writing, for my heart seems dying with the poor old year. The day has been cloudy and dark (as you know) but the stars are lighting now the old year from this world of faithlessness and sin, and a clearer sky than we have had for many a day, gives promise of a brighter to-morrow. But I have *thought my spirit out,* I do believe, for I cannot care for either old year or new. While I am writing, some lingering remains of memory remind me of a thrilling picture in 'Illustrations of the Song of the Bell,' by the same hand that etched that fearful one we saw at Mr. D's. Perhaps I spoke to you of it; it was of the hours coming in, in one long procession from eternity, and receiving their portion either of good or ill to dispense, as they passed through time. What will the hours of this coming year bring us!

Dear C., the foundations of my soul seem all breaking away. I never felt so entirely adrift in the universe, without compass or anchor, as I do at present. All that I thought firmly fixed in my heart is gone, and I shrink from the year, as bringing only new helplessness at a time when I need all my energies. Forgive me, my dear friend, for troubling you with these things. A letter on the eve of another great period which marks off the time of frail, perishing mortals, should be full of hope—of encouragement; and forgetting the past, should look towards the glorious future—the coming existence, when the strife with evil shall have ended. But *thus* I am little able to write now. The few longings I have ever had for the strife, seem all quenched. If I thought this state of mind was to last, I should be miserable. Perhaps I have fallen into some 'slough of despond,' but if so, it must be a very different one from Christian's, for there appears no helping hand. I am not jesting, my dear C., neither am I indulging myself in a melancholy dream; but a conviction of what I am, and my utter inability to be any better, has so weighed upon me lately, as to drive almost every thing else from my mind. Do you know what I can do? If you have any talisman to still the unquiet beatings of my heart, send it to me I pray you.

Why am I so selfish as to write thus to you? I am sure I did not sit down to the unmerciful task of making you acquainted with my utter destitution, but it was with the laudable intention of wishing you a 'happy new-year',—happy in the consciousness of a daily increase in all that is worthy of an immortal and redeemed soul. O, my friend, press on in that glorious path with renewed ardor. Our Saviour has marked the way, and will ever be near, to guide, and strengthen, and to bring you safe to the hills of light. I dare not think of those everlasting hills. It blinds my eyes with tears; for the long, weary path, full of difficulties, snares, temptations, corruptions, comes into my view, and fills me with gloomy forebodings. It does not seem as though I can ever get over them. Evil habits so fixed in the deepest recesses of the heart—love of the world, with its poor perishing trifles, dragging the spirit down to earth. Will they drag it down forever? Can no one break the strong fetters? But this does not sound very much like the words of a believer in all the promises so glorious and precious, written on every page of God's holy word. The very fact that I am a believer in them, makes me still sadder, for if I believed rightly, I should have no more discouragements.

Well, perhaps I shall feel differently when to-morrow's light brings a young, glad year, and the children in their careless glee, little recking of the future, shall come with their joyous greetings, and the world shall go on just as before, whirling and bustling, and our hearts, sorrowing, toiling, rejoicing till the last year comes, and the strife is ended, the drama closed. 'There remaineth therefore a rest to the people of God.' Oh, for an entrance into that rest. I do not feel like giving up yet. There is a Saviour to guide us there. And when the old year is dead, and the bell has tolled its parting; when the new year comes with its life and hope, let us, my dear C., rise, not in gloom, not in despondency, but in the calm and fixed resolve, to go on in the strife, even to the end; to 'learn to labor and to wait,'—'to suffer and be strong,'—to endure unto the end,'—looking to our glorious and risen Saviour, and to the bright company already redeemed, and who circle the throne in their spotless robes.

Dear C., I long to sit by you, to take your hand in mine, and talk of our duties, our labors and trials. There is a rest from sin at the end of all these. · · Mother comes to me very beseechingly to close my letter, it is so late. But she tells me just to put in her love—so here it is, with mine also, and many a wish for your happiness the coming year.'

TO A FRIEND IN NEW HAVEN.

HARTFORD, *Jan.* 18, 1841.

"My dear J. How I wish you had been with me this evening, in our solemn services, hearing Mr. K. discourse from 'When he maketh inquisition for blood, he remembereth them.' As I cast my eye over the audience, and saw the young, the lovely, the gay, the intelligent, and thought how in probability the souls of some, even of those whose hearts were tender, would sink into eternal misery, it seemed to me we were all asleep, to think so calmly about it. To be eternally lost! Oh, what is it! Lost, too, when we might be saved! Do not such thoughts come at times with an almost overwhelming weight? And can we believe them, and yet do so little—scarcely warn our friends of danger?

I had a horrid dream last night. It has haunted me all day. Shall I tell it? I dreamed (it almost paralizes my hand to write it,) that ———'s day of probation was over, and she eternally lost; fixed forever in the land of despair, without one gleam of hope; severed from all that she loved, and condemned to dwell with the spirits of darkness and woe;—and all this when I might have prevented it. Through all the long night I wandered from place to place with my wretched heart, and the image of my friend eternally lost through my influence—and in bitterness of soul, I felt as if I could die too. Pray, my dear friend, for the salvation of this dear girl. Must it be that she die in the midst of so much light from God's word, and with the hopes of the gospel spread out so plainly to her view? What are we about to let our friends go on, day after day, with no warning voice to wake them from the sleep of sin? Has not God promised to answer prayer? Oh, yes, our poor feeble prayers! and I have evidence, blessed be his holy name, that the prayers of some one are answered in her behalf; it may be mine, it may be yours; but no matter, dear ——— is not entirely careless; she does think; she can feel, and by the blessing of God she may be saved. My dear J., could we together supplicate God's spirit to strive with her heart, and never to leave her until her heart is given to Christ, how I should rejoice. But this cannot be. Each in our own chamber, and alone with our God, must pray for the salvation of this dear friend. Will you, dear J., every night at the twilight hour, join me in prayer for this blessing?"

TO M. D.

HARTFORD, *Feb.* 15, 1841.

"My dear M. Your precious letter has filled my heart with gratitude to our Heavenly Father, for giving you in your affliction, such a sweet spirit of resignation to his holy will. Yes, my dear friend, he is an Almighty Comforter, and it is sweet to lie in his hands, and to feel the everlasting arms beneath the sinking soul. Continue, dear M., to trust and love him as you now do, and you will reap the reward of patient waiting on him. Think of the promises in his word. How full of love! A balm for all our woes. O, take them home to your heart. Our Father's chastening hand is upon you, dearest, but we rejoice that you can feel it is in love; and though now it is very dark to you, one day you will be able to rejoice in view of the wisdom and goodness of this trying dispensation. On those hills of light, where all tears are wiped away, where no sin nor sorrow ever come, there we shall look back on our pilgrimage through the world, and shall see how necessary was all the discipline through which we passed. Yet we may weep, for religion does not seal the heart, and forbid us to mourn over our buried joys; but while we mourn, it teaches us to do this, 'not as those who have no hope.' 'The sorrow of the world worketh death;' but the religion of Christ teaches us to look beyond the grave, to that glorious world, where, having been made 'perfect through suffering,' we shall find our rest.

M., how dream-like appears the time when you was here with us. Do you remember the various talks we had of the future? How we whispered our thoughts to each other about this busy, and then bright world? We were novices then in the art of happiness, and worse than novices in our anticipations of it—at least so far as we expected to find it here. Though we warned each other about trusting the dazzle of this earth, though we told how others had found it unsatisfying, there was, after all, a secret feeling—'well, if they were disappointed, we *may* not be,'—and our dreams appeared so rational, we thought we *could* not be. But, my friend, you are *realizing* now the truth that this is a state of trial, not our home, our portion. And is it not best to be taught this early in life, that our affections may be set on heaven? In that world, we shall look with very different feelings upon our earthly joys and sorsows, from what we do here. How much we need trust in God. There is no state in which we do not need his guidance. God, our Saviour, is our life. Oh yes, *our life!* 'Our life is hid with Christ in God.'

March 1. I have been delaying thus, dear M., hoping to have an opportunity to converse with father on the subject to which you alluded in your letter. I think he will write you when his duties become less pressing; but at present he is fully occupied. There is a delightful work going on in our city, of which I have been longing to tell you; for many you knew and loved are hoping in Christ.

It is nearly two months since the commencement of the revival, which has been mostly among the young people. The way had sometime been preparing for this, when Mr. K. came and spent one month here, preaching every afternoon to professors of religion, and in the evening to others, particularly to those who were not Christians.

The remembrance of those seasons is like a green spot in this desert world. We came forth from our dark places, and stood in the light of the Sun of Righteousness; we cast off our garments of mourning, and put on the garments of praise, and already the glory from the celestial city seemed beaming down upon us. It seems to us now, as though we can never go back to the troubled streams of this world, having tasted of the streams which flow from the throne of God and the Lamb. But, dear M., I know not how to tell you half. Many are changed—and more than all, and I have been keeping this to tell you last, our own dear ———;* my heart is very full—what shall I say! She has joined our little prayer meeting, and our intercourse now is so delightful, it seems like heaven begun on earth. It is sometime since she became interested. Before the revival she bad begun to feel that this world could not satisfy the wants of her immortal soul. With all her enjoyments there was still an '*aching void.*' She has had many perplexities and discouragements, since she began to think seriously upon the subject, but our Heavenly Father has been leading her along very gently, and bringing her into the right way. Let us rejoice together in this. Cannot you, my dear sister, even in your affliction, thank God that one more dear one is added to that band who are ever to live and praise God around his throne? Some of our beloved ones are already there; and we are waiting here, in this our pilgrimage, for our Saviour to call us. He will

* The young friend about whom she had the dream.

come in his own good time. 'And them also that sleep in Jesus, will God bring with him.' This verse, M., looks very much as though we shall not only know our departed friends, but that it will also be an addition to our happiness, to have them with us. Does not this seem to intimate that we shall still love and be interested in those whom we knew and loved on the earth, more than those, with whom we are to begin an acquaintance? Nor will this at all interfere with our loving every one. It does not, to my mind, seem requisite to the perfect bliss of heaven, that we should have equal love to all. I have had a little conversation with father on the subject, and he said that 'there was nothing which could lead us to think that friendships begun on earth, and founded in pure motives, might not be continued and increased in heaven.' I have thought much on the subject, dear M., and have heard various opinions about it, some of which have made me unhappy; and I have come to the conclusion to leave the matter with God. He can fill our largest desires. We are in his hands. Our dear departed friends are with him at rest. Let us see to it, that we are prepared for that rest which remaineth for the people of God. This is the *great thing*, after all, that we have a part in the great salvation. Then our cup of happiness will be full in the other world, even though we may not here, know the way in which God will fill it. I long to see you once again, dear sister of my heart, to mourn with you, and to look with you to heaven where Jesus is, and where we may be, if we trust in him. Oh, that we could love and serve him more perfectly. How sweet to feel that in heaven there will be no more sin. We must toil, each in our part of the vineyard, doing what little we can, till we go to our rest in heaven. *There* we shall spend an eternity together. *There* I shall know all that you have known and loved. Let us 'comfort one another with these words.'"

CHAPTER V.

HER RELIGIOUS WRITINGS.

It is with some hesitancy on the part of friends, that the following extracts are permitted to occupy a place in this volume. They were written exclusively for the benefit of the individual who penned them, and are a record of her views and feelings on the subject of religion, with notices of such facts and events as interested her at the time, together with the effect which these had on her religious character. They are selected from a journal which she commenced in January, 1841, and closed in June, 1843, just before leaving home for her residence in the East.

There are those to whom it appears to be a species of sacrilege to expose to the scrutiny of others the private religious exercises of an individual. It will be seen that the manuscript from which these extracts are made, is not exclusively of this character. If it were, this would not constitute the only ground of hesitancy. A difficulty is felt in making from the mass such selections as shall exhibit her character in its true light. The objections against keeping a record of the daily religious exercises of the heart, or rather against exposing this record to the scrutiny of others after the death of the individual who kept it, might, it is thought, be made against any thing which should cause the light of the Christian to shine before men in this dark world.

To make such a record useful to others, it is indispensable that it accord with the traits of Christian experience delineated in the New Testament; and also that there be nothing in the life strikingly at variance with such a record.

Mary is known to have carried her religion into every thing. Her Christian experience was not suffered to lie dormant within, an inoperative principle, confined to herself and useless to others; but it was as a perennial spring, overflowing in its fullness, and fertilizing all around. From the moment, when in her joy at having "found God," she exclaimed, "I am happy," it was her constant, uniform, and untiring effort, to lead others to a participation in the same happiness with herself.

Her religion also was the religion of the Bible. Its sterner doctrines, as well as its milder precepts, were allowed to have their full influence over her. She took *it*, and not the maxims of the world, for her guide. It was a "lamp to her feet and a light to her path," and by it she has no doubt been led to find her home in heaven. But like all other Christians, she was but imperfectly sanctified, and many and severe were her inward struggles, in her attempts to lead a consistent Christian life.

She had a buoyancy of spirit and depth of sympathy which extended to every living thing, and those traits, with others of a kindred nature, fitted her to enjoy life in a high degree. But while they made her more interesting as a friend and more useful as a Christian, they at the same time constituted the principal sources of her trial; and it was through these mainly, that the discipline came, which fitted her so well for usefulness in life, and for a participation in the joys of the redeemed.

As she never separated religion from the active duties and daily enjoyments of life, so in her private journal she has not disconnected these; but while it contains a faithful record of her religious views and feelings, it gives them in connection with the objects and events by which she was influenced in her intercourse with the world around her.

But before making extracts from the journal, it may not be inappropriate to take a brief notice of her earlier religious writings. How early she commenced the practice of committing things to writing for a religious use, is not certainly known; but it was before she felt competent to originate thoughts for this purpose herself, and she therefore made use of the suggestions of others. The selections were her own, and they show a discrimination which is rather unusual in one so young as she was when they were made.

At the commencement of a manuscript which was found after her death, amongst several others of a similar character, is this sentence: "I must remember every day I live that I have a God to glorify—a soul to save."

In the same trembling and unformed hand, were copied with slight alterations, several resolutions of President Edwards. On reading these the first time they met the eye after her death, they seemed to be an epitome of her life, and on this account they are copied here.

1. Resolved never to lose one moment of time, but spend it in the most profitable way I can.

2. Resolved never to do any thing I should be afraid to do were it the last hour of my life.

3. Resolved to think much on all occasions of my dying.

4. Resolved to find out fit objects of my charity.

5. Resolved never to do any thing out of revenge.

6. Resolved that I will so live as I shall wish I had done when I come to die.

7. Resolved to maintain strict temperance in eating and drinking.

8 Resolved never to do any thing which if I should see in another, I should count a just occasion to despise him for, or to think any way the more meanly of him.

9. Resolved whenever I do an evil action, to trace it back till I come to the original cause, and then carefully endeavor to do so no more.

10. Resolved to study the Scriptures so constantly and frequently that I may plainly perceive myself to grow in the knowledge of the same.

11. Resolved never to speak in narrations, any thing but the pure and simple truth.

12. Resolved to strive to my utmost every week to be brought higher in religion than I was the week before.

13. Resolved never to speak evil of any person except some particular good call for it.

14. Resolved never to give over, or in the least to slacken my fight against my corruptions, however unsuccessful I may be.

The foregoing selections are without date, as indeed is the manuscript from which they were taken, but the hand and other circumstances show them to have been written somewhere near the time when she was ten years old. The manuscript appears to have been filled up very slowly, and a considerable improvement is seen in the hand writing and in the Christian character also, as it goes on, or rather there is a more full development of character, both intellectual and moral: but it was not until she was thirteen years old, that she began to date what she wrote. Her first date, in connection with the fact recorded with it, marks a somewhat interesting transaction. On the last page of the manuscript alluded to, in a fair open hand, and standing out prominently so as to prevent the possibility of its escaping the eye of her who penned it, is the following pledge.

"Oct. 19, 1834. I promised that I would read with Miss Chester, my Sunday School Teacher, a chapter every day, beginning at the 7th chapter of Matthew.

MARY E. HAWES."

This promise she doubtless kept for several years, as she often alluded to passages which she was reading in connection with her teacher, and as she had a similar exercise with her own pupils after she became a teacher herself.

As will be seen, she was in the habit of reviewing the year which had just closed, on each successive birth-day. She also did the same at New-Year's; and before each communion season she kept a day of fasting and self examination preparatory to coming to that holy ordinance.

The first extract will be made from a review on the day she was twenty years old.

JOURNAL.

1841. *April* 16*th*. My birth-day! This beautiful sunny spring day makes me twenty years old. Oh, how many are the thoughts which have passed through my mind to-day! The past has been here, and I have stretched my eye to the dim future, as I seem to stand on a mountain in my life, and look back on sunny, lovely childhood, and on my youthful days, half sun, half shade. Oh, how many quiet birth-days have I spent in my much loved home.

Blessings have been strewed thick around my path; *ever strewed* around! Dear, dear home! Friends, much loved parents, religious influences of the purest and holiest kind! New England is my birth place. Here, in the Pilgrim's land, I have ever lived. I do thank Thee, O, my Father, for these thrice blessed privileges.

There is no pageantry nor royal state around my path. There is nothing which the world calls noble or great in this peaceful home; but there is what is infinitely dearer to me, the influence of piety to draw me to the skies; to point me away from this poor fading world, to mansions in Heaven for those who love Christ and His cause. I *know* I am thankful for this, and thankful that so few of earth's temptations are around my way, for O, I have a weak heart, and should have been utterly ruined, had my lot been differently cast.

The past year has been very eventful; the most so of my life. I dare not look forward to what another year may bring. I will trust Him who has so far guided my steps. I will place my hand and heart in *His* care. Why should I fear? Oh yes, the past year has been very eventful indeed. I have had many more thoughts than ever before on every subject, but particularly on religion. And I can humbly say, I do think that this birth-day finds me farther on my course than the last. There is so much sin in my heart that I wonder at myself for allowing that I have any hope, but when I look back at the past year, and watch the workings of my own mind, there does seem to me a great change in my feelings. My views of duty are clearer, and my love of duty stronger. Jesus is my hope and trust, and I think that religion is my daily companion.

I have had *many* thoughts on religious subjects—all the time have been agitating some question of duty, or watching some sin which has crept into my heart and wound itself tightly around my life; and I have had days of mourning because I could not be free from it. I think I have had much religious enjoyment. It seems as though light has been gradually let into my mind, and did I not painfully feel the deceitfulness of the heart, should feel willing to say that an advance does seem to have been made in my views of every thing connected with God, and the Saviour and His cause.

About commencement time, I went to New Haven, and though I passed through many dissipating scenes, I had all the time such a fear of losing myself in them, and of giving way to my worldly feelings, that it did not injure me as much as I feared it would. The week after my return home I count among my most delightful weeks. I had much time alone, and thought I profited by it. From that time my heart was turned more to Christ.

One night during the autumn I remember returning from a party, where the evening had been closed with singing and prayer, and as I laid my head on the pillow, I felt happy. It was the only party I ever returned from feeling better than when I went, and there was nothing of the feverish excitement I had at other times. It does require a great share of grace to attend parties and keep piety warm in the heart.

The latter part of December I had many perplexities. I then passed through a trying season. My wicked heart rose up within me, and there seemed no comfort any where. I felt as though I had no right to call myself a Christian, and I went to work as if I were not one. The fast on the 2d of New Year set me on a little better footing. I thought that my star of hope was beginning to rise, and though the clouds have come over often since, it does seem to grow brighter. My tract district afforded opportunities for doing good, and when the revival commenced I did welcome it with an open heart. Since then I have passed many pleasant hours. Mr. K.'s sermons to Christians I think I derived much good from. My dear ——— can sympathize with me now on religious subjects; and my intercourse with all my dear friends is such as to raise my grovelling heart above this world's delusive excitements.

It was during the midst of the revival that I was called upon to consider a deeply interesting subject, which ever since has absorbed my attention, and agitated me with a thousand hopes and fears. I can trust all in the hands of a merciful Saviour, who has thus far guided me, though in a way I knew not. When I look back on the events of my past life, how plainly can I see the hand of God in every thing! *He*, who has guided me, will still guide, and strengthen me to give up all for Him. I know that as thy day, so shall thy strength be, is a sure promise, and yesterday, while looking round on my home, and my heart was ready to burst at what would probably come in the course of events, and while thinking of my precious friends, and many, many blessings, I could lay all in my Saviour's hand, and let Him dispose of them as He pleases. I do say, "not my will, but thine, O God, be done." And while I yield up *all* to Him, my only desire is to become *wholly* His, and be free from sin.

TO C. C.

HARTFORD, *April* 16*th*, 1841.

"I have been hoping all day, dear C., to find time to write, and think I have fairly secured one half-hour at least, for a little talk with you.

You do not know this is my birth-day. Twenty years of my life have passed—happily, very happily—oh, I dare not look forward. To-day, my thoughts have been half shaded by the uncertain future, and while I have counted over the many happy birth-days which have come and gone, in this my much loved home, I shrink from what the return of this day may bring me. Twenty years! Oh, C., you too have passed them. Can it be that we have bidden adieu to sunny childhood, and are already surrounded with the bewilderment, and bustle, and whirl of life? Yes, we must be borne on by its billows, till death lands us in a world of real existence. I was much interested recently in a sermon of Dr. Cox's, in which he said that *here* we did not live, we only half existed; the other world was to be the scene of our true and perfect existence. The truth of this comes home to my heart every day I live. I never gaze on this earth, lovely and winning as it is, I never listen to the melodies of music, without feeling what is nearly akin to it, the want of perfection *here.* We have each of us, dear C., though in different ways, been led to look to another life, for the development of our being, and happy will it be for us, if these early lessons remain as a talisman to guard us against the many syren voices of this world. O, never, amidst the excitement of life, may we lose the thought of our higher existence.

When passing, an hour since, by an open window through which the south wind blew very fresh, I fancied it bore the fragrance of spring blossoms, and for a moment, May, with all its lovely verdure and opening buds, passed before me; and the vision brought many thoughts of last year. I must live to-day in the past, for I seem standing on one of the mountains of my life, and sunny days of infancy are far behind me, with the half cloud, half sunshine period of youth still nearer, from which I have just emerged; and now, sober and even solemn seems the hue of my coming being. There are some things in my life, which make me look upon it with very different feelings from what I regarded it, when gazing a few years since, in all the buoyancy of youthful gladness, on coming sunny days, in which even the clouds should be of brilliant hues. I do feel, my dear friend, that this life is a deeply solemn concern. 'T is not a merely checkered day, now sun, now shade, but viewed in the light of eternity, it is a period awfully solemn, upon which depend consequences of the deepest moment. O, how could we ever *dream*, my friend? How could we linger mid the fairy lands of earthly fascination, and waste so much of our precious time in beautiful reveries, and entrancing theories, while the preparation for a world of realities was almost neglected? Let us thank God, if indeed we are awakened, and begin with hearts strong in the strength of our Saviour, to press onward in our way to the portals of eternal life.

In our little circle are some mourners, but each of them can say that the afflictions from the hand of their Heavenly Father have been blessed, in drawing away their hearts from this world's good, and leading them to drink at that fountain where eternal life flows full and free. When we see them coming to our quiet gatherings, they who, not a year since, moved in the giddy mazes of the dance, and knelt at the altar of this world's allurement, when their voices mingle with ours in the songs of a holier world, and when we kneel together round the throne of grace, we cannot but send up our thanksgivings, that their trials have taught them the lessons of true religion, and true happiness. Oh, my friend, the blessings from our Heavenly Father's hand have filled us with gratitude—so many that we love are now safe in the fold of Christ, travelling with us to the promised land."

JOURNAL.

Sabbath evening, *April* 18. Here in my quiet seat, I can again spend a pleasant hour alone, with the beautiful blue sky without, and the sunlight on the distant hills. There is something so tranquilizing in such a sky that my feelings are perfectly indescribable while I gaze upon it. Now while I write, there are a few light clouds which add to its beauty, and they are bright with the rays of the sun. Oh, how lovely is this earth! Even under the curse it is full of beauty. But I do not count this tranquilizing feeling as religion. Oh, no. I well know that many may experience the same, and yet have hearts full of corruption and at enmity with that glorious Being who made all things. A natural religion never would do for me. I must be able to call my God a reconciled Father in Christ, before I can hold any true communion with Him in His works. But I do love his works, and I humbly hope that I have loved them lately more because they are from his hand, and that I have in some measure,

"Look'd through nature up to nature's God."

I know the heart is deceitful above all things, yet it is my endeavor to be free from sin in every thing, and to make every thing a means of advancement in holiness. I have, alas, many drawbacks. If it were not for this Saviour, "who can be touched with the feeling of our infirmities," I should sink in despair. My desire is to be wholly renewed. Some things I read this morning in Miss Fry's "Christ our Example," startled me very much, and I only found peace by praying to the Saviour to lead me in the right way.

Monday, 19*th*. While at our devotions this morning, the notes of a robin broke on the still morning air. These early birds of spring, what lessons of piety they are teaching us! All nature smiles around. The hills sleep peacefully in the distant sunshine, and the blue vault of heaven is clear and cloudless, and I am happy—but it is a subdued happiness. I do not think I shall ever again feel the lighthearted buoyancy of youth, or be free and careless again. But I am happy in the thought of doing my Heavenly Father's will, and in trusting my Saviour to lead me into the path of holiness, and far from those sins which make me at times so wretched. Christ strengthens me for every duty.

Evening. Had a gleam of sunshine come across my heart. I felt happy in obeying God, and it left a sweet peace in my heart all the evening.

Tuesday. This afternoon one of my little S. S. scholars came down, and I had a sweet talk with her about prayer, and told her also about my own dear teacher, Mrs. Hovey, and how we always kept the Sabbath twilight as an hour of prayer. It is many a long year since she first proposed our meeting at that time around our Father's throne, to remember each other in our petitions, and it has become the most hallowed and interesting hour to me of the whole week. It is a precious link to bind our hearts, and more precious now that our teacher is in heaven. I proposed that now, as my dear little M. was so soon to be separated from me, that she should remember the hour, and thus we should still be joined in heart around the mercy-seat. Six months' intercourse with this dear little girl, in my class, has twined our hearts closely together, and I have hope that she is a child of God.

Thursday. Our cook is sick, and I have spent all the morning in looking round for another, but returned without having obtained one, and went into the kitchen myself. In the midst of my work came a precious package from New Haven—a little note with an exquisite cushion for a birthday gift, and a long letter from dear Mrs. Fitch, very, very good; but it made me cry hard, and then I prayed for strength. All the day I have been looking to that Saviour, who is able to keep from falling them that trust in Him, and then at my own dark heart, so full of sin, so drawn to this world, that I fear I shall never be able to break away from its enticements, and make an unreserved consecration of my all to Him.

In the afternoon was refreshed by our prayer meeting, and sweet Christian intercourse. These *bonds* will never be sundered. When separated, we can still meet around our Father's throne, and know that the same eternal home awaits us.

O, my Saviour, help me to dwell in the light of thy countenance; to know no will but thine; and to feel happy in yielding all to thy blessed control.

Saturday, 24*th.* I have just returned from the funeral solemnities of the lamented Harrison. At an early hour this morning, the sable robing of the streets commenced. Flags in the harbor were at half-mast, mourning wreaths were around the tower of the Centre Church, and wherever we turned, the appropriate signs of sorrow met our eye. They who, but a month since, rejoiced in the elevation of so good a man to the presidential chair, now appeared in mourning badges among their respective societies. There was something deeply solemn in the sombre light cast on the mourning robes of the church. The speaker's voice seemed to come from a sepulchre of black.

Wednesday, 28*th.* This is indeed a glorious morning—bright with sunlight, and joyous with birds. O, for a heart as full of light as this clear, lovely day! But I am happier than I have been. There is a peace stealing over my mind every day. Is it of heaven? I pray that I may be searched, and that the Spirit may dwell in this dark heart, and the selfishness within be scattered before its gentle influence. Will not this prayer be accepted for Jesus' sake?

Went in last evening to the ——s'. Found the girls preparing to go to E——'s wedding. As I stood in the room, watching the making of their toilette, the thought, that for me, all these scenes were passing away, and that a time would come when I should leave *all*, *all*, filled my heart with mingled emotions. The *parties* I regret not at all; but the social intercourse will go on, friend will meet friend, and the ocean will roll between me and my own home. Yet I was peaceful, and had many sweet thoughts alone, after my return home. A power not my own, kept wrong feelings from arising in my heart.'

"*Friday*, 30*th*. To-day has been, I hope, profitable to me. I have spent it as a day of fasting and examination of heart, before coming to the table of the Lord. I have been looking over the past two months, and think I have been gaining strength and a little light, since the last sacrament. Comparing my feelings with what they then were, I certainly do see an advance. At that time, I felt great trust and confidence in my Saviour; I felt happy also that he was so fitted to be a Saviour to all who put their trust in him. But in thinking of God, I felt almost afraid to think of his sympathizing with us; he seemed so vast, and glorious. My views of him then, were very indistinct. But they have for some time been expanding; and now, the thought that this great Being is my reconciled Father in Christ, is delightful, and the thought of doing his will entirely, is, I humbly hope, the happiness of my life. If I am not deceived, I do turn away from every earthly thing, and make the will of my Father my chief joy; and I humbly trust that I could be happy in it, though all my earthly sources were taken away.

Last night, while here by my window, I had such sweet thoughts, that I felt constrained to say to myself, 'yes, I am a Christian;' and it made the tears come very fast, to think with any certainty, *this may be true;* for all my life long I have feared to admit any degree of hope to my soul. But I do think I love God my Father, and Jesus my Saviour, and I do open my heart to the influences of the Spirit. It does seem to me that this hope is gaining strength.

I am sure I love God, and do really wish to do his will in every thing, and do approve the gospel plan of salvation, and feel earnestly desirous that every selfish and sinful feeling may be taken away, and that every one may know and love and obey God.

My views, too, have changed in regard to enjoying nature, and the various gifts around me. I do not have that same unsatisfied feeling while gazing on the lovely earth. My soul seems to rest in the thought that my Father forms every beauty; and I do not look around with that painful desire I once felt, to have something fill a void which I knew was in my heart, while I enjoy nature more and more every day."

"*Sabbath morning, May 2d.* This holy, blessed morning shines with sweet light on every thing within and around. I have enjoyed a quiet hour in meditation on my Father's goodness, and on the blessedness of his service, and of trusting him. The birds are praising God, and my heart feels like bursting forth in songs of joy. O, this lovely world, what would it be if the smile of God rested on all hearts. This beautiful morning, dear ——— is to profess her love to Christ, and many dear companions are coming forward to take the vows of God upon them. How good is our Saviour! Should the clouds come over the natural earth, as in these changing days they do so often, yet will the Sun of Righteousness remain to cheer our hearts."

TO HER FRIEND, M. S.

Sabbath morning, May 2d.

"My dear M.—I could not think of coming to Sabbath School, without bringing you a little note. How lovely every thing is—full of the beams of divine love—and what gushings of melody come in the songs of the happy birds! Do they not find responses in our hearts, my friend? Never did I feel my heart *leap* in joy as it does this morning. O, M., is it not delightful to live in the service of so good a being as our reconciled Father in Christ? Is it not good to yield all to his blessed control, and know no will but his? Surely there is more blessedness in doing his will, than in any thing else that this life can yield us. If the few scattering joys which have entered our benighted hearts *here*, make us so happy, what must the full glory of that life be, where no sin can obstruct the gushings of peace and joy! I write unconnectedly, dear M., for my heart is so full I cannot give expression to what I would say. I never thought that I could be so peaceful in the service of God, nor have such a sweet, tranquil frame of mind, as I have enjoyed for a few days past. Now I give up every doubt and fear, and trusting only in my Saviour, am willing, I humbly hope, to do all he appoints. Dear M., I did not mean to occupy this note with my own feelings, but they would come out. O, to sing praises to our Saviour! He who has redeemed us from our sins, and given to us the hope of eternal life! But the bell rings, and I must close."

JOURNAL.

"*Seven o'clock, P. M.* I must note down what a sweet, composed, happy day I have had. It was indeed sweet to come with so many dear friends to Christ's table. I can truly say that it has been one of my most peaceful days. *All* is given up to God, and my heart does humbly rest in him, and trust in that Saviour who will never leave nor forsake those who come to him. I have abundant reason to trust him. Yes, O yes; and my heart is grateful; of this I am certain—and though the clouds come over my soul, and sins perplex and distress, and though trials press on every side, yet can I say '*my heart is fixed*,' and I will trust him forever."

"*Sabbath, May 9th.* This is a morning for devout praise. Surely, grateful incense should ascend from every heart to-day. I love to think that while I sit at my window, and drink in the varied beauties of this lovely hour, there are many, in their quiet rooms, who now are sending up to heaven the glad thanksgiving of hearts full of love to God. All nature is teeming with life and joy, and thrice happy are they whose minds are attuned to participate in the gladness of gushing melody from bird and bee. Again the sunlight lies on the fresh green grass and gentle hillside, and the blossoms smile in the light of this glorious morning, and the notes of the sweet robin meet my ear. I love *all*, more and more, every day, and humbly hope I love and adore the Father of all. I think as my love of heavenly things increases, so also does my love of this beautiful creation.

There was formerly, when I drank in the beauty of nature, such an under current of sadness, whence it came I know not, and such a feeling of oppression, as if so much beauty were painful, that my saddest hours were, when gazing on scenes like this before me. It was an unsatisfied mind, looking in vain for something to fill the void; and I did not then realize, as I do now, that it was a *sense* of God's love that was wanting. I thought the feeling constitutional, for as it was in nature, so it was in every thing else that I enjoyed; it awoke the same minor chords to vibrate in my heart. It is not all gone now, but it is so far diminished, that a sweet peace comes over my mind, and a little season alone, where nature smiles, draws my heart right to God, and I go away satisfied and tranquil.

I feel happy, this morning, to leave myself and my dear friends, all in God's hands. There is mercy through Christ. We can trust this good Saviour."

"*Noon.* It is a sweet Sabbath noon-tide, quiet and warm, and the bees are lulling us with their hum around the fragrant cherry blossoms, and the clear liquid notes of a bird, break now and then on the stillness.

This morning, my father went to the Sunday School. After opening it with prayer, he made a few remarks, at the close of which he spoke of the book which was ever open to our view, reading us lessons of love and truth from its beautiful pages. C.* made me understand that she thought it was the book of nature; and I was pleased that she knew so readily. My father's prayers, both at Sabbath School, and afterwards at church, were adapted to this lovely spring day. Dear C. is, I trust, a Christian. It is sweet to have one dear child safe in the fold of the Saviour."

TO E.†

Sabbath evening, May 9th, 1841.

"I hope, my dear E., that this beautiful Sabbath has put many sweet thoughts into your mind, and led you to love our Father in Heaven, with a warm and confiding

* One of the little girls in her class.

† A young friend, in whose spiritual welfare she felt a deep interest.

love. How sweetly the beams of his goodness meet us on every side. Free as the air we breathe, is the love which comes from our God.

Think, my dear E., that this glorious Being, who made the stars in such countless numbers, who keeps them all in their places, who made the birds, too, and each little insect that flies in the sunlight, and keeps them all, watching and guarding them, will also watch over and guard you. Oh, yes,—he has a Father's heart, and not one who lifts even a trembling voice to him will he neglect. He listens to the prayer of the most feeble and timid, and the moment a poor wanderer returns to him, he meets him with a Father's blessing.

Think of that blessed Saviour, who 'though he was rich, for our sakes became poor.' Why did he leave his glorious home, and come to this earth to suffer so long a time, and die in so much agony? Oh, my dear E., we know very well that it was to save us from the misery and the power of sin. He saw us while we were far from God, and in infinite love he came to draw us back to him. Do you know that verse,

'Jesus saw me when a stranger,
  Wand'ring from the fold of God,
He to save my soul from danger,
  Interposed his precious blood.'

My dear E., hear the voice of that Saviour calling you to him. Go and give him your heart—give him the soul he died to save. He ransomed it from eternal death, not with silver, nor gold, nor the precious things of this world, but with a price infinitely more costly, even the blood which he shed on the cross.

Will you not give him your whole heart? And then

your Father in Heaven will love you for Jesus' sake, and will own you as his dear child. He will guide you safely through this life, and should your way ever become dark, yet his hand will lead you on, and bring you at last to that peaceful home where you will join in singing anthems of praise 'to him who hath loved us and given himself to die for us.' No sin, no sorrow can enter that home. *There* our Saviour dwells with all his faithful friends. Many are there whom we have known and loved, and he who guided them safely, will also guide us. Let us go, dear E., together, to that promised land. Jesus will lead us through every temptation. Why should we have any fear when we know that God will help us? Do you know that sweet verse in Isaiah xli. 13: 'I the Lord thy God will hold thy right hand, saying unto thee, fear not; I will help thee.'

Write me an answer, Dear E., and believe me ever your affectionate friend."

A delightful response came back to this note, showing that the individual to whom it was addressed, was already beginning to feel an interest in the things of religion. Mary bore this young friend constantly upon her heart, and there was ever after a free interchange between them of thoughts and feelings on the subject of personal religion, which was interrupted only by death.

"*Saturday, May* 29. 'O sunshine and fair earth,' I say, every time the morning breaks in its freshness. Day and night are telling the same story of love and joy, which, like a gushing fountain, pervades all nature. Morning is for joy and leaping of heart, and evening is for calm and gentle thoughts, but both tell the same tale of a Father in Heaven, ever good and kind.

Tuesday, May 25, was a delightful day. I was in

Farmington on a visit to C. C. We went at 11 o'clock, to Mr. N.'s, where we passed a lovely time, revelling in wood and ravine, and gathering wild flowers in the glen. It is a paradise on earth. The house and grounds are perfect. And there are sweet, Christian hearts, to enjoy God's rich favors there. When I look at them, and feel how much they are enjoying, there is no heart sickness about it, for I know that the angel of peace has spread his wing over their dwelling, and that the other world will but continue and increase their happiness, for its source is in God."

TO C. C.

FIRST DAY OF SUMMER, 1841.

HARTFORD, *Tuesday*, 3, P. M.

"Here I am, dear C., at home, and you are again in your school, and the visit to which we looked forward for so many months, is now in the past, and its events are living only in our memories. But it is a sweet visit to remember, and I love to call up each day, and live it over again. There were many things in it, which can furnish fruitful themes for our meditation. I am glad that we spent the time as we did, for though I brought back to Hartford nearly all the difficulties I carried away, yet I returned with a better heart for conquering them, and have already begun to carry into execution some plans for preserving a quiet, trustful spirit. I feel that I am but just awaking from my childhood's dreams; that I have every thing yet to learn, and all my strength to gain.

My dear C., I count among my chief blessings, that we are permitted to know each other on earth, and to form a friendship which I hope eternity will only strengthen. In coming years, our paths may be widely separated, and our interchanges of feeling be only few. But it will matter little to us, for we can still pray for each other at our

Father's throne, and no distance can ever break the bond which unites us. And while we are steadily pursuing the way our Saviour has marked out, we can look forward to a meeting beyond this life—and O, that meeting! Friend meeting friend, around the throne of God and the Lamb! *There* we can all recount the way in which our God has led us. It overwhelms me to think of it. Many an event now unthought of will pass, before that meeting comes. And our characters, too, will not they have changed? Shall we be the same beings, with hopes, desires, and joys? And shall we recognize each other as friends, who began existence almost together—who wept and rejoiced together in youth?

June 8th. My dear friend, is there not a perfect luxury in these soft summer days? How beautiful every thing is! Praise and thanksgiving, gushing forth in one fountain!—and are not our hearts tranquil? I wish we could spend these lovely evenings together. The foliage is more beautiful here than ever before, and the city has looked like a garden, as I have stood by the window and seen it bathed in moonlight. To me, there is something fearfully solemn in a winter moonlight upon a city; when the din of daily labor has ceased, and a death-like stillness reigns over all the abodes of men—when the spires rise to heaven in their lonely majesty, and the moon passes calmly on her way, over dwellings which hide aching and weary hearts. But though the solemnity remains in the summer time, yet it is of a softer kind, and not what makes me hold my breath.

We had a sweet Sabbath twilight. What a relief it is to meet around our Father's throne."

JOURNAL.

"*Sabbath, June 6th.* My dear C. and I, engaged in a sacred promise, to spend the twilight hour in prayer for three dear friends. May God hear, and answer, and continue to us a praying spirit. The Sabbath twilight is peculiarly dear. It is my sweetest hour."

"*Wednesday, June* 16*th.* Here, by my own window, I have passed a quiet season, and now in these few moments, I must recall the days that are wanting in my journal. So many and so varied have been the scenes of the past weeks, that I have longed to note them down. Perhaps it is best that I am obliged to hurry them over, lest they assume too much importance in my mind."

"*Sabbath, June* 20*th.* Once more alone in my favorite seat, with a sweet Sabbath to reflect upon. Its hours have passed very calmly, and I love to think of the prayers, and sermons, and of my Sabbath-school class. I have, indeed, many sins to mourn over—many wandering thoughts have crept into my mind, and till this weary body of sin is cast off, they will, I fear, ever trouble me. O, I am frail, and sin clings to me; but I can pray and trust in God.

These blessed Sabbath services are my life. May I grow by them in every grace; casting off selfishness, and living to my Father in Heaven. My dear father's sermons and prayers have been refreshing and strengthening to me; lifting my heart above this world. I started with glad surprise when he read the closing hymn. I had been thinking of it during the afternoon, as appropriate. Such pleasant coincidences often occur. My favorite it has long been. 'Nor eye hath seen nor ear hath heard.'

I have a peace this summer such as I never felt before. There are indeed many things without, which do try me not a little. It is a very eventful season, and will, in all probability, decide the destiny of my life. These passing events bring with them many perplexities and trials, which would weigh me down, if I could not look to God and say, 'Thy will be done.' I am pondering many things, and there is a ceaseless rush of thought, which sometimes makes my brain almost wild. And then I have so many duties, that my time is more than occupied—and I have sin and selfishness to subdue within, for my heart is revealing its dreadful corruptions—and I have friends to pray for, whose condition weighs on my spirit—but in the midst of it all, I think I can trust in God, and leave all with him.

I do hope that I live to do his holy will. It is my desire ever to wait on him as *Father*, *Saviour* and *Sanctifier*—to take every duty as it comes up before me, with an earnest desire to do God's will in it—to bear every trial, and enjoy every blessing, in such a manner as will fit me for the other world, whenever God may see fit to call me from this.

Dear Madam Feller has been here during the last week. It was my privilege to see her a great deal. There is a holy influence constantly around her. It is seen in every glance of her eye, and felt in every tone of her voice. She has given up all to God, and now she wants nothing. May not I have the same self-consecration, and give up all to my Father's blessed service? A vacant seat in the carriage which took Madam F. to Wethersfield, it was my privilege to occupy. In spite of our different languages, we contrived to understand each other—talked with eyes, and any way. Returned home feeling as though I had been in the world of angels, so much of heaven breathes in all that surrounds her."

"*Wednesday*, 23*d*. On Friday, walked out to Mrs. C.'s, on the hill. We had been invited there to tea. It was a beautiful evening, and the grounds about the house are uncommonly fine—such a profusion of shrubbery, and so many sweet flowers. But I went, inwardly regretting the loss of my quiet twilight hour; yet I did spend a far sweeter one, than I should have dared to hope for at home. After tea we walked around, and while I lingered alone, *there*, beneath the softest blush of a summer sky, and the fading light of day in the west, I passed some of the calmest and most delightful moments I ever spent. My heart could go up silently to the throne of God, and in Jesus' name, I could pray for all who were then in my heart. I thought of the lines,

> 'Or if 'tis e'en denied then
> In solitude to pray,' &c.

and particularly of this verse,

> 'E'en then the silent breathing
> Of the spirit raised above,
> Will reach that throne of glory
> Which is mercy, truth and love.'"

FARMINGTON, *June* 26*th.*

"Here, in this lovely village, with the meadow land stretching its green expanse before me, spotted with its deep, dark groves, and the misty mountains lining the horizon—here I am, really looking upon it—not dreaming of its beauties—but here at my dearly loved window in Mr. N.'s mansion. Oh, how I should love each tree and hillside, from this window, if it were my own home. I should love to watch each shadow descending from the mountains, and veiling those dark woods. How the whispering breeze, floating o'er these fairy meadows, and bending the soft long grass, would speak in its soothing tones to my heart. What a variety of lessons could I learn from every look of nature. I have seen the morning sun bursting forth in a flood of golden light, upon mountain, wood and meadow, until every thing glowed in beauty. And I have seen the sun go quietly to rest, and a sweet dewy stillness gather over hill and valley; and the stars have looked down in their mild light, and the moon in her calm radiance, has shone on a scene of loveliness, rivaling even the heavens, in its silent glory. I have seen nature here in all her moods, joyous and sad, wild and tranquil, drear and beautiful—shadow and sunlight coming and going, and it has all spoken with a meaning to my heart. I should love it all too well, this 'sunshine and fair earth,' did I not daily pray that its lessons might point me to the skies. They must not speak again of earth's dreamy, fevered enchantments; no, these lovely scenes must lead my heart through nature to its God.

It is two years since I knew this lovely spot, and I have passed many a pleasant hour since then in this dear family. Sweet intercourse I have had with friends here. Charley glads me with his merry frolics. But these quiet moments by my own window, will be my last, for before the sun has gone down I shall be in my own dear home."

HARTFORD, *June* 27.

"*Sabbath evening.* Again in my own precious home, and though wearied in mind and body, I am thankful for a quiet heart. It has been a very warm, damp day. One of those dreamy days, if I were of a mind to dream, but I am not. O, no. There is too much to be done in this world to leave room for dreams. There is a continual conflict to be carried on with sins—a continual watching and striving against them, and need of continued effort, and much earnest prayer for the promotion of holiness in our world. Surely there is enough to do. Oh, for strength, and the willing mind. God will give both, if we only wait humbly on him."

"*June* 28*th.* While at Farmington, I read Byron. I had many thoughts about reading his works; but I wished to know him, that I might be better able to influence some, who love him, and Moore, and Shiller, too well. I prayed to know what was duty—so when dozing time came, after dinner, while all was still, I took down 'Childe Harold.' I read it calmly, for I could do it then—once, it would have made my brain wild. There are some glorious things in it; but through the whole, sweeps the same dark current of thought and feeling. It is fearful to think of his mind enlightened by no ray from heaven; thrilling only to such themes as are natural to ruined, apostate man, brooding over the dark and troubled scenes of earth, and madly rushing on to ruin, with the wreck of faculties, which, had they been rightly directed, would have elevated him high in the scale of being. I read the first two Cantos, after dinner, and each day after, while all was still at the same hour, I made myself familiar, not only with Childe Harold, but many other of his pieces."

"*Friday, July 2d.* I am thankful in the prospect of a few quiet hours, for I need them very much to arrange my scattered thoughts, and know where I am. And first I must take some note of those passing days.

On Tuesday afternoon, I went with a party to the tower. Had a most lovely time, and enjoyed it more than any other excursion I had made there. I have it all in my memory, for it touched too many chords within, to be soon forgotten—but no words can describe the beauty of the scene.

Sweet and calm were my thoughts, almost all the time. I felt free, and happy as a bird. Even the dream-like clouds which lay pillowing in the far north, did not awaken the same feelings of sadness they would once have done. The far off hills, so dim and shadowy, and the sky, stooping so softly down to meet them, as seen from the tower, almost took away my breath.

I had a sweet time down by the boat-house, just at sunset. Some had left it, and were walking in other parts of the grounds, and the few who remained were quiet with the gathering repose of nature. I stood alone by the lake, and watched the thick foliage around it, fringed with the last golden light. The waters were sleeping calmly beneath the o'ershadowing mountains, and I blessed my Father in Heaven for the beauty there is in our fair earth, and holy thoughts of his love came floating into my mind. I was not troubled with vanity, as I had formerly been on such occasions; and yet I feel almost afraid to say so, for I know the same selfish feelings remain, yet they do not give me so much trouble, nor occasion, as they once did, such a ceaseless inquietude within. I know, that if I do God's will, that is all that is of importance to me. I am happy for the visitings of such thoughts, for they help me to increase in my desires for others' happiness, and to put down that towering selfishness, which has gained such mastery over me. A bright moon lighted our way home, where we found ourselves safe at ten o'clock. I thanked God for all my blessings.

A bright moon all this week has been shining, and I have sat alone a few moments every night, that the calm stillness of all nature might speak holy thoughts to me; and I have been, I fear, reading the book of nature more than the book of grace. Oh, there will come a dearth to my soul, if I do not awake.

Next Sabbath is our communion, and my heart is sad to think I have improved so little in these two months. There has been a happy arrangement of things, by which I am able to spend this morning in quiet, for oh, my heart aches, it is so out of order, and I need time to think. I must see where I am. Oh, my Father, wilt thou send thy

Spirit to search me and take away my sins, that I may renew my covenant with thee, and be truly thy child.

During the past two months, there has been increasing distractedness, owing to the varied scenes which summer brings. I thought much of this in the spring, and prayed that this spirit of the world might not creep in with the return of warm days of luxury and beauty.

I feel that I have less of it this season than ever before. It seems less a matter of importance what the world thinks of me, or how I stand in the estimation of those around me in a mere worldly point of view.

Last summer I pined to mingle more in society, and it made me unhappy to see how much I was shut out from it. It seemed to me that comparatively few cared to make my acquaintance. This mortified my vanity, and I was continually thinking of it, and turning it over in my mind. I could not persuade myself that this sensitiveness was wrong; for I knew that it was not mere worldly society, nor worldly indulgencies which I desired; but it was that I might mingle in general society, as the other girls did.* I reasoned thus with myself:—'If it were for sinful things

* Several things contributed at the time alluded to, to exclude her somewhat from general society. Among these, the principal was the lateness of the hour when parties broke up. Her father was an advocate for seasonable hours, and was exceedingly annoyed by any irregularities either in rising or retiring, which broke in upon family order, or interrupted the regular studies and duties of the day. The habits of society, in this respect, were at variance with his principles. If she attended parties, therefore, she must do so at the expense of incommoding her father. If she retired from them altogether, she must do so at the risk of losing her friends. This for a time occasioned her much perplexity, and some real suffering. She knew her father had no wish to exclude her from society; on the contrary, that he chose to have her mingle freely with her young friends, and participate with them in all the appropriate enjoyments of social intercourse. But she quickly found the impracticability of doing this, and at the same time of accommodating herself to his hours. She therefore made up her mind to retire from late social circles altogether. As a consequence of doing so, she was dropped from the acquaintance and attention of some, and those who sought intercourse with her, were such as truly valued her society and friendship: and precious indeed to her was this choice circle of friends.

that I pined, it would be wrong, but how could I feel otherwise than sad, when my days passed comparatively in solitude?'

I know that I am fitted to enjoy life, to mingle in all the interchanges of friendship, and to participate in the various scenes which help to form the characters of my friends; but I now see, that the feelings which I had last summer, were very wrong. I forgot the blessings which God was then showering on my path—those sweet blessings which have been mine for years—and the things which he withheld were not what I needed. They would have drawn away my heart from him. It was best I should be without them. How foolish and wicked have been those repinings! What blessings I have enjoyed! The only thing I can weep about now, is my poor improvement of them. My situation is just the one for the improvement of my mind, my heart, and my capacities for usefulness. I have blessings all around, if I only knew how to avail myself of them. I have enjoyed many calm hours alone, and have felt my heart growing better by them, and also by the precious Sabbaths I have had given me. And then I have communion with sweet friends—oh, so sweet, that I can only find relief for my happiness, by thanking God for them. Then, I have continued opportunities for usefulness. My cup runneth over. What shall I do? It seems as though my Heavenly Father is leading me to him; and in every way of love he can devise, is drawing this stubborn, ungrateful, selfish spirit to himself.

I have no more of society than I had last summer, but I have learned to look for happiness in another channel. And *here* I am in danger—I feel it. I am in danger on many accounts: and first, of being *self-satisfied*—of thinking *I have something within that lives without the world's breath.* This is being *puffed up.* I may thank God that he gives me grace to do so, but any thing like pride will ruin all peace. I am thankful that I have sources within my heart, of happiness. But *here* another trouble meets me. I ask myself whence is this happiness? Comes it from doing God's will? Does it proceed from a consecration to the Saviour? Or is it from a feeling within, which is merely a kind of poetic religion? A meditative pleasant communion with natural beauties? If this be the case, then my peace rests on no safe foundation. Lately I have been troubled about this; and it requires my serious attention. I do not think that my religion is mere poetry, but I fear it may all run away in feeling, without producing any or but little good effect. I must guard against this.

I have many sins—God only knows how many—sins of vanity and selfishness, of listlessness, waste of time, and worldly-mindedness—sins, too, of *unquiet*—for I feel that every moment of *unrest*, that I allow, is a sin. And I could not have believed it possible that I should acknowledge this. I said, Christian principle does not take away feeling, and so long as we are in a state of discipline, our feelings must be often sad and gloomy—and so I sometimes allowed a melancholy to steal over my spirit. But this was wrong, and against the spirit of the Bible. Though I now feel that religion, so far from taking away feeling, only increases it, yet I draw a different conclusion from what I once did. The heart in which the love of God reigns, may feel, and deeply, too, the trials which here come alike to all; but there will be in the mind of such a person, a peace, which as 'an anchor to the soul, sure and steadfast,' will keep it unmoved amidst assailing temptations.

I have had during the past two months, many duties, and I have felt all along too hurried to perform them well, and I am resolved to turn over a new leaf, and keep calm.

I think I have wasted many moments in wandering

thoughts during my times of devotion, making these seasons less profitable than they would otherwise have been.

I have loved to pray and meditate; but has it been in a right manner? In all my feelings, desires and plans, am I sure that the glory of God is my end? Have I engaged in these for myself, or because I love Jesus, and have consecrated all to him? These are solemn questions, and I will try to answer them candidly to my own heart, and pray for God's blessing, that wherein I sin, the blood of Jesus may cleanse it away, that so I may indeed do the whole will of God.

I have not enjoyed the same sweet thoughts to-day that I had before the last communion. I have not had that tender spirit—but now I pray for it. May the world be far away, and holy things occupy my mind. And now I commit myself to God. May I have a calm Sabbath, and be in a state of preparation for its holy ordinances. May vanity and selfishness be far away, and I entirely devoted to my Father and Saviour."

"*Sabbath noon, July 4th.* I have just returned from a sweet season, for which my heart blesses God, my Saviour. O, these are refreshing seasons in our pilgrimage. They come as gleams to our path, even now, though far from our Father's home. He sends his love to us, and here in this lower world, we may sing the songs of the redeemed. This is a day to be remembered. How sweet, how joyful, to rest my all on Jesus, to lean on him, and know no fear. *Here* I can praise him only faintly. In that day, when this mortal robe is cast aside, I will raise my voice in a ceaseless song of gratitude—'Unto Him who hath loved us, and given himself to die for us.'

Last communion, I prayed that three dear friends might, ere the day should come again, be safe in the fold of Christ.

That prayer has often been renewed since, and yet this day is here, and finds them still strangers to God. But I know not what may be now passing in their minds. Perhaps some gleam of truth may have entered their hearts, and be secretly at work within them. Jesus has died for them, and I will still pray, that for his sake, they may be made free from sin, and heirs of everlasting life.

This day, at communion, I thought of four things which deserved special notice, and I resolved to do them during the coming two months. And first of all, to endeavor to keep a heart free from all disquiet, humbly doing God's will, and leaning on the Saviour. Then to converse more on heavenly things with all my friends, particularly those a little younger than myself. Then to continue to pray for the same dear friends who have been on my heart for a long time, and to add one more to the number. And lastly I made a general resolution, to be active in every way of doing good, particularly in my class and tract district."

"*July* 11.—*Morning.* Our sweet Sabbath is again here. I have no words for the loveliness of these days. Their beauty refreshes my soul, and leads me to God. Many things have been going on in my inner world the past week, and I have needed much grace to meet its duties, and to overcome this heart of evil, which I bear so continually about. O, when shall I be free from this body of sin? When will the world cease to have power over me? I thank God, that in the midst of much sin, I have been able to look to him, and my prayers have been answered. But I feel the earthliness of this heart more and more. It is too strong for me; yet I will trust in God."

"*July* 12. Last Monday was the Temperance celebration. I sat alone in the orchestra till the procession entered the church. It was truly a grand and interesting sight. In the procession were the different societies of the city. Each wore appropriate badges, and carried beautiful banners. There was the 'Juvenile,' and the 'Young Men's Society,' and the 'Catholic;' but what interested me most, was the 'Washington Society'—to see those rising from the chains of intemperance, and struggling to be free men again."

"*Thursday*, 15*th*. I did enjoy yesterday. Had a delightful ride to the tower through Farmington. Our conversation was quite lively, though not improperly so. All of us were Christians, and in such a party there is always a certain balance, which keeps us from going too far. From Farmington, we went through Avon, to the mountain. That mountain road, sweeping through those groves, and commanding a view of the valleys beyond, is very fine. There were clouds in the sky—but they added a majesty to the scene. The stillness of the lake before the gathering storm, spread quiet over my heart also. We sat by the shore, and woke the echoes by a few pensive strains, and then the rain came, and we ran for our carriage, which was at some distance; but we were not much wet. The locusts, which line the avenue to the boat-house, give the grounds quite an eastern look—and I always think of the feathery trees, which raise their heads in far-off sunny climes, when I see them. Rode home in a thunder storm. It was not a wild and fearful one, and in our carriage we did not feel it much."

"*Saturday evening*, 18*th*. God has been showing me this vile heart of pride and selfishness, and I have felt humbled by it. May it lead me to make exertions for my friends, not in a spirit of selfishness, but in a true desire for

God's glory. My only wish with regard to myself is, that I may be willing to be nothing, and to have God *all.* Have had a deeply interesting talk with F., for whom I cease not to pray. Many things have come to my knowledge about him, and I am hoping and trembling. There will be revelations made on the hills of light, of which we do not now dream; revelations which will show the everlasting, unchanging love and faithfulness of God our Saviour, who will not let us go, but will watch over and guide until we are safe in the path of life. I will still pray, and will not cease."

TO E.,

THE YOUNG FRIEND TO WHOM A NOTE WAS ADDRESSED, MAY 9th.

July 27th, 1841.

"I could wish, my dear E., that I had time for many words this morning, for I love to write to you very much. You seem discouraged, my dear girl, because you do not always keep your resolutions. But you must not feel so. Try again—try very often, and look to your Saviour, who will certainly help you to overcome every wrong feeling. Oh, do not feel as though you should fail. Is not Jesus Christ stronger than your sins? Cannot he help you to triumph over them? What a blessing it is that he has touched your heart with sorrow for them. If you repent, he will take them away, and will make your heart happy, by shedding abroad his love there.

You ask, dear E., if it was wrong for you to pray about the things you did. Oh, no. Go to your Father in Heaven, and tell him all your feelings, and pray about every sorrow you have, and thank him for every joy, and ask him for what you wish—only say just as Jesus did, 'Thy will be done.' Dear E., you cannot please him more than by doing so. Satan and sin, have driven us away from our

Father, and they would keep us away if they could; but he calls us to come home to him, and be his dear children, and hold that sweet intercourse with him, which children may. Therefore you may go without fear, and in Jesus' name, may lift up your heart to him at all times. And what a blessing! In our waking hours, and in the quiet night, and when the morning dawns, and when we walk amidst the beautiful scenes of nature, we may lift up our hearts in prayer to that good Being, who is ever near us.

And now, my dear E., I must close. Often I pray for you, that God would give you strength to go on in the right path. May you never grow weary in well doing, is the prayer of your sincere friend, M."

TO C. C.

HARTFORD, *Wednesday evening*, *July* 28, 1841.

"Dear C. I scarcely know where to begin, among the multiplicity of interesting topics which have accumulated the past weeks. I have thought out many things, and have longed to seize my pen, but, I blush to say it, I am hurried as ever in this hurrying world. O, if I only accomplished any thing! But I *am* going to do two things, and if one was not that I am to spend a week at the sea-side immediately, I should not be writing you in so anti-puritanical a time as I now am.

I do thank you ten thousand times for your letter. I would gladly take each separate topic, and tell you of the thoughts it has occasioned. When I return, I shall enjoy writing to you. But you are wondering why I should think of being away just now. It could not be avoided. Miss B., one of Mr. Brace's teachers, is obliged to leave town for a few weeks, and it was impossible to get any one to take her place, and I did consent, though with much fear and trembling, to go into the school during her absence.

As my health is not perfectly equal to it, my friends are going to send me on Friday to the sea-side. I shall return in time to commence my new duties on the second Monday in August. O, C., I dare not speak of it. I did but exist before; and those long hours in school, teaching Butler and Algebra to girls older than I am! But it will have an end. If I live through it all, then I will talk about it.

I have no words to tell you of my joy at the tidings of J. N.* Such an event can only be prayed and rejoiced over with tears of gratitude. Surely we can trust and pray with assurance now. If I had seen you a day later than Wednesday, I could have told you very much. Perhaps I had then too many hopes. Yet I was never so overcome as on that day, with the thought of God's faithful love to the poor wandering children of this world, seeking them out, and leading them in paths they know not, till he brings them to that path which conducts safely home.

Pray, dear C., that my heart may be fixed on the Saviour—that I may listen all the time to the teachings of the Spirit. I dread the water-side for fear of the company; and yet I am looking forward with longing delight to days spent 'where the glad sea winds are blowing,' and the blue water sweeps its waves among the rocks. I am going to Sachem's Head, which is said to be delightful this season. On my return, I shall try to stop a day in New Haven, for my dear J. is going south. I cannot bear to think of her leaving us. But I must look forward now to heaven, as the place where dear friends can enjoy intercourse, which must be denied here."

JOURNAL.

"*Sunday evening, August 8th.* Here am I again in my own home, with my beloved friends, and by my quiet win-

* A young friend who had just become a Christian.

dow I am spending these last holy hours of another Sabbath. Another week has past, full of events, and full of subjects for remembrance and prayer. My health is improved by the jaunt, and my heart is, I trust, somewhat improved by the seasons of devotion I have enjoyed at the 'Head.'

This morning I awoke early, and a strange sadness hanging over me for which I could not account, filled me with perplexity. Have prayed much all day for absent ones, and have been ready to ask how I knew that any of my prayers would be answered. But I will always pray and trust in God. Let not my eye become dim nor my steps grow faint. What I need is perseverance. Help me, O my Saviour, to grow in this grace. I want more enlarged views. I want to act from deep, warm principles of piety in every thing. But I will work yet more hard. I will trust in God for sanctification by the Spirit, and will give up all my interests to Him who *doeth all things right.* May I remember that *it is mine to trust and do His will.*"

TO M.

"*August* 21*st.* It was my earnest desire, my precious friend, to answer your letter immediately on its reception, and nothing but the most urgent duties could have prevented my doing this sooner. How my heart did rejoice in your letter. Dear M., we have both been led, though by different ways, to change our views very much with regard to this life, and the life beyond the grave. Let us praise our God and Father that he has inclined us to look away from ourselves to the interests of his glorious kingdom,—let us thank Him that he has enabled us to feel that it is a privilege to live only to do His will, by trying to advance the cause of our Saviour, in this ruined world. O my friend, could we sit down together for an hour, we should find themes enough for conversation. If this blessing is denied us here, yet in Heaven we can "Remember all the way that God has led us." When I think of God, and of Jesus, and of the kingdom of holiness which is arising over the ruins of the fall; when I think of that home, in which all the redeemed of the Lord will at last be gathered together, my heart is too full for words. O, these are themes which awaken overwhelming emotions. Does it not seem, dear M., as though you cannot rejoice enough over the change which has taken place in our hearts—that we who were once strangers, are now children of a Father infinite in every perfection that can be conceived? And when we think of our dear friends, coming back one after another from their wanderings, and received into the kingdom of love and peace, have we not cause for the deepest joy?

I am writing, dear M., on the very table we used together so long, and in the room we called ours for many a day. Like a dream those days have passed, and still like dreams will the remainder go, but there is a world where existence will be dream-like no longer. *There* every thing is real, and for that reality I long more and more every day.

Friday evening, August 27th. You see I write journal fashion, according to my usual plan, dear M., for I cannot command any length of time, as I am at present in school. Miss B. needed a little vacation, and wished me to take her place in the Seminary for a few weeks; so I am installed teacher of eight classes, and though I find it very fatiguing, I like it better than I feared I should.

My time this summer is passing most delightfully. I think I can call it the happiest in my life. Every day, I have enjoyed as it passed. I often ask myself why I am so happy, and I hope I know the reason; and that it is based on a foundation which the changing pleasures of this world cannot remove. I shrink from presumption, but I feel that I should be grateful for the quiet heart God has given me during the past months; so that the enjoyments of life have been gilded by a brightening radiance, and its sorrows robbed of their gloom.

Were you here this evening, by my side, in this still chamber, which has been the scene of many a long communing, in the days that are gone, we would talk of all the way through which we have passed, and bless God for that guiding hand which has led us on till now. As we go on in life, how many dark dispensations are cleared up—how often is the veil lifted from many a mysterious and trying providence! I bless God that I can trust Him. In all His ways He doeth rightly. And in Heaven, if not here, we shall know the reason for every discipline we receive at our Father's hand.

When I think of you, my precious sister, I have such yearnings of heart to see you, that I can scarcely be satisfied. O that we might weep together over your sorrows, and rejoice together over the consolations of the precious Gospel. There is comfort *there.* O, M., I know that you feel it. It is not mere words when you say that God, your Heavenly Father, supports you. I praise him that you know in your own experience what it is to lean on His Almighty arm. No other comfort can compare with this. God only knows how to support the stricken soul. Is it not sweet to look to Him as Father, Saviour and Sanctifier—to feel that He is doing all that infinite love and wisdom dictates—to trust Him in all His ways? That sweet word *trust*, yes, it tells all.

Keep, dear M., that same confiding spirit even to the end, do the will of your Saviour *here* in this world, and peace and eternal blessedness will be yours. There is 'no wave of trouble' to roll over the spirit once safe in its home. Do you remember the song we used to sing, called the 'home of the soul?' How much more do our hearts now feel the sweetness of looking forward to such a home, than when we sang it in those days when we could not feel our need of it? It is not till the changes of life show us the emptiness of earthly bliss, that we turn with longing eyes to that world where our Father and our Saviour dwell. An Infinite Being can alone satisfy our spirits, but *there* we shall find an overflowing fountain of blessedness.

You must not wonder, dear M., that I speak so much of my feelings being changed. No deep affliction like yours has sobered my views of life, and yet those views are so different from what they once were, that I am disposed at times to doubt my personal identity. We are led in different ways to place our trust on what is the only sure foundation; and though it be through dark paths, yet the end is bright.

I rejoice, my precious sister, in the interest you feel in all that concerns the kingdom of our Saviour in this fallen world. We have given ourselves to the cause of Zion. There are our dearest interests, and though we work in different parts, it is the same vineyard. We are beneath the care of the same leader. We are passing to the same gathering place, the gathering place of all the redeemed. There are celestial lands before us. Do not the gleams from the Heavenly Temple come down even now to gild our path? Cannot we catch some strains from the angel choirs above to cheer us on our course? It is sweet to join our interests with the interests of the Church of Christ. Let us, dear M., strive to look more and more away from ourselves, that we may feel and labor for the many who are perishing in their sins. I want more of the spirit of Christ, that I may feel for every being upon the face of the earth. Are we not all brethren? Is not the soul of each infinitely precious? O, my friend, if our hearts are touched with compassion for the wanderers from their Father, let us thank God, and do all we can to lead them back. Blessed be His name that we may feel for them, and that our poor labors may receive a blessing. How sweet a privilege it is to bear our dear ones to the throne of grace, to supplicate for them pardon and peace? It is such a relief to pray for them! For we go to a Saviour who feels for them more deeply and tenderly than we can.

I long to talk with you of our Saviour's kingdom, and to pray with you for its advancement. When shall it be? Must we wait till we have cast aside our earthly tabernacle ere we meet again? It will be sweet, M., to join with you in the songs of the redeemed, but I do earnestly desire to bend with you once before the mercy seat, to unite our petitions for the perishing millions who know not God. When will the day come, when the knowledge of the Lord shall fill the whole earth? When our Saviour shall reign and the whole earth be his? Why wait the days, the days of Zion's glory?

We all love to think of our precious M. Many send love to you, and my dear parents call you their other daughter, and now, my dear sister, I must say farewell for a little time."

JOURNAL.

"*August 27th.* I have much strength to gain for my new and varied duties, and I long for the quiet hours it has been my lot to enjoy for the past months. But that sweet season for growth in grace is now broken in upon by my pressing duties, and again I am in the busy world. But I can trust God still. I must call to mind the seasons I *have* enjoyed, and let their remembrance refresh my spirit while in the whirl of life.

When I begin to think of God, so many thoughts come that I am overwhelmed, and in my prayers I know not whether to *praise* or to *petition.* I have so many blessings it seems as though I must thank God all the time, and yet I have need of so many things that I must pray continually. I want *every shade of sin* to go away from this vile heart. I want every truth in the precious Bible to exert its proper influence over my life. I want to view every thing, both in this world and the other, in its proper light. It is my *one great aim* to bring my soul into entire conformity with God's holy will; yet the duty of self denial in some things is not as readily complied with as I could wish, and then I can only go to God and pray for a right spirit. O, it costs me many a hard battle to endeavor to bring my wicked heart right. But my greatest desire, and for it I am willing to put forth any effort, is, to be a *true*, *sincere*, *active*, *self-denying Christian.* It seems the only pleasant and right way of living. I mourn in secret over my hard, selfish heart; I pray for forgiveness through Christ, and it does seem as though my path is easier. I have some glimmerings of light. I have such sweet thoughts of God, and of Christ, and of the Christian course, that my heart sings often with joy and gratitude. 'Search me, O God, and try me, and see if there be any wicked way in me.' I am afraid of self-deception.

I am at present engaged in teaching Miss B.'s classes in the Seminary. It is very difficult, but I pray for strength, and it is but for a short time. May I fulfil every duty, and do all for God's glory. May I work and pray for the advancement of Christ's blessed Kingdom."

"*September 5th, Sabbath afternoon.* I am alone at home, for I am unable to attend to all the public duties of this day. I am once more by my own window, where I anticipate a quiet hour in thought of Heaven and of my Saviour. It has been our communion this morning, and we have had a beautiful day for its holy duties, but to me it has not been all peace like the last communion. *That* was a day more like heaven than any thing I have since had. I have had a weight on my spirit from which it has been hard for me to arise. I am poor and miserable, and yet I have looked to Jesus, and some faint gleams have been granted me. I will try to trust and do right, then all will end in peace.

Since I have been in school, my mind has been so closely occupied that I could not attend to my religious duties as I wished; and themes on which I once dwelt with delight, have escaped too much from my mind. This has darkened my way. I am so sinful, I need all the help I can have. During the week I have had much excitement, and am worn out with it. I am in a strange state this afternoon; perhaps I am not well; I do very much need support from above. But if I trust in God he will give me strength to meet every duty.

This is a sad account; but I have written down my feelings, and they are a faithful index to my heart, sometimes peaceful and again mourning on account of sin. I want to keep this journal to refer to in after years, when, if I live, I shall be far from this home. The events of this summer have been the touchstone to many hidden feelings. The outer world has been calm as usual, but in my inner world what a succession of events and of scenes there has been! O, my God, if I might not have looked to Thee, could I have borne this ceaseless rush? I should have sunk, might I not have leaned on the Saviour for aid."

"*September* 12*th. Sabbath afternoon.* Again alone, and better prepared, I hope, to spend my hour than I was last Sabbath. I now feel that I was worn out with excitement then. I needed to have been quiet and trusted in Christ. Now all is calm and sweet. I can only thank God and say, 'here, my Father, take me and do with me as seemeth good in thy sight.' I want to keep on in a steady, even course; but there are continually coming up things which deeply excite me, and never till I reach the other world, do I expect to be free from their influence. *There*, we shall be able to bear all, but *here*, joy and sorrow wear away the life.

I am at present in school, and though I love my dear girls very much, yet I find it so fatiguing I shall rejoice when Miss B. comes and I can be released. There will come many duties for this fall and winter, which will require strength and calmness of mind, and I must try to keep my heart quiet.

The American Board are now at Philadelphia, deliberating what they can do in the present crisis. May our churches be ready to meet it. I pray for strength that I may be ready to give up my all. O, I am very weak,—I need to look to Christ for aid in every thing. But I can have a bold heart. I want to have my heart lose its hold on earthly things, and look more at Christ's kingdom. I must use diligently all the means I have for this, and they are very great. I am determined to press on, that so 'Christ may be formed in me the hope of glory.'"

"*Tuesday*, 14*th.* The mists of an autumn evening now hang around the hills and over the trees. The crickets are chirping their songs. I love their voice. There is a *loneliness* in their notes agreeing well with these fading days. These early autumn days are to me the most glorious of the year. There is a hallowed influence in the quiet air, and the vault of heaven wears just the hues which tell of a holier clime. It is a time for elevating thoughts. I love these days more than I can tell. I have loved the summer softness and the young spring's breath, and I love autumn too. Oh, this fair earth, so beautiful even in its ruins, how many looks and tones it has to win us up to heaven. Last year my heart was sick at the thought of autumn. The turning leaves made it recoil. It was not so once, but *then* it made me melancholy to see the trees fading, and the flowers dropping away, and to hear the chill night wind whistling against the casement. I thought continually of Bryant's words on autumn,

" The melancholy days are come, the saddest of the year,
Of wailing winds and naked woods, and meadows brown and sere."

But I thank God, that a year has taught me better lessons. How quickly this summer has passed! Let me see to it that my days are spent usefully, when they fly so swiftly. To-day I have enjoyed, for I am at work on my own plans. My school days are over, and again I am quiet; and can command time for my various duties both at home and abroad."

"*Sabbath, September* 19*th.* Dr. Armstrong of the American Board is here. He has come in behalf of Missions, and though it has been denied me the privilege of hearing him preach, I have prayed that his labors might be blessed.

I have had a dull day in body, but I trust not quite so in mind. Fatigue and excitement have made me nearly useless, but I hope I shall improve as the cold weather returns. This morning I dozed about all the time, have not been down at all to meals, and dozed till after church time this afternoon, but for a little while I have been up, and read 'Last hours of Christ,' and also some interesting papers of Dr. Armstrong, and I have had sweet thoughts of Jesus and His faithful love. So great! It is wonderful! and I so poor and vile. The least thought makes my eyes overflow, for I am weak. I am happy and trusting to-night. When I look in, all is indeed very dark and sinful, but I look away to Christ and all is bright, and I pray for my precious ones, and for this whole world that Jesus may reign."

CHAPTER VI.

SICKNESS AND RECOVERY.

"*Sunday, Oct.* 10*th.* It is just three weeks since I have written in my journal, and I have looked for the first time this afternoon, upon my lovely hills, by my own dear window. I am writing in my own chamber, where I have passed through a deeply interesting and eventful season; for I have been brought to the borders of the grave, from which it has pleased God to raise me, so that now I am fast recovering. I have been down stairs for a little while, and have touched again my dear piano. But I am still very weak, and sit in my easy chair very quietly, reading some, and sewing some, but thinking most of the time. And O, I thank God for the sweet thoughts he grants me.

I can look back on the whole scene, and view it only in the light of a blessing. I had very little suffering—principally weakness; but I was so ill that my parents gave up all hope, and my physicians felt there was scarcely a chance for my recovery. And yet, through the whole, my mind was clear. I knew all which was going on around me, felt my danger, and thought that I should die. It pleased God to give me great calmness, without which it would have been impossible for my disease to have been checked; for excitement was the thing most feared. I left the event entirely in my Saviour's hand. I trusted all to him, and knew that if it was his will, I should recover; if not,

I trusted he would not leave me at the last. It is a miracle that I am spared. I am filled with wonder! I can only say, 'Lord, this life I devote all to thee.'

In this room I have passed, and am passing, some most delightful days. I cannot think of the kindness of all my friends, without the greatest wonder. It makes me very humble. I have had one overflowing stream of blessings, ever since the commencement of my illness. All my wants have been anticipated. The kindest friends have been around my bed-side—the best care has been taken of me. Every thing that love could devise, has been done. My dear Mrs. Fitch came all the way from New Haven, and took care of me a night and a day. O, my cup has been full of blessings! The loveliest flowers have bloomed on my table, and the choicest fruits, since I began to recover, have been before me. But this is not the half.

It has pleased my Heavenly Father to give me a more happy and peaceful spirit than I have ever before enjoyed. I have the sweetest verses and hymns in my memory, and my communings on my bed have been most precious. The dark valley of death, looks not so dark, since I have been so near it, and heaven seems near all the time.

I have yet many sins over which to mourn, but it seems as though my Saviour permits me to lay my head on his bosom, and weep over them there, and supplicate grace and pardon for myself and all my dear friends. I love my friends and every body, and every thing, ten thousand times more than I did before. The sun never shone so brightly, nor the moon so peacefully; and yet I love God, and Jesus, and heaven, as much better. The Bible never seemed half so precious. I can only look to God, and pray him to keep me close under the shadow of his wing, since it seems his will I should live a little longer here. I think this is one of the lessons I needed to learn before entering on my labors in a distant land. Of these I think much. And I have sweet thoughts of my absent friend. I thought of him when I supposed myself dying, and did wish to see him; but I can trust *that* all to my Father's care and keeping."

"*Sabbath afternoon, Oct. 17th.* I have been longing to go again to church. This is my fifth Sabbath at home; yet I have enjoyed my Sabbaths at home very much. To-day has been uncommonly beautiful. The late frosts have turned the leaves golden and brown. I sat down in the parlor after the people had gone to church, and with the bright sunshine looking down through the fading foliage, I committed the fifteenth chapter of John. I had some sweet thoughts then. I do think I thirst for the streams of holiness. I fear to mingle again with the world, for my heart will not be so quiet, when its hum is in my ear. O, my God, never let me stray, but make me abide always under the shadow of thy wing. O, my Saviour, preserve me against the first approach of worldliness. I want to think more of my missionary labors, and cultivate such a spirit, as will best prepare me for future usefulness.

And now, I commit my soul into the hands of my Saviour. I do wish to devote myself and my all to his service. Poor and unworthy as I am, I do love and trust him.

I am still unable to go out, but I sit in my room, doing various little things; resuming my duties as my strength will allow, and thanking God for renewing my life so rapidly. I do bless my Father in Heaven, for the precious hours I have had during the past week."

"*Sunday evening, Oct. 24th.* I hope my day at home has been profitable. Last evening, had a sweet season of preparation, and then a refreshing sleep prepared me for the day's duties. Have thought much to-day of Jesus' dying love, and have prayed over my ingratitude. I have not the joyful frame I sometimes have had; but I am satisfied if I can lay this poor, aching, sinful heart at the feet of Jesus, and know that he will pardon my ingratitude. I can trust him. I do believe on him. I do love him. I do devote my life to his blessed service. May he give me strength to overcome every sinful desire, to renounce every selfish interest.

I have had many delightful seasons alone this week, but last night when I reviewed it, I was startled to find I had been so remiss in duty. It is of His mercy that I am not consumed. A year since, if I had passed such a week, I should have thought myself well off, and should have praised God for it. But now, though I do thank God for the little light I have, I find so much darkness and corruption within, that I can only say, 'God be merciful to me a sinner.' I long to be free from this bondage of sin; but there is contention in my heart, and evil wars with the good. In the midst of all I pray to Jesus, and there is my comfort. Sometimes I think my selfishness is breaking up, and again some new display, damps my hope. But I will go on, and my weakness will be made strength through Christ. Let me remember all who have struggled, and yet have been borne safely through. Let me remember all that Christ has done for me—all that he will do. I can lift up my heart and take courage.

My Sabbath-school class came to see me on Wednesday. Had a precious season with them. O, may they all be lambs of the fold. M. W.* left on Thursday, and I am indeed lonely. I pray God my true comfort may be found in doing his will; then I can look forward to heaven as the place where friendship may be perfected. Dr. Parker, from China, was here on Friday. I was overwhelmed with

* A young lady who had spent several months with Mary.

the welcome and benediction he gave me—a welcome into the missionary field, and a blessing on my labor. I was ready to sink, and could only pray I might be worthy to receive such high honor."

"*Thursday, Oct. 28th.* Yesterday I rode for the first time. The leaves are fast falling, the sky wears its smoky hue—it is our Indian summer. While riding, I thanked God that I breathed in the open air once more. These autumn days, to which I looked forward, I have not been able to enjoy in the open air, but I have watched from my window the fading leaves, and the lovely autumn sky, which seems to shed a radiance so like heavenly light.

I watched for the evening star at twilight, and saw it for the first time this fall. Its gentle light brought thoughts of other days. How I watched that star last winter! My first twilight musings were, when it was looking down upon me, and seeming to woo my perplexed and troubled heart to Him who is the comfort and guide of all. I bless its light again. It brings hours of peace to my mind—hours I shall ever thank God for. I love to dwell on the scenes of last winter. Many a struggle I have had since then, but it does seem, that since that time my course has been onward."

"*Sabbath, October 31st.* This morning, had many precious thoughts, and wrote down a short account of the revival last winter, besides reading a portion in Doddridge. This afternoon, spent the time in prayer, and reading in the Bible—some portions of Isaiah, and also the last chapters of John. Learned the twelfth of Isaiah, a beautiful chapter. I have committed recently, the 14th, 15th and 16th chapters of John, and like to fix these interesting portions of Scripture in my memory. I have been free from distracting thoughts of any kind to-day. I am thankful for the precious season.

We are enjoying some of the loveliest days I have ever known in autumn. While looking abroad, the past, with all its deeply interesting events, comes into my mind, and fills it with strange emotions, which I cannot describe. It is neither pain nor pleasure. It is the spirit of the long gone years, and whether to let it come or not, I do not know. O, my Saviour, do thou purify all my feelings, that my soul may be a fit temple for the indwelling of the Holy Spirit. I do earnestly desire, that every thing I feel and do, may prepare me for usefulness in the cause of Him who has loved me and given himself for me. And while I remain in this dear country, may I so live, that I shall be satisfied in reflecting on my course, from a distant land. Jesus, I give my all to thee. May I make *thee*, *all*."

EXTRACTS

FROM A BRIEF SKETCH OF THE REVIVAL IN HER FATHER'S CONGREGATION, IN THE WINTER OF 1841, TO WHICH ALLUSION IS MADE IN THE JOURNAL.

"*Sabbath morning*, *Oct.* 31*st*, 1841. For a few weeks past, thoughts of that precious season of refreshing, which the Lord mercifully granted us last winter, have been continually in my mind. The return of the evening star to its accustomed winter place, has been one among the many circumstances, to call up those blessed days; for while they were passing, my most delightful hour was, when musing just before service, beneath the light of that one star. Its clear, mild beams seemed to point to the regions of holiness and peace. It was then that I first learned to be truly happy—then, that I first felt the true blessedness of the believer's hope.* I welcome its beams again in the

* Not that she then, for the first time was truly a Christian, but that she took more enlarged views of the Christian's hopes and privileges. See p. 145.

west; they speak of days which I hope to remember with gratitude, from the distant ages of eternity.

As my thoughts have been so much of late upon those scenes, it might be profitable for me to put down such sketches as I can recall, depending somewhat on notes taken at the time, but mostly upon my memory, where they are indelibly impressed. The attempt which I made during the progress of the revival to preserve an account of it, failed through my want of time. My health forbids much active labor now, and I think, while detained from the sanctuary, these sacred hours cannot be better employed than by carrying forward what has been so long neglected, on account of the pressure of other duties.

The revival of last winter will be remembered with the deepest gratitude by many, and will aid in swelling that song which the redeemed of the Lord shall sing on the hills of Zion. Not only will those remember it whose hearts were then first awakened to the beauties of holiness, but among Christians those days will be as bright spots in the past, like oases in the desert; for then, their hearts were refreshed by living waters, and their spirits gathered strength for the remainder of their pilgrimage, while dwelling on the glorious hopes and high privileges, which are the believer's inheritance. We seemed to come out from our dark places, to regions where the mists and vapors were rolled away, and where nothing remained to obstruct the beams of the Sun of Righteousness. The weary distance between us and our Father's throne seemed annihilated, and the portals of the celestial gates already to open upon us. Our hearts rejoiced, and our lips uttered the language of praise; and love, and peace, and joy in the Holy Ghost, dwelt in the bosom. Nor did the precious influence of the outpouring of the Spirit pass quickly away, to leave our hearts more dead than before. Throughout the whole of this past summer, the gentle dews of divine grace have nourished the plants of piety, and though a few have seemed to lose their zeal, a large number have appeared tender and devout, interested in Christian duties, ready to engage in every good work.

The revival among the youth particularly, was extensive; and a large number among these appear truly changed. They are the children and youth in our families, and it is sweet to see them walking in the ways of the Lord. Sixty of them were members of the Sabbath school. At our communion season in May, over one hundred joined our church. That day will long live in our hearts. Though the sun of the natural world was obscured, the Sun of Righteousness shed his beams around. The emblems of our Saviour's dying love spread out before us, filled our hearts with holy gratitude and peace. Earth and earthly things were far away, and the glorious things of the kingdom of Christ occupied our minds. It was a thrilling hour when those who desired to profess their faith came before the altar and gave themselves to God. We saw them, one by one, take their places in the aisle. Many of those we loved, over whom we had wept and prayed, were there—those who were bound to us by the dearest ties of friendship, stood there to join in a nobler and more enduring bond. Some there were, over whose young heads but a few years had passed—they could not be denied the privilege, and they were bidden welcome in the name of the Lord. It was a lovely and grateful company, who gathered for the first time that day, around the table of their risen and glorified Saviour; and long may the influence of that deeply interesting and solemn scene preserve them from wandering away from the fold they then so joyfully entered.

Early in the spring, my father established a 'Young People's Association,' which comprised all the youth of the congregation, who wished to place themselves under his pastoral instruction. These meetings were attended on Sabbath evening, and they have been exceedingly profitable. All classes have attended them, and our lecture room has been crowded throughout the summer. Every one has loved these meetings, and my father said it was impossible not to have his heart awake, and all his feelings enlisted, to see so many young, bright faces, before him. Those who had any difficulties concerning passages of Scripture, or any questions about duty, wrote them down and cast them into a box at the door, from which my father took them, and from time to time commented on them. Very interesting subjects were in this way discussed. Our hour in those little meetings passed quickly away—it was a place very near heaven. The songs of praise in which we all joined, came indeed from the heart. There was one which was quite a favorite with us, and many a time we sang it standing, just before separating:

> "Welcome, welcome dear Redeemer,
> Welcome to this heart of mine;
> Lord, I make a full surrender,
> Every power and thought be thine,
> Thine entirely,
> Through eternal ages thine."

TO M. S.,* ON HER BIRTH-DAY.

Nov. 1st, 1841.

"I could rejoice with you, dear M., and have been happy all day, that your year is opening so beautifully. The skies are smiling upon your birth-day, and may they be the emblem of a brighter sunshine which shall gild your future years, until the light of Heaven's own radiance shall burst upon you. Have we not much to bless our

* One of her earliest and dearest friends.

Father for? Oh, he is indeed crowning our life with goodness. And this day, dear M., the one of all days to you, is a lovely one in which to recall the past, and look towards the dim future; dim, indeed, so far as the events of this life are concerned. M., our childhood has passed like a dream. It seems but yesterday, since you and I were playing together with our dolls; but our dolls died long ago. Those days at the Seminary are more real, and it makes my heart thrill, when any little thing calls them back. Three years have wrought marvelous changes; and our spirits have been growing older, and already we are knowing what it is to live and act in life's drama. Oh, M., must there be this ceaseless change! forever passing on in the current of time; must we go on leaving loved scenes, and treasured events, far, far behind, with memory's picture continually increasing. Well, let it go on, for there will come an end, and we shall pass to another world, more real and enduring.

The past will speak to-day, dear M., and I know you too are listening to its voices, and these fading leaves beneath so glorious an autumn sky are well in keeping with the spirit of by-gone years. Oh, surely it is well to cast some glances behind, while we are hurrying on, even though the retrospect may bring a shadow over us; for the past has lessons we may not forget, and its tones are tones of wisdom, if we will but listen to them.

I would that we could spend this day together, and live over our early years once more; that we could together bless God for the past, and cast ourselves and all our interests, on him who has thus far guided us. Let us give to him our future years, and then indeed will they pass brightly and calmly. Our careless days have all gone by; now we are beginning to think and feel for ourselves. Already have our characters taken the stamp, which in all probability they will bear through life, and through eternity. Oh, it is a fearful, an overwhelming thought; and yet not more fearful than true. We may change in minor points, M., yet I think the future will alter but little the outline of our characters. Perhaps it may not be so; and I would that time might bring something beside maturity to mine. There is one thing in which we may hope to be continually changing—the conquest over corrupt affections and earthly desires must go on. With us, dear M., I could humbly hope and believe, that it is already commenced, and that a Father's blessing even now is resting on our efforts, and a Saviour's hand, leading on in the way. Even now, my dear friend, we can raise the song of gratitude, 'unto him who hath loved us, and given himself for us;' and the past can furnish material enough for a hymn of praise to-day. We raise it unto that God who called us in our wanderings, who remembered us in our youthful days, and led our feet into the path of life. We look back and rejoice in all the goodness which has crowned our years, and forward with unshrinking hearts, to the untried future, for our God is with us. Oh, M., let us ever *trust.*

My heart has been with you all day, and I meant to have written a birth-day note, but I see I must send only an apology for one; and yet if it tells you that I love you, both for the years of friendship which have passed, and for those which I trust are yet before us, and if you make out from it that my earnest wishes are for your increasing happiness, it will have accomplished in part its object. Oh, many an autumn will bring its glorious hues and fading days, and when with them comes also your birth-day, and the many thoughts it brings, think, dear M., of one early friend, who will always pray for a blessing upon each cherished companion of her youth.

Ever yours, M."

JOURNAL.

"*Nov.* 2*d.* Took a French lesson to-day. A gift of mignonette from my teacher, is filling my room with its fragrance. Yesterday took a lovely ride. Oh, so beautiful was every thing! It was M. S.'s birth-day. Wrote her a note, and thought much of early days. We are growing old fast. Well, let the years pass, if we are in the way of duty.

"*Nov.* 6*th.* The blessed Sabbath approaches, and I am expecting to attend the service to-morrow, and come around the table of our Lord, which is to be spread. What a two months this has been! I have an overflowing cup of mercy—brought down to the borders of the grave, and now raised again to life and health. May this life, so wonderfully spared, be all devoted to that Saviour who has died for me.

I have enjoyed, during the last two months, many precious seasons of prayer, and have read the Bible with more interest than ever before, and I hope I have improved in a calm and trusting heart. The voice of the world has been in a measure hushed here in my quiet room. But, alas! my heart is still weak, and now that I am no more alone, I find that sin is still striving, and I must watch and pray all the time. O, this spirit of worldliness, how I long to sweep it from my soul. Where should I hide my guilty head, if not at the foot of the cross.

I have not been to church since the Sunday after my last communion. And now, my Father, and my Saviour, wilt thou pardon all that has offended and grieved thee, during the intervening days, from my last communion season. My heart rises in thanks for thy ten thousand mercies. May I hide myself in the dust, and give all the honor to that Saviour who has loved me, and died for me—to whom I surrender my all for time and for eternity, and consecrate myself anew to his blessed service.

And now may the blessing of God rest upon all who will come around the table of the Lord to-morrow. May it be a day long to be remembered, and in its strength may we go many days."

"*Sabbath afternoon, Nov. 7th.* I have indeed enjoyed the precious privilege to which I looked earnestly forward. Again I have entered that dear church, and partaken of the emblems of our Saviour's dying love, and have had refreshing thoughts of God, and of Jesus. O, I could utter songs of praise for the sweet peace of this day. I spent an hour of preparation in my room, and went early with my dear mother to church. How delightful it was to go again to the house of God. I do know that it is a precious place. My dear father's prayer was indeed elevating, and my thanksgivings went up with his, for my being permitted to enter the holy courts again. The sermon was from the text, 'Unto you who believe he is precious.' I did feel comforted by the train of thought, and my two favorite tunes were sung in the morning; and then at the communion season, my mind was calm and happy. There I renewed my resolution of trusting in Jesus, and keeping a quiet heart; and thanked him for the calmness I have for the past two months enjoyed. I renewed my resolution of praying for four dear friends, for whom I feel much anxiety. May I persevere in prayer, and never faint. And lastly, I resolved to turn my attention more particularly to my future labors, and to try every day to learn something which will be of use to me in a foreign land.

And now may Jesus accept these resolutions; and give

me grace to keep them, even to the end—and whether living or dying, may I be the Lord's.—*Amen.*

"*Four o'clock.* What a day this has been. This afternoon, my dear father preached to the children. I could not go twice, though I wished it very much. So as soon as all were gone, I came to the study window and looked off on the charming hills, so beautiful, so calm in autumn sunshine! And then the sky so clear, and of so soft a blue; it led my heart in gratitude to heaven. 'O, religion is a reality,' I said, as I looked on the calm Sabbath scene before me, 'Jesus does live and reign, and heaven is the home of the Christian.' And I have prayed, and rejoiced, and read my bible here by this window, with no sound to break on the stillness. I have been reading in the Prophets of the future glory of Zion, and I have longed to burst the bonds of sin, and to be perfectly holy. Unto thee, O my Saviour, I turn. Hear my humble prayer. May I give my all to Thee, and never turn away from Thee who art my best beloved friend, my hope, my trust, my all. I want nothing else but to abide forever under the shadow of thy wing."

New Haven, *Nov.* 11.

"*Thursday evening.* I am enjoying a quiet, delightful visit here. Every thing is lovely; music and fragrant flowers, and in an adjoining portico, a sweet canary is pouring forth its melodies—and books, and above all, the society of one, whose judgment, and taste, and Christian principle, make her friendship invaluable. I feel the blessing. May God give me grace to improve it. Already I have many valuable hints from her, with reference to my future labors. There are many questions of duty constantly occurring to my mind. Of one thing, however, I am certain. Whatever tends to perfect character, I must attend to. My great duty is to prepare for the other world, my own soul, and the souls of those over whom I have an influence.

My motives must be drawn from God's glory, and Jesus' love. Oh, these are all-powerful. Vanity and selfishness, my two great sins, I must try hard to overcome. Watchfulness is what I need very much, and I try to cultivate it. A tender and enlightened conscience will be my greatest blessing, for then I shall not be led into any wrong course. And now may God bless all my efforts throughout this day."

"*Saturday evening, Nov.* 13*th.* Last week, at this time, I was at home, and passed a sweet evening. May this be equally pleasant and profitable. This week has passed very pleasantly, more quietly even than at home. I can thank God for the happy state of mind I have enjoyed. The holy communion has remained in my memory with a sanctifying influence, and my Heavenly Father has seemed nearer to me than at some times.

I have this week learned many valuable things about my future course; and I hope to improve on the hints I get from my dear Mrs. Fitch. Her views of duty, and of this world, are so enlarged, consistent and reasonable, that I am disposed to lean favorably to them. Yet I want to bring all to the test, and I need to examine, before I adopt views, which at this time may affect my whole future course. I trust in God, that he will lead me in just the right way. There, a learner at his feet, I am safe."

"*Monday, Nov.* 15*th.* I have been watching the bold front of West Rock, on which the sunlight streamed. This lovely city of elms, and its two sentinel rocks, and the broad bay stretching at their feet—can I ever cease to remember them, or think of them, without a thrill of emotion? I have spent so many happy hours here, that it seems like one of my homes; each spot is familiar, and its nearness to the sea makes it doubly dear. How favored has my life been—full of mercies—may I improve all to God's glory."

"*Sunday evening, Nov. 21st.* I have had some sweet seasons of prayer to-day, and have got many interesting ideas from dear Dr. and Mrs. Fitch. Here, in this dear family, some of my happiest hours have been spent. May God reward them for all the kindness they have shown me. My heart twines around these dear friends, and the thought of parting with them would be insupportable, if I did not hope to meet them in another world."

"*Nov. 23d.* Here I am once more, writing my farewell to this lovely place, and to morrow evening will not find me here. Farewell to the sweet flowers, and the good old piano, and the table where I have sat many an hour, and the quiet sunlight scenes, and the window seat, and the noble West Rock. I love them all. My most light-hearted and careless days have been spent here, and more thoughtful ones too. Here I have learned many things to remember, when my spirit has grown old."

HARTFORD, *Dec. 2d*, 1841.

"*Thursday morning.* I am spending a day in my room, which I have long wished for;—a day in which to look over my future course, and endeavor to adopt those principles upon which I can safely act in after life. This is a deeply responsible act, and I tremble when I think how much is pending upon the conclusions I now come to.

May God direct in the plan which I now write down, and may it be formed with his blessing, that so I may in peace carry it into my daily life, and reflect upon it with pleasure when I shall view this life in the light of eternity.

God has placed me in this world to glorify him, by preparing my own soul for his kingdom, and by doing all I can to lead others to do so. He is sparing me in this world, that my character may be formed into a likeness to his own perfect character, that I may continually increase in holiness, and receive those blessings for which the Saviour died. All that I have belongs to God. My time, the mind he has given me, my desires and affections, all are his; his by creation, and by the covenant of Redemption. And may I ever act as if I fully believed these great truths. God has so constituted us, that we cannot live without exerting an influence on those around us; and in forming our plans for life, we are to remember that we are responsible for the effect which our conduct will have upon others; and we are to form such habits, and act on such principles, as will best promote the welfare of those over whom we have influence. God is calling me to a deeply responsible work—that of glorifying him among those who know him not. I need therefore a double portion of wisdom, to know how to do God's will, and what preparation to make in order to fulfill the duties which will fall upon me. I will not be undecided, but trusting in God, I will be settled and firm in the course I am to pursue. I know that God will direct my steps, and though my earthly friends may not be able to lead me, there is *One* who knows what is right, and who will direct my steps in that path which will secure the greatest good. I trust in God. I look to him to teach me how I shall best promote the cause of Christ in my own heart, and in the hearts of others. May God give me grace so to use all the powers I have, that his will may be accomplished concerning me, and the kingdom of our Saviour advanced, even though it be in a small degree only.

1. My *motive* in all that I do, must be the love of God and Jesus; and my *object*, the glory of God, and the advancement of Christ's cause in this world.

2. In order to glorify my Father in Heaven, I must give all the faculties of my mind, and the powers of my body, their proper uses—neglecting none of them, and using none to excess.

3. I must take all proper means for the preservation of my health; such as keeping regular hours for sleep, exercise, &c.

4. In intercourse with others, I must recommend religion by all suitable means;—a cheerful and gentle deportment.

5. I must place *self* very low, and put *God* on the throne; for only in this way will my plans succeed.—Altered Feb. 21st, 1843.

5. I desire to put *self entirely down*, and God only on the throne of my heart.

6. In all doubtful cases of duty, I must consider the subject with prayer, and when *once decided*, go on *without wavering*.

7. I must keep a *quiet* mind in every duty. *Trust* must be my watchword. In the midst of all duties, labors or trials, let a quiet mind be carried.

8. An observing eye must be mine upon all which is around me, ready to engage in any work for God; and a listening ear, also, to learn whatever I can.

9. Sympathy with the whole human race I must have, in order to do them good. I must not arouse their prejudices, but win them to God, in the gentlest way which my conscience will permit.

10. In pursuing any course of conduct, which I believe right in the sight of God, I must not be turned from it by others' opinions, unless clearly shown that I am mistaken."

TO C. C.

Dec. 20, 1841.

"Do you believe, my dear C., that it is just a fortnight to-day, since that good snow storm which gave me your company? And so it is only six weeks before your school closes. But I must not look forward. How long it takes us to learn that *living in the present*, is the only wise course, so long as we are dwellers in clay.

* * * * * * * *

We are reading, that is, M. S., mother and myself, every morning for the present, 'Schlegel's History of Literature,' and find it very improving. Indeed we make quite a study of it, and it gives me a great deal of satisfaction to be so thorough in a work so valuable as this. I have 'Mrs. Smith's Life,' to read, and an essay on 'Living for Immortality,' by Foster; besides several little books which I am dispatching as fast as possible. Then we have commenced French, and I am more interested than ever. Fitting dolls' clothes, and patch work for the society, and making calls, fill up the fragments of time. Here I have given you a list of my occupations. My time never passed so pleasantly, so free from care, as it does now; and I feel these are golden moments which I must improve. I have made it a rule to see some of my friends every day, and generally spend a portion of the afternoon in calling. It is very delightful to mingle once more with my dear friends, and to enjoy their society. My father wishes to have me in society as much as possible. As there was no service, I spent the last evening with him, and he gave me many a good hint about my duties, &c. I find that he observes little things much more than I thought he did. His not speaking often of them, has deceived me. But I believe now, that he is a careful observer of habits and manners.

Shall I make any apology for such a note of egotism? I will not, because I think you wish to know what I am doing during our separation. And I expect just the same of you. Remember, dear C., all you see and hear, and tell me when you come. I want to know if you have forgotten our promise about drawing a sketch for one another. I have thought of it many times, and once had my view selected. The little bag, which I tried so hard to finish, I send now, and hope you will carry it for my sake. I have made a little silk case, lined and wadded, for your sweet Testament to live in, and another for M. W.'s Bible. Did you have a pleasant Sabbath yesterday, dear C.? I had a very refreshing one, but a part of it was spent at home; for my Sabbath-school services are very wearing, and yet so interesting, I cannot think of giving them up."

JOURNAL.

"*Dec.* 21*st.* The return of this season, reminds me forcibly of the days of last winter. Last year at this time, my spirit was shrouded in a gloom, which hid the light of heaven from my eyes. The corruption and sin of my heart, was staring me in the face. But for all those miserable days I can now only thank God. I did indeed pass through a dark way, but I humbly hope it was for my good. The first day of this present year, I began to see light, and since then, my mind has gradually become more peaceful, and my purpose of obedience to God, more and more confirmed.

This morning I have been spending a season of prayer, especially for our dear church, that we may be prepared for the approaching fast. And I have been looking over also the year now drawing to a close. How much I have, over which to rejoice; and yet it is not all, nor chiefly because my way has become so much brighter, as regards my temporal concerns,—but it is, because my heart can look up in the midst of all my sins, and can trust in God, and own him as Father, Saviour and Sanctifier.

I long for a time like that of last winter. The dissipation of summer, and the traveling of the warm months, has now given place to a season of quiet. O, may we all improve it! Those precious days! O, that they might return again. Many of my dear friends then found a Saviour. But there are yet many who are without hope in the world. Will not our Father send his good Spirit to touch their hearts, and lead them to him.

I have many duties to perform before New-Year's. I am making some little gifts for my friends, have society work to prepare, and in addition to this, I have to spend some portion of my time, each day, in Mr. F.'s room, to have a portrait of my poor self taken. With regard to the *principles* of my life, I do try to be governed by them; but the one I find the hardest, is to be firm, after I have decided a difficult question of duty.

My *plan* I try to pursue, and have reason to think that it is the best I can have; but I have to hold myself back, for I am continually undertaking too much."

TO C. C.

Dec. 26*th*, 1841.

"Well, my dear friend, this is a most beautiful day, with which to close our Sabbaths of this year; and now I know you are enjoying this glorious moon, and thinking, (but I hope not too much,) on the varied events of the portion of time we are now closing. I lingered in our church after service, to watch the sunset light upon the pillars, and our noble organ; and I would have staid, had I dared, to review there, in the house of God, the Sabbaths of the dying year. There are many thoughts which come crowding on our minds, and our hearts are back in the passing days, those days which brought so much trial* and affliction, but which brought, too, the comfort and the blessedness of a Father's love. Let us think, dear C., of the blessings which have crowned the year, and of the mercies which have, even though under disguise, come to us. Let us think of those, who forever released from the sin and corruption of this world, are tuning their golden harps on the hills of Zion."

"*Monday evening, 27th.* I have just returned from a pleasant evening meeting, the first I have attended since my illness, and it was very good to be there. These precious privileges make a Christian home seem very delightful, and if we prize them so highly, will it not be our highest happiness to extend their influence to the whole family of man? Oh, for a spirit of benevolence, that shall embrace the whole human race. I hope to derive much benefit from Mrs. Smith's Life, which I am now reading. How much we have to learn. I do not mean of mere worldly science, but of the things pertaining to God and our own souls. When thoughts of that blessed kingdom, which our Saviour is setting up in this world, come into our hearts, how every thing which does not aid it, sinks into insignificance! And yet I feel that very many things in which we are engaged, though perhaps not bearing directly on the great work, do so advance the cause by the influence they throw around us, that it is part of our Christian duty to engage in them.

Oh, the time is so short for 'all we need to do.' We have just heard a vague report of the death of a beautiful girl, formerly a member of our family. How strangely sorrow and joy, death and life are mingled! Another of

* Miss C. had buried her father during the year.

our beautiful flowers is this week to be married. The wedding is to be at our house, so I expect to be very busily and pleasantly occupied; and this, with the approaching solemnities of the fast and communion season, will fill up the week.

Do you remember a sad, gloomy letter I wrote you, just a year this week? I think of those days, as among the most miserable of my life. But I feel very differently now. Thanks be to God, that darkness has given place to trust in him."

JOURNAL.

"*Dec.* 31*st.* The last rays of the sun are gilding with a rosy hue, the light clouds above the horizon. There is snow on my distant hills, and they are sleeping as in summer days. My heart is far back in the days of this now dying year.

My character has undergone a greater change in this, than in any preceding year, and yet perhaps the events and experience of earlier ones prepared for the change. A certain peace and trust, in a Christian hope, has carried me through all the changing and deeply interesting scenes of the year. To God, my Heavenly Father, be all the glory. I do repent of every sin. May his pardoning mercy blot out the guilt, the worldliness of the past year, that it go not over into the year which is coming.

This morning, I felt rather stupid on account of the excitement of yesterday. S. M. and Mr. F. were married in the afternoon at our house. A few friends came in. S. looked most lovely, and F., noble and protecting to the gentle being, who has given him her all. She is a lonely orphan—but exceedingly beautiful—and every one loves her. May God bless them, and make them truly happy. After the bridal party had gone to take the cars for New

Haven, we all prepared the cake to send round to the friends. A beautiful group of young girls knelt around the table, as they tied the white ribbon around each little parcel.

And now farewell to the hopes and fears, joys and sorrows, of this year. There is a world 'where time is not measured by years,' and no change comes. May I trust in Jesus, and do his will, then may I hope for an entrance into that blest abode."

CHAPTER VII.

A YEAR OF PREPARATION.

"*Communion Sabbath, Jan. 2d.*, 1842. Just two months since I began to go to church after my sickness. I have had a sweet season of prayer. The communion season also I enjoyed, and hope it may have been profitable to our church. My Sabbath-school was very pleasant; the sermon on nearness to God, and the communion, precious; and I felt a happiness in surrendering myself to Jesus. But this afternoon, remaining at home, because too fatigued to go again to church, I read in Mrs. Smith's life, and have been in an agony of tears. O, how poorly I can control my feelings. I read all about the parting from her parents, and thought about another parting that will come, with such bitter sadness, I knew not what to do. O, my Saviour, though I am weak, I turn to thee.

7 o'clock. I feel calm now, and trust in God, that he will give me strength to do his whole will;—that he will help me overcome my selfish inclinations, and consecrate every thing to him who died for me. I have had a sweet season of prayer. How good is my Father in Heaven! I will trust, for he knows best."

"*Jan. 9th.* How fast has the first week of this new year flown! This day I shall count as my sweetest, for I have been freer than usual from wandering thoughts, and from distracting cares. Had a pleasant season with my class, and listened to a deeply solemn and interesting sermon from my dear father, on 'the influence of the Spirit.' May we all pray for a blessing on the labors of this day. I find it very sweet to look over the notes I have taken, concerning the season of religious interest, which we enjoyed last winter. Cannot those precious days return? Oh, what can I do? Lord, teach me.

It has been a most lovely afternoon. The soft sky and golden sunshine, gilding every thing, remind me of the beams of the Sun of Righteousness. If this earth is so beautiful, what must Heaven be, where the presence of God gladdens every spot, and illumines the celestial hills! I thank God that I can look to him, and call him *Father*, through Jesus Christ, his only Son."

Wethersfield, Feb. 20th. "This is my second Sabbath in this place, where I am visiting my dear M. W., and I hope that both have been spent profitably. My seasons alone during this week, have been unusually solemn. O, I feel my deep ingratitude a little more than I once did. Spent last evening alone, looking over the past week—found cause of sorrow that I had not been as spiritual as I might have been. O, my Saviour, fill my heart with gratitude; may *thy dying love* be my *watchword*, and sweetly constrain me to spend and be spent for thee.

I am making many precious friends here. Can I do them any good? If I have the heart, Jesus will open the way.

At the window where I am sitting, I have spent many sunset hours in prayer; and henceforth will the view from it be associated in my heart with some of the pleasantest and holiest hours I have ever passed. I love to connect natural scenery with devotion. Even in winter our earth is fair, and is a temple sending up its praises to God. I shall think of this window when I am far away,—of the sunset colors and morning rays, which have lighted the lovely meadows spread out before me, through which our Connecticut is flowing—and there is the same fine skirting of hill and sky, which I always love to watch.

Went into the Sabbath-school—had a class of three little girls. It was a solemn work, for I shall probably never meet them again till the judgment day. They, too, appeared interested."

"*Tuesday, Feb. 22d.* Beautiful day! Soft mist on the mountains, and in the valley the river twinkles with a smoky light, such as I often saw last Spring. Surely nature, in all her features, is lovely—What must be the character of that Being, from whom come all these works? My heart is quiet and trusting, and I can go cheerfully on in the performance of my many duties."

"*Thursday, Feb. 24th.* This day has been usually observed as the fast for colleges. This morning, spent a few hours alone, and hope I had a profitable season. And now I want to commit my own soul, and the souls of all for whom I pray, to the keeping of our God and Father, that he may work in us all that is acceptable and holy in his sight."

"*Friday, Feb. 25th.* Went in, with M. W., to the State Prison. We were just in time to see the prisoners assemble for evening prayers,—a most solemn and affecting sight. I shall never forget the measured tread of these poor beings, as they came in files from their workshops; nor the slow and earnest voice of the Chaplain, reading the portion in Ecclesiastes, commencing, 'But if a man live many years,'—nor the singing of the prisoners, 'There is an hour when I must die;'—all has made too deep an impression ever to be effaced. The services were peculiarly solemn, for the coffin of one of their number was before them. Without name or date, there it lay, reminding them, that, though shut out from the world, yet death could find an entrance through prison bolts and bars. They bore him away without the walls, and thus has closed, in darkness and gloom, the career of one who began the world with feelings of buoyancy, of hope, but unchecked by religious principle, soon sunk into shame and sin, and now his end is come. We saw the guard and four of the prisoners bearing the coffin to its grave behind the prison walls. Mr. B. is well adapted to the station he fills. His manner is sincere and solemn."

"*Hartford, Sabbath evening, March 4th.* This afternoon my dear father has been reviewing the twenty-four years of his ministry, of the commencement of which, this day is the anniversary; and our hearts have rejoiced in view of the goodness and mercy which have followed us all the days of our life. Thanking God for the past, we have looked forward with humble trust for the future, and there in his holy house, have left our offerings of praise. The prayers, the music, and the sweet hymns, were all in keeping; and when the last one was joined in, 'On Jordan's stormy banks,' I am sure no heart there but thrilled with emotion. And the doxology, 'Praise the Lord,' ending in its hallelujah, amen, the rich organ notes swelling in full harmony, seemed, as my dear mother said, like the anthems of heaven. Almost all the congregation who were here when my father was ordained, are now sleeping in their graves. Many have died in the hopes of the gospel. They will not return to us, but we shall go to them. My father offered the fervent prayer of his heart, that when we were gone, others might be here, who should form a spiritual and living church to the end of time.

Our new and deep-toned bell rings this day for the first time, calling us to that church we love so well. I shall love this I know, though 'tis not the bell of my childhood. That good old bell! connected as it was with so many of the happiest seasons of my life—whose tones were the familiar ones of my earliest moments; could I help loving it? My father says, I shall not hear that bell in Smyrna. No, its tones will not reach me there. There will come a time, when I shall no more go up to that sanctuary, which has been my Sabbath home from my earliest years; when I shall no more join in its holy services. But I am not cast down; through my tears, I can look to a more glorious temple above, where God and the Lamb forever dwell. No, no; this dear place of worship, that has nurtured so many plants of piety, will be called mine no more, when I depart from the home of my youth; but if I humbly walk in the ways of piety, and lean upon Jesus for strength, may I not hope that he will go with me in all my wanderings, make me bold and faithful in his service, and that he will cause the truths which I have here heard, to spring up in my heart, and bear fruit forever?

In the strength of this day's services, I hope to go many days; and now I go to my twilight engagement. May my Father meet a poor unworthy child, and give her a blessing through Christ."

"*Thursday, March* 10*th.* I am writing by an open window, my own favorite one, and the sun is really oppressive. It is a beautiful spring day, and brings to memory those of last year. There are mild winds without, and the blue-birds sing on the trees around the window. So faithful is our Father to bring again the sweet spring time. Would that it were spring in my heart! And why may it not be?

I have been endeavoring, by a morning spent alone, to prepare for the solemn services of the approaching communion. I feel that I have need of much prayer and fasting, for my heart is not in such a state as I desire. I look back on the year which has passed, since my mind began to place a new confidence in my Father in Heaven, and felt a new emotion of love and trust in my Saviour, and I could weep that I have made so little progress. Those days last spring, I can truly call happy days, and I know that I might enjoy far better ones now, and ought to, but for this evil heart."

"*Thursday afternoon.* We have had a sweet prayer meeting. These seasons must be improved, for this summer is the last one we may ever spend together. In the fall our beloved H. is to be married, and then we shall no more meet as we have done.

We are beginning to get strangely accustomed to the scenes of active life. Marriages, and engagements, are almost a matter of course now. But we can never be accustomed to the thought of partings and separations. These are the sad hard things.

O, my Father, help us all to realize that the thing for which we live is, to *glorify thee.* That these passing scenes in life are chiefly important, as they help to form our characters, and to fit us for a higher state of being.

My daily portions of Scripture are now about the closing scenes of our Saviour's life; and this morning I read his last prayer, that beautiful, touching prayer, which none but the Saviour could pray. And now I commit myself to my Father in Heaven. May he work in me that which is holy and pleasing in his sight, through Jesus Christ."

"*Friday morning*, 11*th*. Went last night to hear the Rainers;—voices most exquisite, and singing in fine taste. 'Rock'd in the cradle of the deep,' was perhaps the most beautiful. Their native Tyrolese costume, and their sister with her guitar, swung gracefully over her shoulder, added much to the effect. But while such a concert could be attended with truly Christian feeling, I am almost ready to blame myself that I went. I think it is better, on the near approach of the communion, not to attend any thing which diverts the mind. One so weak as I am, is easily drawn into the world, as this little incident has shown me. I did pray before I went, and the thing was not of my own seeking. O, my Saviour, wilt thou help me to keep a steadfast mind; fixed only on Thee."

"*March* 13*th*. Have had in some degree, I trust, a profitable day. I *felt* during the administration of the sacrament, that I must live at a less 'dying rate.' I resolved to live nearer the Saviour—to look more entirely to him, and to endeavor to feel more the great truths of the gospel; and this afternoon, while reading and meditating alone, I have had this *feeling* much deepened.

I have been becoming, of late, too well satisfied with my own state—have been contented with going on, having a little pleasant feeling, dropping a word now and then, and have not thought enough of the importance of doing 'with my might.' I know that calmness is necessary to the profitable performance of duty; but that heart is the calmest, which is steadily fixed on the one great object of following Christ in all things. O, my Saviour, hear Thou my prayer for a steadfast heart."

"*Thursday, April* 7*th*. To-day, Mr. B. gave me a Greek lesson. Oh, why is this heart sickness, when I am reminded of my future course! I love the friends far away, I love their country, I hope I love my work; but 'tis the thought of leaving this dear, dear place! O, may my heart feel so great a desire to do good, that I shall feel strong in the thought of separation, looking beyond this life to our happy meeting."

"*Sabbath, April* 10*th*. One of the most beautiful days of the season. The buds are fast opening, and the grass is green all over the fields. How lovely is returning spring! May my heart feel it, and be happy in these delightful days, because it is fixed on Jesus, and on doing his will. I am ready to burst out into praise and grateful joy with every thing around. Every thing speaks a Father's love. I do give up my heart to Jesus, to be devoted entirely to his service. How often I write this in my journal, yet not so often as I feel it. It is my habitual desire to be devoted to him.

This is my last Sunday before I shall be twenty-one. O, my Saviour, cleanse away the guilt of the past. My dear father preached from the text, 'I would not live alway,' and I hope that in some little measure, I could enter into the meaning of the sermon. At the close, he read the hymn which expressed the sentiment in the text; and Mr. M. played as if he felt it, while it was sung most sweetly."

"*Monday noon*, 11*th*. Just like a summer's day, reminding me of Burleigh's exquisite poem on June—

'Hiding the sunshine in their vapory breast,
The clouds float on like spirits to their rest.'

I have been out walking this morning, and have been oppressed by this beautiful weather. How true it is, that often, when every thing is bright and beautiful around, our hearts are listless. Perhaps it is because the greatness of the beauty overpowers them, and that they are too contracted to take it all in. It is this which makes them so poorly able to take in the sublime truths of Redemption. Yes, our hearts are contracted. O, God, wilt thou open mine, and may I feel as I should on every subject."

"*Friday, April* 15*th.* I hoped to have spent yesterday as a day of prayer and fasting, but domestic duties prevented; yet all day my thoughts were more tender than for a long time past. And although my time for meditation has been very much broken in upon to-day, yet just before tea, I had a season of prayer, that the sins of the past might be forgiven me, and that I might begin my new year with entire devotion to God.

When I look back to the sweet birth-day last year, and think of the mercy that has followed me all the time, how I was permitted to pass a pleasant summer, and how in the fall, when brought to the gates of death, I was raised up again, and carried in peace through the winter; when I think of the intercourse with beloved friends, growing more delightful every day; and of the many precious seasons in private, which, throughout the year, I have enjoyed, I am filled with gratitude. Surely my cup overflows!

This is the bright side of the picture. On God's side every thing has been mercy. On my own, I can only write sin, sin, a mere blank. I fear very much that I have let the prevailing lukewarmness around me influence my feelings also. Should it be thus, with one for whom so much has been done? And now in taking this solemn review of the past, I can say, first of all, that my great sin has been in not striving to live each moment of time for the glory of God. How sweet it would have been to have done this. And secondly, in not leaning entirely on the

Saviour for aid, on whom my all depends; and lastly, I have not felt as I should with regard to the missionary work, nor willing as I should be to deny myself. This grieves me. Over this I pray in bitterness of heart. Over these sins I have been mourning. I have taken them to my Saviour. O, that he would have pity upon me and remove every sin, and grant that in penitence and peace, I may close this year, and awake in my new one, with new life."

" *Saturday, April* 16*th.* This beautiful morning makes me twenty-one. How sweetly it shines. I look upon the same hills, and soft sky, which one year ago shone so brightly, and many thoughts come stealing over my heart. Twenty-one years! It is a long time to look back upon. I think of my childhood days, so sweet and happy, of the friends who have risen in my path, and made my life so pleasant, of the blessings innumerable which my Father has showered upon me, and I can only bow down, and in deep repentance for the past, give up my heart to him anew.

O, God, wilt thou take this life which thou hast spared; wilt thou grant that throughout each moment of the coming year I may be wholly thine, and act only from motives drawn from love to thee, as Father, Saviour and Sanctifier. Thou only canst tell what lines are written for me in the future; but I have trusted thee in the past; shall I not also for the coming days? When I look to this poor wayward heart, I despair of ever attaining the only worthy end for which to live—but when I look to thee I say, great God, all things are possible with thee. And now I do sincerely and unreservedly give up this heart to thee. I feel that I shall be safe under thy eternal guidance—and supremely blessed, if I may be under thy control, throughout every moment of this life. May my *aim* be single. May *self* be put far away. May I live with direct reference to Jesus, and the concerns of his kingdom, striving that my *every act* may tend to its furtherance in this world. This is my prayer. May it be heard only through Christ.

Have received beautiful birth-day remembrances from some of my friends. May I live so truly to Jesus, as to be worthy of their love.

April 17th. After going to S. S., where I met my dear class, who all appeared interested, unusually so, in what we talked about, I felt so fatigued that I came home; and here by the study window I have been thinking, and looking over my last year, and praying too.

O, I thank God for many things I find in the retrospect, and mourn over many things also.

I have very many feelings of the past now in my heart. This birth-day has called them up, and I have been comparing them with my present feelings.

I fear that last year I let my religion assume a too poetic character—rather dreamy—looking too much for natural beauties, and letting my thoughts be governed by the world of beauty which was around. I thank God that he made me to receive enjoyment from every thing in nature; that he gave me a spirit to respond to all the loveliness around; but I desire, that as my mind has been open to impressions from natural objects, it may be now open to those far more glorious objects that exist in the spiritual world, of which Christ and his great work are the foundation. And I humbly hope this may be the character of my meditations this year. O, my Saviour, open my heart to these blessed truths.

The day is uncommonly fine, the air is bland, and the bird notes exquisite. My heart loves these. Yes, I may love them. 'Love not *these the less*,' but *God* and *Christ more.* I feel that I am in danger of placing these first. It must be God and Christ first.

I must now try to form some kind of plan for the summer. My studies this winter have been very light, and I have not done much, as my health requires I should live easily.

I shall endeavor to spend some time over Greek and French every day. O, I rejoice that my mind feels more interested in the Mission cause. This has been my great trouble, that, when God was so graciously pleased to call me into his vineyard, that I, instead of leaping and taking hold of the work, should have had so many misgivings about it. I can only go and mourn before Jesus, and ask him to forgive the past, and give me a heart to feel for poor lost souls.

I can rejoice now in a little better spirit. O, my Saviour, keep that which thou hast put into this heart. It is all of grace. Yes, every thing is of grace. I have more reason to feel this than any one else, for I have sinned against greater light and greater love. I do now rest all my dependence on the Saviour. I cannot look away from him one moment. I will keep in his presence—there alone is life and safety.

The principles I laid down last December, I desire should govern me now that my plan will have to be different. Indeed I cannot form one quite yet, until I look round and see what is to be done. My letters from the East tell me many things, and throw light on the preparation for my work. May I have strength for all that needs to be done.

Thursday, 20*th*. Most lovely, sunshine all around, and

music of the birds very sweet. These beautiful days should fill our hearts with gratitude.

Yesterday went to the consecration of St. John's Church. A beautiful Gothic, yet not equal to the old one. The scene was imposing and solemn. The priests in their robes kneeling in the chancel and round the altar, made a beautiful picture, and carried my thoughts back to the old Romish days, when

> The marble floor was swept
> By many a long dark stole.'

And then the glorious strains of the organ swelling along the arches, made my very heart leap. There is that in the forms of the Church which is exceedingly imposing, and there is thrown a veil of both poetry and mystery over its rites which fascinates the eye of the imagination. Oh, yes, it does fascinate, and there is the danger. 'Tis a veil to hide the simplicity, and, to the unrenewed mind, the *severity* of religion. It throws around the plain, self-denying, humbling precepts of the Gospel, a drapery very graceful and beautiful, and having also a devout air, the mind becomes contented to rest in it, without looking deeper for the spirit and power of godliness. I have indeed the best reason for believing that there are many pious and sincere worshippers in that church, but that its peculiar forms and tenets have the tendency to foster pride, and quiet the conscience, I have also very good reason to believe.

The service of yesterday made a deep impression on my mind. I am glad I went. It may be useful to me hereafter, and help to form my opinion of matters and things. I fear I was too much taken up with mere curiosity, and did not pray as I should, that that place of worship might be the gate of heaven to many souls. Yet so much of the service seemed merely formal, that my curiosity was excited more than any thing else.

"*Tuesday*, 26*th*. Feel deeply the state of beginning declension. Last year, how different we were. All interested and happy in the love of God. Now we are cold. 'O Lord, wilt Thou not revive us again?' Thought yesterday morning of asking a few friends to a special prayer meeting, and spoke to one about it. And now I pray for a blessing on this plan. May it succeed, and our meeting on Thursday warm our hearts and turn again our backslidings. Many of the dear girls joined the church at our communion in May, last year. The coming Sabbath, is the anniversary of that event. They will grieve that it finds them so little advanced.

Saturday, *April* 30*th*. The evening before our holy communion has at last come,—and beautifully its light is fading, while a sweet bird is singing his vesper song among the blossoms. My work in the early morning, and afterwards, with my singing and drawing school, has wearied me, and I sat at home this afternoon sewing and thinking. It was beautiful without—the sun shining brightly, and greenness and freshness all around. I have some sweet thoughts, and all this week have been more than usually tender, but I have not that sweet peace I enjoyed last year at this time. I cannot tell to what it is owing. Outward things affect me much less than formerly, and I have nothing to trouble me. Yet my heart does not flow forth freely and gladly, delighting in doing God's will, and resting in the sunshine of his face. Yet I think I feel more willing to give up every earthly thing. I can call God *my* Saviour. I do love him. O for a heart that entirely rests in him. I can tell my Saviour all my wants and he will help me.

Sabbath evening, May 1st. A delightful Sabbath within and around, and I do bless God for it. Since meeting, a thunder storm has been refreshing the earth, but now it is clearing, and the sun is gilding with a most peculiar crimson light, the trees and chimneys and masts of vessels, and a soft glow is cast over the eastern sky, where the clouds are passing away. Oh, how lovely is nature in all her moods! A flood of amber streams around the setting sun; and now I can see a faint bow just where the hills are peeping out of the mist Bright and lovely even in tears, this fair earth always seems. I shall love it till my latest hour. But O, there is a more glorious one where the redeemed shall dwell—one which shall never lose its freshness and beauty—on which the eye can feast and never grow weary!

That sweet bow, just in the spot where I gazed oftenest, just over those hills I have watched most—did it not mean something for me? I will learn its lesson of hope. Though these earthly scenes are hidden from our view, there are others more lovely, more spiritual, to be discerned by the eye of faith, and I will turn to them, for they can give me more true happiness.

The communion I did enjoy, it was refreshing. I thought over the whole year—so full of mercy to me—and I can say with thankfulness that I have enjoyed more refreshing seasons in my devotions at home, more comfort in the ordinances of the gospel, especially in the communion, more quiet in my Sabbaths, than ever before, and I can add, than in all my life put together.

I did give my poor heart all away this day at the communion, and now I do it again. I want to have more conversation of a Christian nature—and this has been turned into a resolution.

Tuesday, May 3d. Yesterday, in looking over the "Missionary Herald," thought how much need of self denial on our part to carry forward the great plans for the promotion of Christ's kingdom. I thought much of this yesterday. Oh, how much I need a heart filled with benevolence and ready to do my all in this work! which I cannot but feel to be glorious, and alone worth the energies of an immortal being. I pray God that he will so direct me, and so fill me with his love, that all I am and have may be devoted to Him, without one selfish reservation.

Wednesday, 4th. After dinner walked to Aunt M——'s, found a May-day party there. I had hoped they would have deferred their crowning till a warmer day, but there they were, and in spite of the showers they were a merry and beautiful group. S——, their lovely queen, fairer than most of her companions, did the honors of her station with grace and dignity. Her wreath was beautiful, and they had all shown much taste in the arrangement. It brought to my mind the time when I was a little girl, crowning May queens in that same grove. I went and played with them, and tried to be young again among their bright faces.

TO MRS. FITCH.

HARTFORD, *May* 16*th*, 1842.

"*My very dear Mrs. Fitch.* Your note, so full of kind words, deserved an earlier answer; but you know that to you, I do not need to make apologies. I should have written a very plain matter-of-fact sort of note last week, and I should have told you that you certainly mistook my character in supposing I was looking forward with very bright anticipations—but I have since then received a letter from the East, and after the reception of every letter, I find my heart looking forward more and more. And yet, my dear

Mrs. Fitch, though I make this confession to you, I feel that I do not anticipate so much as you seem to think I do. I do not dare to build my hopes of happiness on any thing which is in this world, for I feel too deeply in my own heart, that *this life*, however happy, cannot satisfy.

I am free now from any *morbid sense* of the vanity of this world, and I should be the last one to plant 'yews and cypresses' on the path-way through life, for I shall ever feel that there is enough of enjoyment mingled with the sadness, to make this state of being far more than passable—and to the Christian it surely need not be a gloomy way; for while he passes on, trusting in his God, there is many a ray of sunshine, and many a bright star, to light him to his home. But I do feel that there is nothing earthly on which we can place our *dependence* for happiness. And is not the true difference between the worldling and the Christian this? The latter may enjoy many things which the former does, but while he enjoys them he looks to a higher source, and feels that his portion is more enduring. I pray God that I may take the good and evil just as it comes, patiently submitting to the one, and thankfully enjoying the other, and striving to do his will, whatever it may be."

TO ONE OF HER EARLY FRIENDS.

HARTFORD, *July 5th*, 1842.

"My dear A. Since I heard of your marriage, I have wanted to send you my most sincere wishes for your increasing happiness. I little thought while your bridal day was passing, what was then taking place; and even now I can scarcely realize that you are no longer A. R.

And so you are now a wife, a happy one too, I imagine, rejoicing in the love of one who is more to you than all the world beside. My prayers have gone up to heaven for you, that God's blessing may be upon your union; that he may direct you in all your future path. Wherever your future lot may be cast, may His eye watch over you, guarding you from every evil; leading you to choose him as your everlasting portion.

I did not think, when you left my sick chamber last November, that I was bidding my good-bye to A. R. Had I known it, my dear friend, I should have urged you, even more strongly than I then did, to have settled one subject, which has for a long time been pressing on your attention; that so God might have been with you as your friend, in the important step you have taken. But it is not too late now. Can you not, joined by him with whom your destiny is linked forever, now in the commencement of your married life, give up to God, your Father and Redeemer, the hearts which should be his, and devote your lives to his blessed service? These are not mere words, dear A. I write what are the deepest feelings of my heart. You may have all the happiness which this world can give, and yet without *love to God*, you will find in the end that you have trusted for happiness in something which cannot satisfy an immortal being. But I believe that you are willing to assent to all this. The trouble with you has seemed to be, that you could not do what you felt was required of you. I wish I could make it seem plain to you. It does seem to my mind the simplest, the easiest and the most blessed thing in the world, to give up the heart to the control of God, and by daily looking to him for strength to conquer our corrupt inclinations, to grow in every thing which will make us like him. The act is one of simple, delightful trust, in one who knows just what we need. You have your Bible, dear A.; you can go to that. You will not forget, I am persuaded, in the midst of all the scenes through which you are now moving, that you have higher and more important interests, which demand your most serious attention.

I feel, my dear friend, that it is a fearful as well as a blessed thing to live in these days. It is a time in which we cannot take neutral ground; we must either take our stand as defenders of the truth, or shut our eyes to it, and be against it. Will you not inquire for yourself where right is? Do not be content to glide on with those who are around you, but ask yourself, 'are they right?' Take your Bible, dear A., and in the view of the glorious things which are being accomplished in these latter times, ask God to direct your course in life, that so it may be onward and upward, and brightened by his approving smile. You are now in the busy scenes of life; no longer a young, careless girl, acting without any thought or fear of the future, but engaged in more sober duties, which will tell on your everlasting condition.

May God bless and keep you. My heart is almost too full to write, while I think how years may pass away, and I shall hear but little of that early friend with whom many happy hours were passed. Our spheres will be widely different. May we each pass our days in the love and service of our God, and at last, may we meet in joy, to mingle our anthems of praise 'unto Him who has loved us, and washed us in his own blood,' and hath redeemed us from sin. Yes, to that glorious Redeemer, may it be our eternal happiness to ascribe all honor and glory. Good bye, my dear friend, my heart often prays for you

Your truly affectionate M."

TO THE SAME.

HARTFORD, *July* 21*st*, 1842.

"I feel, dear A., in parting from you, more than I can express. You are going to a far distant land, where the gospel ordinances to which you have been accustomed, will no more be present to draw you to God. You will be where the religion of your fathers is despised. Dear A., may the Lord keep you, and place around you his protecting arm, so that the adversary shall have no power to harm you. Your future course, perhaps, does not look to you as it does to me. I have deeply felt, ever since I knew you were going to ——, the coldness that would imperceptibly creep over you in regard to spiritual things. They will not be the less important because you may be insensible to them. The world may draw you into its whirl, until you forget that there was a time in your youth when you felt the importance of having a portion in the Saviour, and the scenes in which you will mingle may so engross your thoughts, that the whispers of God's spirit will not arouse you. But there will still be a God in heaven, whose eye will follow you, and the day of account will be ever drawing nearer and nearer. Dear A., there may come a time when the world shall be unfolded to you in its true light, when you shall see it is not worthy of your soul. O, then, when weary and sick at heart of its vanities, will you not remember the Saviour, whose love it may not then be too late to receive?

I know not how to close, dear A. I feel more than I can tell you. I shall pray for you 'without ceasing.' May God give you his blessing, and follow you in every path you may take.

I have one little favor to ask, my dear A., in parting. This little 'Daily Food,' I want to give you, with the request, that you will learn a verse each day, and think that your friend M. is learning the same. It will be a pleasant bond of union, when the ocean wave rolls between us, to know that the same bortion of Scripture is the comfort of each. Farewell—God bless you.

Ever yours, M."

JOURNAL.

"*New Haven, Tuesday evening, August 30th.* Once more in my dear New Haven home, after a week full of interest. Last Monday evening, in company with Dr. and Mrs. F., left this place for Philadelphia. The full moon was shining most gloriously over the dark waters of the sound. When we were fairly started, I began to feel that we were really going to our friends. It was too warm for sleep, and all night, as I lay in my berth, I could look out upon the waves and see the distant lights on the sound; and I continually thought of that song, 'Rock'd in the cradle of the deep.' Early morning found us at New York. After breakfasting on board, we went to the ferry to take the cars for Philadelphia. Saw, in crossing the ferry, the British ship 'War Spite,' a noble vessel. I had made up my mind to look at every thing I could, and to learn all I could; and certainly there never was a journey better fitted for the furtherance of such a purpose than that.

The day was uncommonly fine. The clouds floated over the deep blue sky, and were reflected from the waters beneath. It was a day of beauty and of glory. Our ride in the cars was full of interest to me. Every thing seemed novel. We passed through many places, and I enjoyed looking in the highest degree. Then we took the boat at Bordentown, and passed down the noble Delaware. 'Tis a most beautiful river, lined with green trees, and verdant meadows, and then the country seats and villages peeping out, were so picturesque, I was never tired of gazing at them.

I shall never forget the beauty of that day—the light sails floating on that sunny river—the soft clouds above us—the lovely scenery all around—peaceful, but never grand. We were approaching Bridesburg, and sat anxiously looking for the boat which was to take us on shore. It was a pleasant change from our large steamer into that little boat, and to skip lightly over the water to the shore, where Mr. D. was waiting for us. I was overjoyed to reach that place, to which I had looked forward so often; but it was far more beautiful than I thought.

I have no words to describe Pine Grove, the residence of Mr. D. The old venerable trees, tall, so tall they seemed to rest upon the sky,—the house, so antique, and just the one to people with visitants from the spirit land,—the beautiful opening to the river—the willows sweeping their long branches over the lawn—all combined to make it one of the finest places I ever saw. Then the perfect stillness reigning there—for the grounds are arranged so as to hide every other house, even the most distant; and it seems as if there was no house within a mile. I stood by the window, gazing out upon its beauty. Never before had such majestic trees greeted my eye. We were all entranced, and dear Mr. and Mrs. D. enjoyed our delight. Of the happy days spent there, I can say but little. The remembrance of those friends, will live like a fresh fountain of gladness in my heart; and of them I need no pen and ink memento.

Thursday was very beautiful. Rode to the various scenes of interest around the city. We saw in Germantown, old mansions, which must have stood before the revolution—and went through the valley of W., a most wild and romantic spot. Then to Laurel Hill, the cemetery on the Schuylkill, with its beautiful trees and solemn monuments—a most interesting spot. The monuments in white marble were exquisite: one of a little boy sleeping; another, a rose-stalk with six buds, in memory of a mother with her children resting there."

"*Hartford, Oct. 13th.* I have been looking over my state of mind for the past few months, and I felt that a day spent in this manner, and in forming such an estimate of the duties to which I must attend, this coming season, would not be unprofitable. My time has indeed been broken in upon very much since the warm weather commenced. Constant company until the last week in July. Then I prepared to go to New Haven, and the third of August found me there. Four weeks spent most delightfully in New Haven and Philadelphia, passed quickly away.

Thursday, the 15th of September, S. and M. W. spent with me. In the evening, their brother T. came in, and after staying a short time, took his sisters to pass the evening at his cousin's. Little did we think it was the last time he would pass our door. Friday morning, early, the girls were up, for M. was to start for Salem. We parted with kind and happy words, and no thought of the bitter to-morrow sent its shadow over us.

After dinner on Saturday, came the sad, dreadful shock. Poor W. and another young man were drowned. Mysterious and deeply afflictive this bereavement has been. After tea, went and staid with S. all night. Sabbath was a day long to be remembered. Oh, it seemed to us all, as if life never could be any thing again. The body was carried to Wethersfield at noon. A prayer was made by my father at the house, before its removal. Never can we forget that day. May we all remember the impressions which sank into our souls, while we stood around the bier of him who was so lately with us, in all the flow of life and health. He was the only son of his widowed mother.

This solemn event saddened us all, and the approaching wedding, where he was to have been, could not call back our thoughts to gayety."

"*Wednesday, Sept 21st.*, was dear H.'s bridal day. Spent the morning there to assist in arranging flowers, &c. When I went again at evening, they were just putting on her veil. There she stood for the last time as H. D. She was very calm, and looked most beautifully. Then we descended to the library, where Mr. P. and our groomsmen waited, and we prepared to go into the parlor—pinned on the white favors, and all was ready. I felt what could not be put in words during the ceremony, and prayed with my whole heart for their happiness, in the path in which they should walk. Then came the wedding party, and we were in a crowd of company, while H. met them all with sweet dignity and grace."

"*Nov. 6th.* Our communion. We have passed a precious Sabbath. My heart rests itself, and all its interests, on my Saviour; and I can look in and around, and feel calm in the thought of his love, of all my blessings, of all the gracious things in his kingdom, and in our eternal home. My communions will be few in this dear place, but may they prepare me for the more perfect communion in heaven. Since tea, spent an hour in prayer for all the dear friends who appointed to meet with me. What a comfort to remember them, though far from us. Oh, God is full of mercy to grant me these blessings.

And now I commit all my cares to God. My desire is, to do all I can for him. *Forgetting self—persevering in what I begin—feeling humble—trusting in my Saviour.* These are my resolves. Oh, for grace and strength."

"*Nov. Thanksgiving day.* There are many thoughts in my mind. I have been thinking all the morning of the innumerable mercies which crown my life. I have blessings in friends, in opportunities for improvement, both mental and moral, in ways of usefulness, and last, though not least, blessings in a spiritual sense. There are mingled feelings this day.

Great God, thou art pouring upon my poor, unworthy head, such blessings as fill me with shame, when I think of my poor improvement of them. Wilt thou give me strength to use them all in the way which will best glorify thee.

One thing fills me with anxiety. Not one of all my dear friends, who were not Christians last year, have become so this. Some of those over whom I have prayed, are interested in religion, and will, I trust, show in future, that their attention is not transient. But some who are dear to me, remain yet away from Christ. O, may I work while the day lasts, with a becoming zeal and untiring spirit of love, for those over whom I have influence; and may I, should another thanksgiving find me in this world, have the joy of seeing my desires fulfilled, in beholding them safe in thy fold.

This may be the last I shall ever spend in this dear home of the pilgrims. But ever shall I praise God, that he cast my lot in this land,—in these New England scenes, among these glorious privileges.

And now, in view of all my blessings, I come, and with grateful heart commit all my way unto the Lord, fully persuaded that he will do all things rightly with regard to the future. I can say that my *chief desire* is, so to use the good and the ill, I may yet receive from his hand, that he may be glorified, and his own perfect will be fulfilled with regard to me.

My dear father gave us a delightful sermon—'Who maketh thee to differ?' Just the right kind of sermon for the day, and the best way to make us feel truly grateful. When he closed, with the earnest hope and prayer for the continued prosperity of our beloved country, and looked forward, too, to the time in which we should meet around that throne where no sin would mingle with the voices of praise, my whole soul responded its amen to all, and I felt I could gladly go forth from my native land, to labor and die on a foreign soil, and cheerfully could trust my dearest interests in the hand of God.

Immediately upon the close of his sermon, the last word scarcely dying from his lips, the full organ swelled, and the choir struck up the anthem, 'Blessing and honor, glory and power, be unto Him who sitteth on the throne, and unto the Lamb, forever and ever.'

When I went to my room at night, I felt that it was the pleasantest thanksgiving season I had ever enjoyed.

Dec. 4th. Talked with my dear mother of the future, and had happy thoughts of our parting, and of my future work. Much impressed with what *Charlotte Elizabeth* says of private journals. She thinks they cannot be faithful, and may deceive us. Oh, may this not injure me! I write for the fixing in my mind events which I shall love to recall, and I pray God I may never, by reading these pages, be led to indulge a self complacent spirit. Let me remember the sins which I have but imperfectly noticed, and while they look me in the face, may I seek for peace only through Jesus."

"*Thursday*, 8*th*, 4 *P. M.* I thank God for putting it into my mind to keep this afternoon of the week as a time for meditation, and the special reading of the Bible. I have commenced studying the Bible anew, and can truly say that I find pleasure and profit thus far. If I look to God, he can give me such knowledge as I need. May I find him here in this season! I long to know the truths which lie hidden in his word, and I have been praying for light, and also that I might come fully under *Divine influence*, and be in all things subjected to God's holy will."

"*Sabbath evening, Dec.* 18*th*. These precious days which are passing, how can I improve them aright? When life is only for once, and is so short, how full of importance! Eternity only will make us realize these things. But I long *here* to see things as they are. What I want is a *true* interest in the souls of my impenitent friends. I feel that I have not yet learned the way to pray and labor for them, and I am trying now to find out what Jesus would have me do. Something seems to me wrong, for I have been praying a long time, and yet see no results. And oh, the time is so short!"

"*Fast-day, Dec.* 30*th*, 1842. In reviewing the year, I can truly say, 'goodness and mercy have followed me all the way;' and while I am deeply conscious of my own ill desert, I hope I do not deceive myself, in thinking, that I am on the whole in a better state, than when I wrote my fast-day account one year ago. I would hope that there is some more steadfastness; not so much blown about; that I am some nearer Christ, and feel his *dying love* some more, and the preciousness of redemption. I have had my mind turned more to the Holy Spirit of late; and I do hope I feel better about my missionary work. Yes, I do thank God that it does seem delightful to be engaged for Christ, and working in his vineyard, wherever he appoints. I hope I feel a desire to go wherever he directs me, and do whatever he thinks best, and if he would only go with me, that I would be willing to go far away for the sake of his cause.

There is a change, but oh, the work is far from complete, and yet, that it is begun, is cause for joy; and I will continue to trust my Saviour, and look more earnestly to him alone, and ask him to search my heart, to root out all evil, and fit me to do his holy will. If in any thing I am more peaceful, and am better in my feelings, it is all owing to the grace of God. Oh, I thank him, for bearing so long with me, for preserving my life and my privileges to me. I am resolved to keep my eye fixed on Jesus. Each year makes him more precious, and shows me more clearly, that he is my only hope. I am ready to sink without him, but his love does encourage me to continue the conflict. One side of the picture looks dark, but the other does look bright; but I will look alone to Jesus, who can make all bright."

"*Saturday, Dec.* 31*st.* Yesterday was a good day. Our church in a good state, and some encouragement to hope for a revival. On God's side all is ready; may he take every obstacle from our hearts. The prayers were solemn and the crowded room seemed filled with the presence of God.

It may be the blessing waits even now. God knows what the year will bring. My prayer is, O let me be fully devoted to Jesus and his cause, and may my ——— be a Christian. Yet my desires stop not with his conversion; my dear class, my friends, this dear people, the whole world. How sweet to think, that though our fondest projects may fail, yet Jesus' cause will go on, and will come to a complete accomplishment. Yes, 'The kingdoms of this world will become the kingdoms of our Lord and of his Christ, and he shall reign.' And in this kingdom let me and my dear friends cast all our interests."

"*Jan.* 1*st*, 1843. This morning was our communion, and it did seem pleasant to have it come on the first day of the year. We sang 'Our God, our help in ages past,' a sublime hymn, and 'On Jordan's stormy banks I stand.' My dear father's sermon was from Colos. i. 12; showing what was necessary in order to be prepared for the happiness of heaven. I could answer all the solemn tests with some satisfaction.

It was sweet to be around His table, and I did enter with my whole soul into the consecration of myself to Christ; and I did pray, that when the year came round again, I might be engaged for him far away among the heathen. These precious privileges, these dear friends, are very dear to me, but I do hope I can leave them all, and I pray God that I may not be in the slightest thing deceived about my state. I have resolved to go no step alone. I consecrate to Jesus, *my time*, *my studies*, *my friends*, *my earthly store*, and ask him to guide me every moment. O, he whose love brought him to die for us, will he not give us all things necessary to enable us to live for him? O, I know he will. My only resolution, or rather all my resolutions, are comprised in this one thing, '*trust in Christ, daily and hourly.*'

My class were all present this morning. We spent our hour in serious personal conversation. I talked with each one of my dear girls, and tried to get them to begin this day to do right. I have trembling hope for three. May God guide each one. I fear they may be suddenly called away. May I be faithful the little time that remains.

And now I give up myself, and all my dear friends, and my interests to Jesus, praying that *this* may be a year of the right hand of the Most High; that his kingdom may come, not only here, but in all our world. *Amen.*

I must notice the beautiful day which smiles upon us. The sky is bright and softly blue, and the snow lies upon the ground, and gives a sweet, home-like aspect to all the dwellings around. Yes, all is calm and bright and beautiful. My Father makes it all. And He who makes the natural world so lovely, is making the moral world shine brighter and brighter, and all the dark clouds of pollution shall be chased away. One thing I like, and 'tis that I am learning to read the *revealed word* of God, as well as the *natural word*, and I am thankful that I am beginning better to comprehend and love its sacred pages.

I must notice also, that on Saturday, I received from my dear friends such a testimonial of their love and interest in me, and of their love to the cause in which I hope we are all engaged, that I was overwhelmed with emotions. How sweet to have these dear friends, and sweet to spend an eternity in heaven with them."

"*Jan.* 15*th.* I have refrained from writing in my journal, because it wearied me—but I think these few weeks have been among the most interesting of my life. I wish I had a connected account of recent events, for I should love to remember them when far away. I intended to have squared off old accounts the last year, and begun afresh in my journal, but many duties prevented. On Friday, Jan. 6th, I was invited to spend an evening in a large circle of friends, where they were to dance. I felt sorry to have these circles just now, when we are hoping that there is a little revival. Could not go—feared I was *getting severe.* O, to think of my setting up for a censor! It troubled me to stand aloof from my friends, and to be obliged to show them I did not approve of dancing. Several times of late have been so tried—very few of my friends think as I do. In time past I have had much perplexity, and much thought on the subject, but my mind is made up.

Sabbath, heard a solemn sermon from father, from the text 'He is joined to his idols, let him alone.'

After dinner, as I sat in my room, mother opened the door, and told me with tears in her eyes, that F. had come to see father, completely overcome, in an agony of feeling, impressed during the sermon. How I then hoped with trembling. I could only pray—and when I thought how many conflicting feelings were in his heart, the *pride*, the *world*, I could hardly believe it would be possible for him to change. But what is impossible with man, is possible with God.

On Tuesday evening, on returning from the lecture, we found F. with my mother, in the parlor. But how changed! Gentle, subdued—his voice tender, and he appeared completely absorbed in the one subject. Mother had been reading to him, and he had been several times in tears. As he retired with my father for private conversation, we spent the time in trembling thought and prayer. I could only think of this verse; and it was in my mind, with a power before unknown,—'With God all things are possible, but not with man.'

That night, at evening worship, some expressions of my father's showed that he hoped that F. had at last found rest. O, this was too good to be believed! That F. was now a Christian—a ransomed one—could it be true? That night, the prayers of months, of two years, had been graciously, most wonderfully, most sweetly answered. I speak not of my own prayers. Too much sin had been in mine, for me to hope much in regard to them. But others had prayed. There had been some, who had had their thoughts turned particularly to this stranger in our midst. Has not

God something for him to do? How wonderful is his working!"

"*Thursday*, 12*th*. F. came in, so happy, so changed, that I could not believe it was he. He gave us some account of his feelings. The case is truly wonderful. May God give him grace to hold out. He played and sang 'Return, O wanderer, return,'—told how unworthy he was, how wonderful it was that God should change his heart of sin. His eyes were full of tears many times. He could not think of Jesus' wonderful love, without thinking of his own sins. 'He long'd to devote his all to him.' Said 'it was the sweetest enjoyment to kneel down and pray;' 'to take his Bible and read.' All looked well—still, felt how much he needed God's strength, to keep him from falling.

On Wednesday, the 18th, T. called to see my father. She was indulging a hope—was impressed by the same sermon, and same part which had affected F. Surely, God is wonderful in working. She is very intelligent, and the workings of her mind are very deep. Had a few words with her. She told me how differently she felt towards me from what she used to. She once almost hated me, because I wrote her a religious note in school. I had forgotten the circumstance. It was some years since—five, I think."

"*Wednesday*, 25*th*. This day is set apart by the North and Centre Churches, as a day of fasting and prayer. We need such a season very much, for we feel our churches are not in the best state for a revival. We are hoping and praying, and doing something, but we feel that we need to be converted anew ourselves, before we can enter, as we should, into the work. It is very evident that God is ready to bless us, if we do not, by our coldness, hold him back. Oh! this must not be!"

TO M. S.

Sabbath, Jan. 29th, 1843.

"My dear M. I have felt, this morning, that I must write you a note just as we used to do long ago. Does it not seem as if God has a blessing for our classes, if we will only be faithful, and pray and labor without fainting? May he give us strength, and the willing, earnest mind, to engage in all that he points out for us. We can commit these dear children to him, and beseech him to receive them as his own. But O, I tremble, lest we may not feel and act as we ought. Dear M., let us continue to join our prayers for their conversion. I am sure we may pray with the expectation of a blessing; for does not Jesus love their souls far better than we do? Yes, and we pray to One who not only loves, but who has given himself to die for them, for us all. He can raise us from our ruin, and make us free from sin. Oh, blessed emancipation! To be free from sin! from all which separates our souls from Him who is the fountain of holiness and life."

JOURNAL.

"*Monday, Jan. 30th.* The reading, yesterday, of 'Edwards' Life,' has awakened new feelings, and caused me much sorrow. I found my love to God and Christ so far below his, that I determined to go directly and search the matter out in my heart, and see whether I had any reason to hope, and whether I had not been deceived all my life.

I have had a solemn and heart-searching time. I have been in bitterness of spirit, but I am glad and only glad that I read this book. I long to be a whole Christian, not a *half, undecided* one. Oh! how dishonorable to God, how ungrateful to the Saviour who died for me! Sometimes I think I have not yet seen enough of myself, and these trials are to show me. I think it is only doing God's will, which will satisfy my heart. I remember his sweet promise of the Holy Spirit to those who ask. Will he not grant it to me?

Dear Saviour, here on this day I long to give my whole being to thee, without any reservation. I shall be happy only when thou takest me, all that I am, and all that I have."

TO C. C.

HARTFORD, *Feb.* 20*th*, 1843.

"I have thought much of you, dear C., during these weeks in which the Spirit of God is blessing your town. I wish that we were enjoying a refreshing from on high—but I hope you are careful not to do too much. I never would do again as I did during our revival two years ago; and yet I cannot be sorry for what I then did, for I would not for worlds give up the experience of that blessed winter. It is very hard indeed to keep in the right line. A fear of not improving the peculiar blessings of a revival, leads on the one hand to a constant activity; and on the other hand, the fear that nature will sink under it, makes us want to rest some; and so we are continually wavering, (that is, I am, I hope you do better) between the two. I sometimes think that the old saying, 'we may as well die one way as another,' is the best one for me to act upon, and so be relieved from this constant struggle. Happy indeed shall we be in that blessed world, where there will be no sinking, decaying nature to trouble and draw away our thoughts. Till that world is reached, we must toil on, sometimes mounting joyfully to heaven, and sometimes drooping, and sad, and weary in this land of sin and temptation.

I must tell you, that last week I had a most lovely letter from my dear Marion. I shall never in this world see her again—and yet I have become strangely accustomed to this thought. Is it because I really feel heaven to be near, and this life's separation a short one? or is it because I have become indifferent to these partings? We were as near sisters as we could be, and when she went away it seemed as if the best part of my life had gone with her. I wish you knew her.

This is the day that Isabella* is to be married, and the next week on Tuesday, she sails in the Emma Isadora, for Smyrna. I have lived all this month in thoughts of her. I am reading Harriet Newell's life too. So young! only nineteen—and such a sweet, happy Christian. Does it not require great grace, to turn away from every earthly thing, and say, 'Whom have I in heaven but thee? and there is none upon the earth I desire beside thee.' It is this entire devotion to the Saviour which animated the first heralds of the Cross, that I long to feel—and yet I am only groping my way along, through toils and through tears; sometimes feeling the love of Jesus, but often full of sorrow at my poor attempts at loving and serving him, who is worthy to receive the affections and the homage of all hearts in the universe. For this I daily strive and watch and pray—and will you not, too, pray for your friend?

I want to thank you in my piano's name for your remembrance to it. It is ready to return the sound in the sweetest manner it is capable of, if you will only listen. Will it be waking the echoes of a foreign land next year? I suppose you would say, 'this is a question M. can answer better than I.'"

* Now Mrs. Bliss, at Trebizond.

JOURNAL.

"*Feb.* 21*st*, 1843. To-day I have been looking over my state, and trying to give up myself anew to God. I have been looking over my past life, and I feel the deepest sorrow in view of my continual vileness, and my preferring my own will to God's. Though my outward conduct has been correct, yet this has been manifested in a thousand different ways. When I view my life, and think how it has been filled with infinite love and goodness on the part of God, and with continual sin and ingratitude on my part, I am overcome with sorrow—particularly that when called to the Missionary work, I did not rejoice and devote myself gladly to it, but shrank back, and preferred my own ease. For this I can never cease to feel the greatest shame and sorrow, and, I trust, the deepest penitence. I have wept and prayed over it many times—and to-day it has been again in my thoughts, standing out among the dark lists of sin in my past life. I do beseech God, in his infinite mercy, for Christ's sake, to blot out the past; and I earnestly entreat him to give me now a sense of his pardoning love.

I have been endeavoring to yield up my soul into the hands of Jesus, that I may begin *now* with *full purpose of obedience to be the Lord's.* I desire to place him *first*, and I do not know of one single thing that I am not happy, or at least willing, to give up, and my heart approves of it, and I feel I cannot be happy in any other course. To God my Father, my Saviour, my Sanctifier, I do now yield myself entirely, desiring only to be in his hands, to have no will of my own, but to do his own blessed will, from this time forth and forever more. And now, trusting in atoning blood to wash away the guilt of the past, and trusting in an Almighty friend to keep me with regard to the future, I commit myself and all my interests to his safe keeping.

I renew my resolutions, my principles of action I would rather call them, made more than a year ago. I have lived *very poorly* indeed in accordance with them, yet I do desire still to be guided by them—and by God's help I will keep them—but oh, by his help alone, for I am all weakness.

And now I have given up all to Christ. I have made a full consecration. I hope I am no longer *half persuaded*, but all persuaded to be his, entirely and forever; and yet, I never felt my weakness and sin as I do now."

"*March 5th.* The light is fading of a precious communion Sabbath! How much has happened in these two months! What encouragement have we to go on, still hoping, toiling, trusting, till the end come! In the midst of the various and conflicting feelings, which for these two months have been agitating my mind, I think I can see the leadings of God's blessed Spirit. I hope I find in my heart this day a more ardent desire to be wholly devoted to Jesus.

During these two months, F. and T. have become Christians. How little did I think, last communion, that I could count this among our blessings, when next the day came. Surely, God is full of love, and shall I not go on, and have strong faith that all my dear friends may be led to the Saviour, until our circle shall be safe in the fold, and not our circle only, but millions of others, until this whole world knows the Lord our God? Several, too, of my young friends, are becoming more decided in their Christian feelings, and exhibit pleasing evidence of being God's children. May Jesus take them and lead them straight to heaven. And the good Spirit is gently touching our hearts, reviving the graces of his children, and calling those who are far away from God to return.

These two months have been marked by mercies outwardly, and the inward strivings of my heart have been marked by mercy too. And now I do commit myself to a Saviour, who can save me. And I surrender to him all I am, and all I have, to be his forever. With God I leave all my friends and myself—and in his hands we are safe."

"*Saturday, March* 11*th.* I am here in New Haven, with my dear Mrs. F. She is very feeble, but we trust her in God's hands."

"*Sabbath,* 12*th.* This morning heard the blue birds singing. How pleasant is the returning spring! may it bring spring to our souls. May God's Spirit breathe upon us, and awaken us to a new life.

I have had some interesting conversation with my dear Mrs. F., but she is very feeble. I feel continual solicitude in her behalf. She is hardly out of my thoughts night or day. I watch her every moment, but her physician thinks more favorably of her case."

"*Hartford, April* 16*th,* 1843. My birth-day, and I am twenty-two years old. I have many thoughts to-day, and yet I see that time does soften and chasten our feelings; for I view the past and the future in a far calmer manner than I have ever been able to do before. The past is full of blessings on God's part, and I hope I have some gratitude. And it is indeed full of sin, and I hope I have some suitable sense of it. May I from this time forth make a holy use of all that God grants me, looking only to Jesus for pardon, for strength, for happiness. I have many sweet blessings to notice in the past year. Oh, how good is my Saviour. To him I do indeed surrender all. May his kingdom come, and his holy will be done in this sinful world, and may all I learn, and all I do, be for the furtherance of this great object. The future, all to us unknown,

I commit to his care. He will bring events as seemeth him good. I am not anxious. This is probably my last birth-day in this dear home; but God gives me strength to contemplate it peacefully; and I hope I can say, my chief desire for myself and all my friends is, to be employed in doing God's will."

"*June* 30*th*. I had not intended to write any more in my journal, for it occupied so much of my time—so I closed it on my birth-day. But I think on such occasions as the communion Sabbaths, &c., it would be well for me to note a few of the more important events which occur, both in the inner and outer world.

These two months which have passed since our last communion have been marked by innumerable mercies. My time has passed for the last few weeks in a very even way, both without and within, but before that I was some of the time tempest-tost. Yet it does seem to me I have advanced some. Since the last communion, I have learned more what it is to *abide in Christ*. I have been helped some with regard to my selfishness, and find it easier and pleasanter to live for others, than ever before. There is still trouble in my heart, that the Bible is too much a sealed book to me. Over this I pray daily and earnestly. I feel that I have but begun, in every thing. I do hope that God's Holy Spirit has renewed my heart, but I am very faint and sinful, and can scarcely keep along in the path in which it is my earnest desire to walk. But I try to look at Christ. And what I have been resolving on is, *to abide in him through all things*.

I am happy in seeing my young friends coming one by one into the kingdom of Jesus. E. joined the church last May, and next Sabbath C. will also. The others of this young circle continue their interest in divine things—and the number is increasing. O, may God keep them, and lead them all to heaven.

I have been able to accomplish many things, and there are some more which I wish to finish before H. comes. But I try to be patient about them all, trusting in Christ, that he will help me in every thing needful. Oh, I long to be fully devoted to this blessed Saviour.

May I and my friends be engaged in doing his will; then, whatever comes, all will be right."

Here ends the journal; a manuscript of about five hundred pages, compactly written, in which the principal events of two and a half years of her short life are briefly noticed, together with the influence which these had upon her Christian character.

She seems to have had two reasons for keeping it. One was, as she has said, that she might have the satisfaction of recalling scenes and events contained in it, when she should "be far away." And the other, that she might be able to mark with more distinctness, her progress in the divine life. The foregoing extracts are, of course, but a small portion of the whole, but they are sufficient to show the tenor of her daily life—with this exception, however, that she judged of her conduct by the motives which influenced her, and not by actual results; and has given her own impressions of herself, rather than the impressions of others with regard to her; and while she has treated with unsparing severity, her faults and imperfections, she has scarcely noticed the daily routine of active and benevolent duties which graced her life.

CHAPTER VIII.

PREPARATIONS FOR LEAVING HOME, MARRIAGE AND DEPARTURE.

TO M.

HARTFORD, *June 9th*, 1843.

"MY dear sister,—Since I wrote you last, I have had time to do a great many things. I wish I could send you a daguerreotype likeness of my life for the year past, for there are many things in it I want you should know. My winter was taken up in preparations for leaving home. Thanks to good friends, I have had very little sewing to do, for they insisted upon doing nearly every thing for me; and you may be sure it has been a great relief to mother as well as to myself. I wish you could see the beautiful gifts I have had. Not a week passes without bringing some token of love from some one or more of my friends. They have remembered many things that I had not thought of as necessary, so that my Eastern home will be most beautifully supplied with articles for my personal comfort.

I spent nearly all the month of March in New Haven, with my dear Mrs. Fitch, who is very ill indeed. Death must come into these happy circles; but it is blessed to look at this world only as our state of trial, and to remember the world where rest will come. And is it not sweet to trust ourselves and our friends in the hands of One who metes out all our changes in wisdom and in love? He has His own blessed designs to fiulfil; is carrying on his own cause in our world; and if He sees it to be necessary for the triumph of truth and holiness that we suffer, then let us trust ourselves in His hands, and feel that He will give us strength to bear all which He sees fit to lay upon us in this our mortal life.

I scarcely dare look forward a few weeks. H. is probably now on the ocean. Dear M., were you by my side, how much we could recount of all the way in which the Lord our God has led us. When I think of all that has passed in my life, I can only thank my Father in Heaven for all his mercies; and I feel that I am the least of all, and the most unworthy of such blessings.

* * * * * * * *

I find in closing that I have not begun to say what I wished. I intended to have told you about my missionary work, but that I must leave till a future time. We shall be engaged chiefly with the Armenians. I feel an increasing interest in that part of the missionary field, and O, I hope, my dear M., that I shall have strength to consecrate my whole life to the service of Christ, and may be the instrument of some good to that benighted people.

During the past month, I have been seeing many of my dear friends, and O, my heart twines around them so, that if I did not trust in Jesus to bear me through the parting, I could never leave them; but I look to Him, and I can trust all that I love in His hands, and feel that we are all united in the same glorious cause, and have the same heavenly home in view. You, my dear M., will ever live in my heart of hearts, and the memory of those days which we spent together I shall ever cherish as among the sweetest of my life."

TO MISS B.

"My dear Miss B.,—It would very poorly accord with my feelings to write a formal note of thanks to the friends who have so kindly united with you in your labor of love; and yet I wish in some way to express my gratitude for the unwearied efforts which have been made to render my home on missionary ground comfortable and pleasant. Will you tell the ladies from me, that I shall ever carry the remembrance of their kindness in my heart, and that I do not cease to pray that God may reward and bless them? It will be a comfort to me to know that I am remembered in your prayers, for I feel more and more every day my need of strength from above to prepare me for the duties which may soon devolve upon me. Life is of so little importance unless spent for the glory of God, that I long to have every moment of mine occupied in doing His will.

Oh, how sweet it will be, when this life is over, and when all the redeemed are gathered to their home in heaven, to meet those we have loved here, and spend an eternity with them in the praise and service of Christ. Then, it will be joy to us to reflect, that in our feeble manner we were able to do something for the kingdom of holiness and peace which God is setting up in this world."

When Mary was called to contemplate the missionary field as the scene of her future labors, before deciding to enter upon it, she examined her qualifications for the work with great carefulness and fidelity. The work of missions was in her estimation a great work; and the preparation which she deemed necessary for entering upon it, was something more than external accomplishments, or piety even; she felt that there must be a love for the work itself; a preference of it to any other work, and a willingness to make personal sacrifices whenever the salvation of souls or the cause of Christ should in any way require it. As has been seen by notices in her journal, she had a constant sense of her dependence on divine aid in all her efforts to promote the spiritual welfare of others; especially was this true when contemplating her qualifications for the work of missions. She had from early youth been a devoted, self-denying laborer in the vineyard of Christ at home, but now that her field was about being changed, and God was calling her "to the deeply responsible work of glorifying Him among those who knew Him not," she felt a new and increased sense of dependence upon Him for aid; and under a deep conviction of utter helplessness if left to herself, she "resolved not to go one step alone, but if Jesus would only go with her, then she would be willing to go far away for the sake of His cause."

But her preparation was but in part completed when she decided with regard to her qualifications for laboring in a foreign field. Another and a heavy responsibility she felt to be resting upon her—a responsibility which she might not put off lightly, or lay aside without seeking counsel and strength from above. Providence had opened before her a wide field of usefulness in her native place, and had qualified her well to fill it; and she loved to labor in it, and was daily seeing results which brought joy to her heart, and encouraged her to go forward.

Her Sabbath-school class, how could she leave this without knowing that each dear pupil was safe in the fold? She had a trembling hope for three of the youthful members of her class, and she must find one who would be able to watch over and guide these; and who should also have warm hearted piety, that so she might win to the Saviour those whom she herself must leave strangers to Him.

The dear circle of intimate friends who met weekly in her room to unite with her in coming to the throne of grace, would these continue to meet together in another place of prayer, to remember her as well as themselves, when she should no longer meet with them? and the friends who were still out of Christ, for whose conversion she had been laboring and praying a long time, how could she leave them thus?

Among other benevolent objects was one which was dear to her on many accounts. It was a youthful sewing circle, who met at stated times to work for the "Grand Ligne Mission." In this circle she felt at home; each member was to her as a younger sister; and she had presided over it with untiring cheerfulness from its commencement. Finding it impossible to obtain one to take her place, she continued to preside over it until near the time of her leaving home, and then was obliged to commit the dear little circle to Providence and their own efforts.

A number of young girls met with her weekly to unite in prayer. Several of these were members of her class in the Sabbath school. It is delightful to recollect that some of the number continued to meet at the same hour, and in the same place where she so often met with them, until after her removal from this world; and there is reason to believe that having knelt with her here at the throne of grace, they will one day bow with her before the throne of glory.

When she committed to God the interests which were dear to her, as she so often was wont to do, all these, and more also were included, and there was a deeper meaning than the mere words implied.

But these interests, dear as they were, and difficult as she found it to dispose of them, were yet in her estimation not the greatest which she was called upon to resign. Ties stronger than these must be broken. To a friend she writes thus; "I find that my heart clings so strongly to my home, that I shrink from the future. I could bear it for myself, but for these dear parents, I feel every day, that I cannot go and leave them." But the leadings of providence were direct and clear, and the parents of Mary thought it right and felt it a pleasure to smooth the path before her, and to yield her up to the call of duty.

Mary was married to the Rev. Henry J. Van Lennep, a missionary under the patronage of the American Board, Sept. 4th, 1843, and sailed with him, accompanied by her father, in October following, for Smyrna. A few extracts from last letters to friends, will give the reader some slight idea of the events attendant upon her leaving home, and also of her feelings at the time.

TO M.

HARTFORD, *Sept.* 22, 1843.

"I have seized my pen while H. is marking our trunks, to tell you in some hasty lines what I have been longing to tell you in a whole sheet. Dear M., you can imagine, without my telling you particularly, the occupation, and excitement, and overwhelming care and thought, which have attended these few months; and you will not wonder that in the midst of it all, I could not sit down and write to an absent friend.

You probably know that Sept. 4th was our wedding-day. We started the next day for the 'Falls,' taking Rochester and the meeting of the American Board on our return. The meetings at R. were very interesting, and we formed some delightful Christian acquaintances. Our journey was, as you may well suppose, full of deep interest. And now we are lingering for a few days in our beloved home, with the precious circle of our relatives and friends around us, soon to bid adieu to all. O, may God strengthen them and us for the parting.

You will not forget to pray for your friends who are so soon to be removed from the privileges of a Christian land. May we be faithful to our God, and to the cause to which we devote our lives. Dear M., pray for my poor father and mother. There is a world where we may all be happy together. We try to fix our eyes on that world. May those who have been the light and support of my way through all my early years—may they reach that home where all the redeemed shall rest in peace.

Dear M., we are both united in the best of causes. Let us trust our Saviour. O, M., remember my father and mother; write to them often. Don't forget our Sabbath evenings. Good bye. God bless you.

Ever your friend and sister,

M. E. V. L."

TO MRS. F.

Sept. 27th, 1843.

"My dear Aunt S. We are on the eve of our departure, and the day after to-morrow, we take our last look of our dear home. The piano and my little bureau are now being packed, and our house is very sad indeed. I have come to my room to say my parting words to my dear, dear friend. How much I shall want to see you! How often my thoughts will fly back to New Haven, and will seek your room; and when we are tossing on the ocean, I shall turn to the quiet homes of my friends and give them many thoughts, but not regrets. Oh, no, I am not sorry I am going. I am not afraid of the deep. dark waves. I have committed my way to the Lord, and my trust is in Him; and my prayer to Him is, that my selfish heart may become pure and disinterested, ready to take hold of any labor that will advance his kingdom and glory.

My dear aunt S., you know how I remember your words of counsel: how I have laid up in my heart all the treasures, which intercouse with you through many years has collected. May God reward you for the good you have done me. You and dear Dr. F. have been precious friends to me.

I have not begun to tell you what I wish, but I shall try to find time on board ship to write you a long letter. May God take us all safely through this changing world, and bring us to His heavenly kingdom. To Him I trust the future. To His care I commit my dear parents and brother; He can supply all their need. Oh, you know what we all feel now. Pray for us.

Ever your affectionate,

MARY E. V. L."

The parting from the home of her childhood can never be put on paper. Often as the scene occurs, it comes with a first painful freshness to every one who passes through it; and to one who has not felt what it is, it can never be described with any thing like the overwhelming reality.

After leaving home, Mary spent a week very pleasantly amongst friends in Boston, and from that place, sailed for her eastern home the eleventh of October.

The morning of that day rose clear and bright—adieus had all been spoken; the last parting with the parent who was to be left behind had been anticipated; the secret chamber and the presence of God only having been witness to that scene; and now only the public exercises on board remained to be performed.

At 10 o'clock the deck of the Stamboul was thronged with sympathizing friends, who were there, not so much to give and take the parting look, as to commend the little company who were to encounter the perils of the deep, and some of whom were to take up their residence in a far distant land, to the protection and blessing of God.

The prayer was offered, the parting hymn was sung, the vessel was loosed from her hold, and bore away on her outward course. As she swept by the projecting wharf, Mary was seated on the deck, her husband and father standing protectingly by her on either side; but her heart was not with them then. One object on the shore riveted her attention. It was her mother. A friend who witnessed the scene, in speaking of it afterwards to that mother, said, "She looked as if she would, have taken her heart out, and left it with you." A mother's feelings in parting from a daughter in such circumstances have been expressed by the poet in a manner strikingly true and beautiful:

"Yet go, my spirit goes with thee!
Yet go, thy spirit stays with me!"

One white signal seen through the shrouds of other vessels, marked the path of the Stamboul, as she gently glided along amidst the dense forest of masts which lined the harbor. At length she was seen through an opening vista, in bold relief on the clear blue sky, all her canvas spread, and every sail filled. Another turn, and that bark with its precious freight disappeared from the straining eye.

TO HER MOTHER, BY THE PILOT-BOAT.

BOSTON HARBOR, *Oct.* 11*th*, 1843.

"My dear Mother. I write in full view of Boston, where you are, and am sitting where last you saw me, looking on the waves, the clear sky, the city—all is beautiful! and God is with us, and with you, and He will keep us united in heart.

Dear mother, my own dear mother, you are not sorry we are going. You know why we go. It is not for our own pleasure; it is God who has appointed our way;

and I do think we go for Him, and shall live for him in every thing.

Dear mother, pray that we may be wholly devoted to our Saviour; that the salvation of all may appear so important to us, that we shall be always earnestly engaged in leading many to Christ. Pray that we may never forget the object of our mission. Good bye, my precious mother, we are all in God's hand, and he can sustain us. I have not a fear if God will only enable us to do right.

Two o'clock. My dear Mother. The beautiful breeze which took us from the wharf died away soon after, and now we are becalmed in the harbor. I remained on deck a little while after writing your note, and then came down and arranged the things in our state-room. Then H. came, and we read together the 14th chapter of John. Isn't it a sweet chapter? Since then I have been on deck till just now, looking at Boston—at the State-House, and I knew that Mrs. B.'s, where you were, was near there. It is a dear land, and I could not bear the thought of leaving it and you, if I did not feel that God had ordered it, and that He would go with me and make me useful. When we sat on deck, I heard the waves dashing on the shore with a ceaseless rush.

My mother, when you go back to H. and the house seems lonely, do not think you are alone, for my heart is with you. God will keep us, and we shall meet again. Blessed thought! we certainly shall meet again, if we trust in Christ and are faithful to Him, where there are no more partings. Dear E., God keep him and make him a Christian.

Once more, my dear mother, good bye.

Your own daughter,

MARY."

CHAPTER IX.

EXTRACT OF A JOURNAL KEPT WHILE CROSSING THE ATLANTIC

Bark Stamboul, *October* 21*st*, 1843.

"My dearest mother,—This evening is the first time I have been able to succeed in commencing the journal to which we have looked forward with an interest both painful and pleasant. And you see by my writing that the motion of the vessel prevents my doing it very easily. But I do *so* long to write you what is passing! I have *thought* so many long letters to you since we parted, that I must begin, spite of all the difficulties. Oh, how beautiful my home looks! How blessed all the days that I have spent there! My heart returns to it with such a longing that at times the separation is almost insupportable. But I do not want to fill my journal with these things, neither for your sake nor mine. Dear mother, it is God's will, and he will render this discipline useful to ourselves and to others too.

While I was writing your second note in my state-room, I felt very dizzy, but I was determined to finish it, so that Mr. Hill could carry it to you; so, as soon as I had sealed it, I ran up on the quarter-deck and stood by H., to breathe the fresh air. We watched the land, all the islands about Boston, and the beautiful shores. Several gentlemen went with us, and returned in the pilot-boat called the Breeze. Between three and four o'clock, they shook hands with us and wished us a pleasant voyage, and then one by one descended to the little boat, which took them to the Breeze. Then we were all alone, our little company, shut up for a long voyage.

We had dinner about four, but I could not go down. I sat on a cannon and leaned my head against the side of the ship, while H. brought me the old cloak. But soon I was too ill to sit up, and I went down to my berth. Thursday morning I was still sick, and could not bear the thought of eating, and heard to my horror, as the gentlemen were talking around the breakfast table, that eating cured sea-sickness, and eat, a person must. Steward brought chicken tea, but it made me very sick, and then H. took me on deck a little while, and then back to my berth, where I passed the afternoon dozing and thinking of home, and of you, and of the good cold water in the well. Oh, how often I tried to imagine that Clara was bringing me a glass of fresh water; and then I longed for ice, till I almost thought I had it in my mouth.

Oh, how much I thought of you that afternoon, and prayed for you, and thought of your reaching home. Dear mother, did not Christ support you?

I counted the hours, and thought when you would take your tea. I am continually imagining what you are about. I follow you in all your daily duties.

Sabbath my heart all went home. I heard the church bells, saw the bright faces of the Sunday school girls, looked in upon you at your Sunday dinner, and imagined you reading to E. afterwards.

As M. was able to be brought on deck, we sat together and talked of home. I forgot to say that on Friday evening we commenced family prayers. The crew are not present. In the afternoon we had preaching on deck. I wish a painter could have drawn the group. It was a clear afternoon, about four o'clock. Some of the gentlemen leaned over from the upper deck. The crew sat in a row and looked intently at father, and the two mates sat on the raised place where you and I stood together; you remember it. Dr. A. and father stood near the cabin door, and then we sang, and father, who had suffered much from sea-sickness, prayed, and preached a short extemporaneous sermon, and it was quite like Sabbath day. I had thought the day would not be very profitable nor pleasant, but it was both. In the evening we sang sacred music in the cabin, all the good tunes that you love, and I retired with that quiet feeling which a sweet Sabbath always gives.

Monday, the 16th, was a wild day; our first hard wind, and a head wind too. We reached the outside of the gulf stream, and the weather is always warmer there, and apt to be stormy. Our introduction was rather a hard one. I attempted to sit at dinner, but was obliged to remove with my plate up stairs, for the ship rolled and pitched in a remarkable manner, and the spray came washing over the deck. O, what an afternoon and night we had! There was no rest for us. We heard the wind screaming through the cordage, and while we lay in our berths, the heavy tramp of the sailors, and all the sounds connected with a storm, kept us from sleep. Tuesday passed in a tossing manner, cloudy, and I think showery too; but Tuesday night passes all my powers of description for discomfort. O, our rolling and tossing, and the sliding about of every movable thing was wonderful. I wish you could have seen our state-room on Wednesday morning. In the course of the night every loose article had toppled down, and lay in a mass of confusion on the floor. The bowl which had been used for arrow-root, was rolling from one side to the other, and the two spoons were following it. Bang, went the folding doors every few moments, like cannon, and bang went the backs of the settees, also, and creak, creak, said the rudder, while a confused chorus of movables filled all the spaces of time. In the morning, our 'intellects,' to say nothing more, 'were all up in heaps.' The only way to cure such things is to go on deck; there the fresh wind generally puts all things right. There was one day we could not go on deck at all, it was so stormy. The only thing to do at such times is to lie still in our berths. Those days we could do very little. I tried now and then to open my crewel work, but the least motion seemed a burden, and sitting up below made me sick.

Friday, the 20th, was a glorious day. During the night it had cleared off, and in the morning a grand breeze was carrying us between ten and eleven miles an hour. The waves were magnificent. It was very hard to keep our position for a single moment; but in the afternoon, though they tossed us still, they were not quite so high, and I came down and took out my things, and arranged my state-room in nice order, without feeling sick at all. I have not been able to do it before, since I came on board. Saturday morning, as I awoke early, I tookmy crewel as I lay in my berth, and had an hour to work in before breakfast time. The only tedious hours are from daylight till breakfast, which is not till half past eight. It makes the night seem very long to retire as we do about nine, but all the rest of the time flies."

"*Tuesday, 24th.* Sabbath, 22d, was not clear, but the rain was most providentially detained till after our service, which was at ten in the morning. Father preached from the text "Behold I lay in Zion," a written sermon, but he made selections from it. We sang Ariel, 'Oh, could I speak the matchless worth,' and Ward, to the words

'When I survey the wondrous cross.' After service it rained, so we all came down stairs.

We have an Italian on board, a servant of Mr. F., who is an excellent cook, and sometimes he makes us very nice dishes; but our cook, who is a miserable one, is quite jealous of him, and Guseppe cannot do as much as he would. But last Sabbath he cooked our dinner, and though I felt very sorry that so much time should be spent in cooking an extra dinner on that sacred day, I could not help relishing his dishes. Our poor bodies occupy, at sea, the most of our attention. We are continually contriving for our appetites, for we become more and more dainty. Our cook tries to make bread and pastry, but both are miserable, so we eat ship crackers. Every day steward roasts apples for the ladies, and these are very fine. The best part of our dinner is the fine dish of apples that always appears last. Our water, as you may suppose, is not good; I can scarcely be willing to taste it; but we put the currant jelly in sometimes, and sometimes the soda powders, and sometimes go without."

"*Wednesday, October 25th.* We have had a fine wind to-day, and after the bad winds of the last few days, it has done our spirits good to know we were going so fast to Gibraltar. That is the point to which we are now looking, and where, if this wind continues, we can be in a week or ten days. We are already 1600 miles from America.

Monday, the 23d, was a very mild day. I never before felt the sun so hot in October. At times it would be oppressive were it not for the winds. That day, I began reading to H. in French, and trying in earnest to speak it. The nearer we get to Smyrna, the more I long to be able to speak it easily.

Yesterday was again warm and beautiful, but the wind

was unfavorable. After dinner we had our trunks brought on deck, looked over our things, and got at last fairly settled for our voyage. Our state-room is in nice order, and we are as comfortable as we can expect. Our captain is uncommonly kind and attentive. Every morning he has had a matress spread on the deck in the stern, and a covering spread over it, where the ladies can sit or recline at their pleasure.

To-day our fair wind has made all our hearts happy, but it has made some of our company sick. It has been impossible to walk on deck, or even stand, and I sat on the little bench on the quarter-deck, where the chickens are kept, and while H. read, succeeded in spite of the winds, in making a bag to put some of our articles in. After dinner read French, and then H. told me many things about Smyrna, until the sun had gone down, and the new moon, like a silver thread, looked now and then from among the clouds.

Dear mother, I never was so far from you before. But here, on this mighty ocean, our Heavenly Father is as near as when we are on land; and it is very sweet to remember our absent friends, as we do each evening in our prayers."

"*Thursday, October 26th.* To-day, my dear mother, has been, not only the most delightful day on sea, but the most delicious day for October that you can imagine. Warm as early September, and the clouds floating in a clear blue sky like summer weather. We are about three hundred miles from the Western Islands, and from there to Gibraltar is nine hundred miles. All our invalids are better to-day; every one has been on deck. For several mornings Mr. T. has said, 'Steward, we can't get our ladies up till they have their roast apples,' but this morning we took them on deck.

We go at the rate of seven miles an hour, but as the wind is directly aft, we feel almost no motion. Our stern windows are open, and the pleasant music of the waters comes in continually, and we sail along as smoothly as if no storm had ever ruffled the gentle billows. I have had the luxury of sea life to-day; and to-night feel quite contented with my ocean home and ocean life. But how soon the scene may change, and storm and darkness come back again! As I sit on the deck, in the warm sun, with my sewing, I have nice times to think. O, it seems good to recall my poor scattered thoughts, after the whirl they have been in so long. But I have many things that need attending to within.

M. has been on deck most of the day. I sat by her during the morning, on the quarter deck, by the mizzen-mast, and while I sewed, we talked together about many things. After dinner M. came on deck, and again we sat in the same place, and H. read to us, while I worked on my crewel. Our afternoons are very short, for dinner is not over till three, and the sun sets quite early now. We watched the beautiful sunset, and then the new moon shone out softly, and M. saw the first star she had seen since she left land. How beautiful the stars are on the ocean. The evening is lovely as the day has been. We have just had our family prayers, and here, on this wide ocean, we find these seasons very precious. I cannot but hope that this family worship will do good to some on board. The crew do not attend, but the passengers must, I am sure, be benefited. I am getting to like my ocean life very much. I have plenty to do, and then as every thing about the sea is new to me, there is no monotony.

My time is fully occupied with a pleasant variety of duties, and there is no want of society.

"27*th*. During the night the wind freshened, and to-day we have enjoyed the consciousness that our rolling home was going very fast to Gibraltar. We have had quite variety enough to-day, and some sport too. The motion of the ship was so violent that it was hard to keep our position, and father, who was sitting with us in the cabin, felt it very much. Suddenly the ship gave a great roll, which upset every thing which could be upset, ourselves, too, nearly, and the water came pouring in through the port-holes in our state-rooms. Plenty of work we had and plenty of fun. Fortunately our own was nearly closed, but Mr. T.'s berth took a large quantity of salt water. All but the steward enjoyed the wetting highly, but he, poor fellow, had too much to do with the drying part to feel very good natured about it. About one o'clock I took my book and tried sitting on deck. H. tied me and my chair to the mizzen-mast, and I was able to read an hour, spite of the rolling of the ship.

"*October* 28*th*. About twelve this noon, the wind, which had died away during the night, began to freshen, and continued to do so all the afternoon, and now we go at an astonishing rate, I think twelve miles an hour; H. says faster than he ever sailed before in a vessel. We are passing the Western Islands, though they lie nearly one hundred miles south. We are to pass between them and the main land, but shall not see them.

"*Oct.* 31*st*. Since I wrote we have had wild times, which I can scarcely describe at all. The gale which was blowing when we retired on Saturday night, increased so that sleep forsook us, and we could only lie and toss and roll with every motion of the ship.

To-day things have become quiet, and I have been able to return to my work, and my usual ship duties, so that the sorrows of our stormy days are fast receding, even from memory. In a warm sunny sky and smooth sea, all traces of tempests disappear. But I do dread a storm again; not for any one thing in particular, but for the all things in general. The exceeding uncomfortableness of every thing. It is impossible to keep our position, either sitting, standing, or in our berths. There is nothing to be done but to roll with every motion of the crazy ship, till all one's bones ache. Then the cabin has such a gloomy and deserted air; the doors are all closed, except one half, and through that comes now and then, splashing down the stairs, a large wave, to wash the floors of both cabin and state-rooms. Every thing gets damp and wet, the air becomes stifled. Every body feels the languor and uncomfortableness of being obliged to stay in a narrow berth. Even if sea-sickness does not add itself to the catalogue of evils, the mind becomes gloomy and dispirited, and it seems as if one would feel forlorn to the end of life. I do not say that all the company felt exactly so. I believe two or three of our gentlemen passed through our trials quite comfortably.

" *Wednesday morn., Nov. 1st.* When I bade you good night, I intended to spend a part of this morning in writing, but I can go on only very slowly, the motion is so great. We are now about 300 miles from the coast of Spain. Do you not think my imagination must be filled with thoughts of the old Spanish days of chivalry and renown—of Grenada, too, and its thousand associations? How strange it is that I should be here! and yet I am so far from realizing that I have left America, that I continually, in conversing, use the word *here*, when I am speaking of persons and events at home. It seems as if I have only stepped from the wharf into the vessel, and am still in America. But when once I get sight of the coast of sunny Spain, and see its old castles frowning on the sea, my dream will vanish, and I shall feel that I have indeed left the land of my birth.

I have a confused recollection of the days when the wind was so violent, and I only wish to remember it long enough to tell you about it. The sun shone brightly on Sabbath, and the sky so beautifully blue and serene, was a great contrast to the dashing scene beneath it. Now and then, a shower would for a few moments obscure the sun, and then all would be bright again. Between three and four in the afternoon, H. urged me to go to the cabin door, the sight was so fine. It seemed almost impossible to do it, but with much exertion I managed to get my things on, and with H.'s assistance went up the stairs. Then, mother, and not till then, I saw the ocean. You have read enough descriptions of "ocean waves," and "ocean tempests," and any thing that I can say, will not make them any more vivid than they now are in your mind, but to really know what a storm is, you must with your own eyes witness it, and then you will understand what mountain waves mean. The decks were lonely and deserted, and the waves ran over them in undisputed possession. Occasionally a sailor in his oil-cloth dress, dripping with water, would appear at the vessel's side, stooping to escape the waves which broke momently over the ship. We stood on the stairs, looking out at the door, only half of which was open, and when the waves came we hid our faces from the spray. You remember there is a step from the deck upon the cabin stairs, which prevents the water from running down, excepting when a wave is borne directly over the ship's side down through the cabin door without touching the deck. There we remained about an hour, watching the most magnificent scene which my eye ever beheld. Above, the sky was beautifully blue, and the clouds dazzlingly white, or tinged with that delicately yellow light which we have so often admired in our sunsettings at home. Around us the ocean dashed in its fury. I could not resist the impression, that some of its long waves, like vast hills, were land instead of water. We had scarcely reached our state-room, when a large wave came rolling down the stairs into the cabin. We were safe. That night I slept from extreme fatigue, but had sad and troubled dreams. About midnight we were awakened by hearing the water rolling and dashing into the cabin. H. sprung to close our door, and then we lay still to hear what would be done next. We heard Mr. T., whose berth is next ours, calling out in a tone almost desperate to the captain. "What! you wet?" captain exclaims. "Up to my knees in water," rejoined Mr. T. The captain was also nearly swimming in his room. But pails were brought, and carpet bags, trunks, shoes, &c., were fished up out of the water, amid the laughs and jokes of the poor sufferers; for the only way is to take things merrily. One must be good-natured if he is soaking in his berth.

Monday the wind was still wild, and we sped along our course, while the sounds in the cordage were as if the full ocean band were busily at work at their wild harmonies. Yet in the course of the day the sea became calmer, and faces became a little more bright, while our company, one by one, crept on deck towards evening, to get revived by some fresh air. That evening we had prayers, and retired quite comfortable.

Yesterday was beautiful, and we enjoyed the deck, though occasionally a shower would send us below for five minutes. It is surprising how quickly a shower comes and goes on the sea. You scarcely perceive the clouds till you feel the drops on your face, and a moment after the sun appears bright as before. The storm has made sad work with M. and Dr. A. and father; they all want cheering. After dinner I sewed in the cabin, striving to cheer M. Then H. came for me to see the sun set. It was a golden sky, and after the clouds faded, the moon looked calmly down on our bark, as it danced on over the waves. Just after tea I sat with H. a short time on deck to enjoy the moonlight, and in the evening I talked with dear father of home, and the friends, the loved friends there, and after prayer, I wrote in my journal.

The nights in my berth I am very weary of. To lie in such a narrow space is very hard. But we have many comforts, and I do not complain. A fine breeze is now carrying us on our course, and we are all in good spirits.

While I have been writing, Guseppe came below and announced a ship, and another one is just now on the verge of the horizon. They are the first we have seen for seventeen days. Now as we are near the coast, we hope to see them. I wish we might see an East Indiaman. This is M. S.'s birth-day, and I intend writing her a note. She marked it in my 'Daily Food,' and father thinks of using the verse for a text for a sermon.

I shall begin to-day a letter to send from Gibraltar. Capt. says H. may go ashore with him there, though we shall stop only two hours. Oh, to see Gibraltar!

" *Thursday morning.* I have just finished a letter to send you form Gibraltar. If our wind continues we shall reach there day after to-morrow I have filled a sheet, and yet I have said almost nothing that I wished. I wanted to tell you my thoughts and feelings, and to say something about Boston, and about your home plans, and to send some little word to my friends. My heart was too full to put down on paper, and I have said almost nothing I wished. As soon as tea was over, I went and sat by father in the back part of the cabin, and had a long talk with him. How much his heart yearns for home! He has not borne the ship part well at all, and suffers for want of exercise. We talked, too, of the passengers, and how much it was to be desired that some good should be done while with our company. Soon we separate, never to meet till at God's bar.

My dear, dear mother, we are in sight of land—all on deck looking, but I have just run down to tell you. Spain is in sight before us, real land. My heart is too full to write. I could cry hard, I don't know why. Oh, how good God has been! Now indeed I feel I am away from America. How strangely looks that long line of misty coast, and very strange are my emotions; full of pleasure, and full of pain, and full of deep, deep interest. This is Spain—and soon we shall distinguish the old convent which for ages has stood looking down on the sea, where the nuns have chanted their matins and vespers, and its bells have mingled their voices with the waves. How little I once thought that my plain Yankee eyes would look on such scenes! Dear mother, I have been praying that I may look on all these interesting shores with the feelings of a Christian; and may all that I see and learn prepare me for my work in that dear country which comes nearer every hour.

"*Nov. 4th. Saturday afternoon.* I have just closed your letter, and H. is directing and sealing it, and Mr. T. will take it on shore to-morrow. O, I hope it will reach you safely. Father is writing at the table, and nearly all our gentlemen have been so engaged these few days past. I wrote C. C., after closing the journal for you yesterday, and as soon as tea was over we went on deck to watch Cape St. Vincent, which we passed by moonlight. We saw its high bluffs, and with the glass distinguished the two convents, one on the extremity of the cape, its white walls shining in the moonlight. The other, of reddish brown, is not so distinctly seen. It was very interesting to watch them. What a wild, lonely place to which to retire from the world! Probably they are monasteries, not nunneries.

We stood in the moonlight by the helm, and while there had a long conversation with Guseppe on the nature of true repentance, to which the man at the helm also listened. The conversation accidentally, I hope providentially, commenced by my picking up a tract which fell from his pocket, and as he took it, he said 'Oh, this is mine, I am going to be a Christian.' I fear no impression can be made on his giddy mind, for he is an old, playful, reckless fellow.

We went very fast until four o'clock this morning, when the wind died away, and it became decided that there was no more hope of our reaching Gibraltar to-day. So many new sights are continually coming, that I must go on deck, and shall continue my journal afterwards. 'Africa is in sight!' is the cry. We are wide awake. These are new sights and sounds.

We have a few moments now before tea. Oh, what a day this has been to me! You may imagine my feelings, but words cannot express them. I have stood gazing at these shores, till thoughts innumerable, of home, of childhood, of Spain, of Africa, dark, deluded Africa, have all floated vaguely, dimly in my mind, and I am oppressed by them, and turn in prayer to God, that he will be my Father, and make me a Christian in all things, and will prepare me for my work.

This morning was beautiful, and that every thing might be ready in honor of our arrival at Gibraltar, I staid in my state-room and cleaned out all the dirt, which dust-brush and dust-pan could gather, and then brushed the paint from father's coat and cap, with cologne water and clothes-brush, and afterwards mended them; in which I succeeded admirably, to father's great delight; then I went to M.'s room and told her the Daily Food verse, and read to her, then on deck, which was about 12 o'clock.

While we were at dinner, Guseppe announced a city in sight, and we ascended, when dinner was over, quite incredulous, but not one only, many were visible. Cadiz rose from the sea, and the low range of mountains which stretched along, bore many a village and house, whose white walls shone in the sunlight. Farther inland, the high mountains of Spain towered, and soon Cape Trafalgar came to our view. How many thoughts these shores awaken! I can scarcely write, my heart is so full. I came down stairs about four and finished your letter, and then tried to write in the journal, but it was impossible to stay below. The sky was somewhat overcast, but a brilliant sunset shed a flood of violet and rosy light over sea, and shore and sky. Far off to the south, Cape Spartell, on the African shore, rose dimly, it seemed to me sorrowfully, from the water. Long we gazed on every side, while the sailors drew from the hold the chain cable to use if needful. A fine breeze and strong current carry us rapidly through these green waters. We are about thirty miles from Gibraltar, and shall have a fine moonlight view, if the clouds pass.

These are deeply interesting days to me, and indeed to

us all. To-morrow, while our dear friends at home are gathering round the table of our Saviour, we shall be gazing on the Rock of Gibraltar, and on the blue waters of the Mediterranean. My heart is almost too full to write! How good God has been, and we can trust the future with him."

FROM MR. V. L.

"*Nov. 4th.* We have had thus far a pleasant voyage in many respects. It is true, that it is only a little more than one week since we began to have fair winds; but we have often, during that time, gone with great rapidity. Now that Spain has come in view, it really seems that we are advancing on our course; but until yesterday, our progress was rather a matter of faith: we credited the calculations by the sun, the stars, and the chronometer, and yet it seemed to us that we were stationary.

Mary makes the best sailor of the new hands. She has been on deck more than any other lady; even more than one who crosses the ocean for the third time. She has not been sick much, and when she was so, had nothing of that depression so common in sea-sickness. She has enjoyed the voyage more than she expected, although we have had unusually rough weather. We have, indeed, many enjoyments here on the broad ocean; enjoyments of the sea, the sunsets, the conversations, the reading, the religious services, but in the midst of them all, we have thought of the dear friends who are receding farther and farther from us every hour."

CHAPTER X.

BARK STAMBOUL. MEDITERRANEAN.

Tuesday, Nov. 7th, 1843.

"My dearest mother. I feel quite lonely since I sent off my journal, for it seemed almost like parting with you. But I had so good an opportunity, I hailed it with joy. Now I must go on regularly again—and I would it were possible to give you any thing like a true description of these few days; so unlike the rest of my life, so full of interest and excitement. I closed my journal to you the evening before reaching Gibraltar. I longed to sit up and watch our entrance to the Straits and Bay, but it was not thought best. When I retired for the night, I felt little inclination to sleep, and by two o'clock was wide awake, and as the moon was shining, I could not resist the inclination to rise and peep through the port-hole, but saw nothing except water, for our side of the ship looked only on the ocean. So I laid me down, and as a sudden squall came, and the men were running hither and thither among the ropes, did no more than have several short naps, before the gleams of the dawn came in at our window. Then rose again, and saw the majestic Rock of Gibraltar directly in front of us, and we went on deck to see the sun rise.

Dear mother, how gladly would I present the view to you, which we then witnessed. H.'s painting of the Rock is the best I have seen, and that, you probably remember; but no pen nor brush can give a true idea of the glorious light which tinged the clouds, and shed itself over distant mountain land, and misty shore, and wave, and vessel and rock. That mountain land was more interesting than any thing I had ever seen before, realizing all my ideas of lofty, wild summits, so distant, so towering, they seemed like giant shadows among the clouds; so beautifully covered with violet light, and so completely shorn of all trees or shrubs, that the effect is entirely unlike the mountain land of America. During all the day I found my eye wandering from the interesting sights amongst which we were, to seek those dim and distant outlines, over which the shadows slowly passed. They were the mountains of Spain, where the wild Moorish battle cries had often echoed, and Spanish knights had wrought their deeds of valor and renown.

We were in the Bay of Gibraltar. Directly in front of us rose the barren rock, covered with its fortifications and frowning upon the sea. The town, with its houses of a light yellow or brownish hue, lay all along the water, and was guarded by a wall, strong and massive. During the night there is no entrance to the town, for at the firing of the evening gun, soon after sunset, the gates are locked. A number of vessels lay in the harbor, some steamers and an English man-of-war. But it is an unsafe harbor, and is subject to sudden gusts of wind, very dangerous to vessels."

"*Wednesday evening, Nov. 8th.* I have been sea-sick for the last three days; for the night we left Gibraltar, a miserable head wind came, and our ship has pitched nearly all the time since; while we are kept almost in one place; I mean as respects advancing on our course.

To-night we are quiet for a little season, and I am glad to come, dear mother, and talk with you again.

How strangely that Sabbath passed at Gibraltar! While you were quietly enjoying the privileges of communion, we were anchored in a foreign bay, gazing upon a city, in whose streets mingled some from nearly every nation on earth, and viewing that noble rock, around which so many associations cluster.

Very busy times we had in the early morning. We were coasting up and down the bay, hoping that the officer would come out from the port, and give us permission to land. In the cabin, Mr. T. was arranging his baggage to send ashore, and there was much passing up and down the cabin stairs. As no officer made his appearance, the captain concluded to go on shore, and Mr. T. went with him, but they came back in about a half an hour, saying that they would not let them land. Then we took breakfast, and our poor passengers, who were hoping to get a nice meal on land, were forced once more to partake with us of our ship food. Soon a boat came, and a man in it told the captain if he would drop anchor and go ashore, he could get a permit for his passengers to land. Again our little boat put off, and we waited in suspense another half hour, when we saw it returning. It was now near ten o'clock. The captain remained on shore, and sent the boat for those who were to land. Right glad were they, and they bade us good-bye, and descended one by one into the boat. Mrs. T. was lowered in the arm-chair by the sailors, an operation which we shall all have to endure. When they were gone, we sat quietly on deck, where the rays of the sun beat down, becoming quite warm as the day advanced.

The town seemed an abode for the dead; not a donkey, nor man, nor soldier could we see. We did not expect to, in the town itself, but we thought we ought in some of the numerous paths leading along the side of the Rock. I believe, though, they were hid by walls which were built along the paths. Every thing had a Sabbath-day look, and the most perfect quiet pervaded the whole scene. The only signs of life were a few odd-shaped Spanish boats, which appeared and disappeared among the shipping.

It was a day full of deep interest. We sat on deck, and many were the thoughts which floated through our minds. After some time our boat returned, bringing delicious grapes in baskets, such as we see pictured in views of warm climates. They were entirely unlike ours, but more like those white Malaga grapes which come done up in cork dust.

The rest of the baggage was then sent ashore, and one or two boats came from other American vessels, bringing their captains to visit ours. Our second mate, G., concluded to return to America in the Manto, for he has been sick ever since we started, and I prepared my journal to send by him. What a long day that was! The longest I remember to have spent, since the memorable day that father sailed for Europe.

The captain did not return till late in the afternoon, and he brought with him a new sailor, and also some very fine melons snd olives. It was very difficult for him to obtain fruit, for the market was closed, being the Sabbath. Our captain was tired out. He had eaten nothing since morning, and he was so busy trying to get off, that he could only take a little dinner on deck.

We were so troubled to raise our anchor, that it was not till after sunset that we could get under way. Our sunset was truly Mediterranean, very unlike the sunsets of America. A beautiful violet hue, melting into rose, tinged sky and cloud and mountain and wave. Our hearts were filled with the glory of the scene. Far off, the African shore raised its bold front in the evening sky, and on the side of the bay opposite Gibraltar, several little Spanish towns and Moorish watch-towers, were bathed in violet light, while directly over the Rock, rose the moon, nearly at its full, making a combination of glory and beauty, which surpassed any thing my eye had ever seen. We sailed by moonlight slowly out of the bay. One by one shone lights from the town, and from the top of the Rock we saw and heard the sunset gun fired. Our ship had got free, after some difficulty. The captain of the Manto, a fine generous man, came with his second mate and several of his men, to assist our weary sailors. Our poor men had been up all night, and during the day, too, had been hard at work, and though they sang their wild, merry, sailor songs, to make the work go lightly, it was evident they were tired out. It did our hearts good to see captain L.'s men, fresh and ready to lend their aid; and so before the rays of the sun had faded away, we were ready for sea. We walked on deck beneath a glorious moonlight, and sailed by a fair breeze on the waters of the Mediterranean; while my thoughts were with the dear friends far off over the Alantic. We began to look forward to our journey's end, and to rejoice that our sea trials were so nearly over; when, alas! the wind changed during the night, and the next morning we pitched about in a head sea, sea-sick and cold, and very uncomfortable—so unlike our ideas of the Mediterranean.

After dinner on Monday, I sat nearly all the afternoon on deck, looking at distant scenery. Far off, rose from the sea the Sierra Nevada, or snowy mountains of Spain. The sun shone brightly upon them, and I would it were possible for me to describe the magical effect which those Spanish mountains produce. They tower above the clouds, and are seen in every variety of light and shade. Their barrenness, so far from injuring their picturesque appearance, only heightens it. We watched them all the afternoon; and at evening we remembered the monthly concert.

This Mediterranean sea seems a very sociable one to me, we have so much land in sight, and its tall cliffs come down so protectingly to the shore. Then the motion in a fair wind is delightful. The vessel glides on smoothly, and we have none of the heavy Atlantic swell; but a head wind is very trying, owing to the short waves, which makes the ship pitch and toss sadly. I think the ocean is far more interesting when land is in sight. There is a peculiar feeling when far from land, which I shall always remember with deep interest, and I rejoice that I have been on the wide waste of waters; but there is a magical beauty about the sea when a distant shore bounds the horizon, upon which the breakers dash their white foam. We had the happiness last night of retiring, with the consciousness that a fair wind was carrying us gently along on our course. In the morning, just at sunrise, we were passing Cape Degata. Its brown cliffs, on which stood lonely Moorish watch-towers, frowned upon the sea. These Moorish towers are a very interesting sight. They are placed along the shore on very high-points, at the distance of about ten miles from each other, and command a very extensive view of the sea. There, in ages back, they watched the invading foe, and lighted their alarm fires upon these mountains.

I have had many sweet, quiet thoughts here on this ocean. On the deck I have been looking into my heart many an hour, and striving to get ready for my work in Smyrna; of you, too, dear mother, I think at morning, noon, and evening."

"*Tuesday evening*, *Nov.* 14*th*. On Friday, after closing my journal, a storm which had been gathering for some time, came over, and the lightning was more vivid than I ever knew. The quantity of rain we have had is very surprising. It has rained every day, though we have had long hours of sunshine. Saturday was a gloomy, cold day, and we were sailing in the broadest part of the Mediterranean, between Majorca and Sardinia, so that no land was to be seen.

During the night there was a great deal of rolling, yet I contrived to sleep nearly all the time; but on rising in the morning with a strong resolution not to be sick, I found I must yield, and in my berth, notwithstanding the motion, I had pleasant Sabbath thoughts and conversation with H. We regretted being deprived of service on deck. Only twice have we been able to have service there. Towards noon the weather became fine. We had been all along going on our course, but the motion was in consequence of the north wind which blew down the Gulf of Lyons. As soon as Sardinia should shelter us we should be free from that. After dinner, talked with H. on many interesting topics, and particularly about desiring to be in Heaven, and being willing to leave this earth at any time. H. said he thought it was a Christian's duty to be looking forward joyfully to the time when heaven would be his home. I told him how lovely this earth appeared to me, and that it troubled me that the thought of leaving these scenes forever should make me unhappy, and that I felt I needed to place my affections more upon the other world. I had been thinking and praying over these things, which had been suggested to my mind by my shrinking from dying at sea, and my earnest desire to reach Smyrna. H.'s views of heaven are much better than mine, and I hope that they will make mine more what they should be. I pray over this subject, and already my views are brighter.

Dear father came and talked with us a long time about heaven and the privileges of Christians. We talked till the daylight faded and the stars came out. The sea was calmer, and in the evening we had service in the cabin. Father read his sermon, "Life and immortality," &c.

Yesterday was calm, nearly all day, and we sat on deck, beneath a pleasant, warm sky, and worked. Just before tea, walked the deck for exercise, and in the evening netted my mat. The breeze was fresh and fair, and during my sleep, I dreamed very vividly of reaching Smyrna. O, mother, how strange it seems to be so near the place to which we have looked so long.

This morning, when I went on deck, I found we had passed Sardinia in the night, so that only a faint blue outline remained to be seen. The waves have looked beautifully to-day, and the sky has been bright. Father is in fine spirits at the thought of soon reaching Malta, from which we are now only about one hundred and seventy miles. What a small company we shall have from Malta to Smyrna. Four of our number leave at that island.

After dinner, just as I was going on deck, a storm came up and it rained very hard. Captain has taken in sail, for the night is very dark, and he does not like to pass without some care among these islands. There is a great deal of motion, and we all dread the night."

"*Wednesday evening.* Our breeze has been so very light to-day, that we are still some distance from Malta. We slept last night notwithstanding the motion, and under the good providence of our Heavenly Father, came safely through all the shoals. As soon as the sun shone into the cabin we went on deck. The coast of Sicily looked very dim, far to the north of us, and the small island of Pantelaria, a place famous for its donkeys, lay on our western horizon. We had passed it in the night. During the forenoon, went on deck to see mount Juliano, the highest land on the southern coast of Sicily. After dinner, had a general overlooking of trunks, and a grand preparation for landing at Malta.

Sometimes when the thought comes over me that I am really going to Smyrna, you can imagine how strange and yet how pleasant a reality it is to me. Could we only all live together! My dear mother, let us all be ready for that blessed home where we shall have no separations—that home where our existence will truly commence. Shall we ever reach that home? O, may Jesus make us faithful to him and to his cause. May he prepare us to meet him and all our dear friends in the abodes of eternal rest. Good night, dear mother. Father is going on deck, and I will go too, and have a few parting words.

"*Thursday evening.* We are moored in the harbor of Malta, and shall pass the night within sound of its many bells, and in full sight of the spot around which so many associations cluster. We passed a very quiet night, but this morning, though the sun shone brightly, we found the wind just opposite the quarter we wished it to be. I went on deck before breakfast, and we saw the coast of Sicily, on one side, with the snowy peak of Etna, distant from us one hundred miles, and on the other side lay the low, rocky island of Malta, and its two adjacent islands. The morning was very warm and bright, and the sky a glorious blue, and our gentlemen sauntered about, unable to attend to any thing but watching the sails, in hope that our calm might give place to a fair wind. We were passing slowly along, without any hope of reaching Malta until to-morrow, though we were not thirty miles off. About dinner time our wind became fair. Captain's eyes brightened, but we kept it from our company, for fear of disappointment, as it might not last. However, during dinner the fair wind became too apparent to be any longer hidden, and the sails were made ready for Malta. Our gentlemen put on clean clothes and hats, and looked so land like, it did our hearts good. On we went, beneath a bright sky, while every moment the rocky shore, with its houses and scanty trees, became more and more visible. We were making for Valetta, the name of the port. We passed St. Paul's bay, and thought of the shipwreck of the inspired apostle. H. read me the chapter containing the account, and if it really were the spot, how interesting it would be! It is very probable, though not certain, yet it is enough so to make it an interesting place.

Every thing was in readiness for landing. Our flags floated in the breeze, and we all stood on deck, viewing each object as it became defined to the eye. A glorious sunset added to the beauty of the scene, while the curious Maltese boats made me think of the "Maltese Boatmen's song," and almost involuntarily we sang,

> "Then haste, let us row till the daylight is o'er."

A Greek vessel was slowly passing into the quarantine harbor near us. We saw the Lazaretto buildings, and directly in front rose the old storm-beaten fortification of the knights of ancient days, and rising above these were the light brown buildings of the town. The sunset gun fired just as captain was setting off in his boat, and we waited anxiously the result of his visit to the shore.

The sunset colors were fading on the horizon, but we stood gazing, while light remained, on the massive walls and churches, which filled our minds with strange thoughts, and told us we were indeed in the old world, in the midst of scenes which before had to us existed only in our imaginations. Strange music floated across the water. I thought it was a full, deep band. It was the tolling of the hour. The light grew fainter, and then the bells all woke and rang for vespers. The island seemed but the abode of bells, for from every quarter they rang out upon the breeze, some making merry music, and some sounding in such solemn tones, that all I had ever dreamed of a vesper bell, was embodied in the strain. There was one heavy one, that tolled slowly amidst the merry peals, as we listened in silence, while our hearts were sad for the deluded worshippers, who were then kneeling at their evening devotions; and we prayed that a true and holy worship might ascend with their vesper prayer.

Our captain returned, and told us nothing could be done after sunset, no officer could be seen, no permission given to land; and so we remain here quietly, losing very much time; and yet I am half reconciled to our detention, for I long to hear the matin bells. It seems very pleasant to hear land sounds, and yet the sounds which float to us are by no means home-like. They carry our thoughts back to days when Rome ruled alone over the consciences of the nations, and they remind us that her veil of darkness still blinds a large portion of the earth's population. We presume some festival is causing the continued peals we hear. Music, too, of drums and trumpets, is passing along the streets. The stars are shining gloriously, and the dark walls before us are partially illuminated by the lighthouse, and here and there other lights appear, while almost every moment the bells are chiming, and mingle their voices with the ceaseless roar of the sea as it breaks along the shore. These are strange and novel sounds to lull us to sleep. Our company have retired, and I must retire too, to be up 'bright and early.'

"*Monday afternoon, November 20th.* I have come, my dearest mother, to try and give you some account of the many things which have taken place since last I wrote. But first, let me tell you we are scarce one hundred and twenty miles from Smyrna; and to-morrow we might hope to tread on that shore to which we have so long been looking with earnest expectation, but a strong head wind forbids the hope, and we know not how long we may be detained among these islands of the Archipelago.

How I wish I could give you some account of last Friday, that would make you feel just as I do in looking back upon it. It seems like a strange, troubled dream, and as though I had been for a few hours an inhabitant of another world.

During all Thursday night, you know, we lay in the harbor of Malta, within sound of its many bells as they tolled the hour, and at four in the morning they commenced again, and continued ringing more or less until between seven and eight. We were up early and saw the sun rise, and then captain went on shore. We were on deck, watching all that could be seen, eyeing the town with our spyglass, and the health officer came along side to look at us. This gave us much amusement, and he too seemed quite good natured about it, particularly when the steward in his comical hat looked over the ship's side at him. Soon came innumerable boats, some to sell things, some to bring people to our ship, and to take our passengers ashore.

The consul came, and Mr. and Mrs. Buel, Baptist missionaries, very pleasant people. They knew H., and Mrs. Buel brought me a beautiful bunch of flowers, which I am still keeping—some fine carnations among them.

And then, mother, what do you think we did? We went on shore and saw Malta, and the wonderful sights and sounds nearly turned my head. There is so much motion

I cannot write. Oh, I have so much to tell you, and we are so near Smyrna, too!

"*Wednesday, Nov.* 22*d.* The lands near us are full of interest. On one side lies Asia, so soon to be my home, and on the other, Scio rises to our view, and already the mountains around Smyrna are distinctly seen; but a head wind still detains us; we can only slowly tack along, up the channel of Scio, with the faint hope of reaching to-morrow, the city to which our hearts have gone. How do you think, my dear mother, that your daughter feels in looking upon what is now her adopted home? It was yesterday, that the first faint, blue outline of the continent which is the cradle of our race, rose to our view, and I could only pray when I looked upon it. Now we are very near it. We can distinguish its Turkish villages, and we turn alternately from them to the island, where, among its groups of trees, once stood the mansions of so many happy families whom the fire and the sword destroyed. These lands are full of interest, and you may easily imagine what recollections they call up, and what associations they awaken in our minds. It was you, dear mother, who taught me to feel for poor Scio. Do you remember, too, how, when I was a very little girl, I went once to sew for the Greeks? But if I am going to write a regular journal, I must turn back to Friday.

It was quite an unexpected pleasure to be able to go on shore. Mr. and Mrs. Buel urged our going, and the consul told us the captain would be detained some hours, so we thought we would venture to go. Father and Dr. A. thought it would be a refreshment to us; so I flew down and begged the steward to get my band-box, and H. got my shawl, and in my great ship shoes and gloves, I was in rather a funny garb to appear on land. H. was in a somewhat similar plight, yet in a land where we were total strangers, we did not mind our medley dress. They had the arm-chair ready to lower the ladies, and I found the operation easy and pleasant. We reached the landing time enough for me to have the pleasure of welcoming father and Dr. A. to Malta, for they came after us, with the consul, in another boat.

And now, mother, if you want me to describe Malta, I will tell you that to give you a true description is out of the question. Valetta is the name of the port, and there are streets and houses, and plenty of people, making racket enough for three or four of our cities, but every thing is so different that description can give you but a faint idea.

But I will begin at the beginning and go on to the end of the little I saw of Malta, and perhaps I may be able to give you a better idea than a man who writes travels, and does not know, what you in particular, would like to know.

The whole island is composed of a rock of a yellowish brown color, or rather a very light drab, so soft when first it is hewn, that it is very easily cut into beautiful vases, &c.; but it hardens on exposure to the air. All the fortifications, and houses, and pavements, are of this stone, so that they have the same color, which makes a good contrast to the blue window frames and balconies.

The Moro, or St. James' Castle, hid the place of the landing from our ship, but as we came round its high old battlements, where the knights in olden times fought, we caught a view of a scene of indescribable bustle and activity. It was by the custom-house; and as we neared the shore, innumerable boats surrounded us, and our own little Stamboul boat was the only thing that looked familiar.

My dear mother, H. has just called me to go up on deck, and see the town of Scio, which is so near that we can distinguish the people walking along its shore, and the dismantled villas, which are standing desolate and sad among the trees. Upon these very waters the Turkish ships floated, and on these very shores they landed their soldiers, and spread ruin and sorrow all around. The centre of the island is very bold, and the mountains tower, naked and barren, over the green and cultivated slopes which come down to the sea. We can discern many cypress trees and several minarets. My eye has, in a little measure, become familiar with strange scenes. But I must go back to Malta.

By the iron railing round the yard of the Custom-House, a soldier in the splendid costume of the Highland regiments, was leaning, watching all who came and went. Several of them stood around, and they are most splendid looking men. Tell E. their dress is more grand than the picture of one in my music book. Their black plumes nodded in a perfect forest over their caps, and it was singular to see their limbs bare, both above and below the knee, for a little space. I felt all my childish awe of soldiers coming back, when I gazed on these Scotch Highlanders, and I verily believe E. would have bowed down to them. But they had very pleasant Scotch faces, and I did not see that they bore any arms, though I presume they must have had them of some kind.

We landed on steps cut in the rock. There were two or three of these steps, hewed not very even; and then we walked along the shore, while on one side the city walls, and a large convent with grated windows, towered above. We then turned from this street, which is called the Marina, and entered a steep, walled pathway. My eyes gazed with wonder and astonishment on every thing. There was enough on the Marina to excite my amazement, but we hurried along amongst groups of Maltese, and on turning into this narrow pathway, we found ourselves somewhat more quiet, though our Maltese attendants were sufficiently noisy, and a dirty little dog annoyed me very much. From this steep path, which we ascended by long steps, we turned into another a little wider, and then into St. Paul's street, which is long, even and clean, and nearly as wide as Grove street.* A part is very steep, but where we passed to the hotel, to which the Consul took us, it was quite level. How strange the people appeared to me! Most of the lower classes hurrying about their work, with burdens on their heads, and some who could afford it wore black silk mantillas on their heads, which fell over their shoulders. Priests were walking here and there, and mules dragging carts with immense wheels, toiled along. Those carts were the most outlandish things you can imagine, and the harness of the mules seemed made up of bits of rags picked from the streets.

But our Hotel was my admiration. We entered by a long entry, and ascended by flights of stone stairs to the third story. In the corner of the landings, stood pedestals about three feet high, supporting vases, where were planted house plants, such as geraniums, &c. The pedestals and vases were of Malta stone. The hall, where we stopped at last, was quite spacious, and looked down into a court in the centre of the house, and upon one side opened the room appointed for Dr. A. and father. The parlor and bedroom were very large and airy, and exceedingly high. The floors were stone; the chairs what we have been accustomed to, cane seats, and the sofas, or divans, looked quite natural also. There was a piano in the room, and the walls were adorned with Italian paintings. In the centre stood a very large table, and a smaller one, with a vase of flowers on it, stood by the side of the sofa. Between the two sofas a tiny stove was placed, and the pipe went up

* The street in Hartford in which had been her own home.

to the ceiling. An old-fashioned bookcase, with a few old books, stood between the two windows which opened on the balcony, and two oranges lay on the top of the case, with their stems and a leaf or two remaining. On the side opposite the sofas, the bedroom opened, and the beds, the frames of which were of iron, looked neat and comfortable as at home. The wash-stand looked natural, with its vases for soap and tooth-brush.

While we stood in the hall, looking at the baggage, music struck up 'Hail Columbia' and 'Yankee Doodle,' and we found it was the custom to salute strangers with their national airs. We had been followed by a blind man and one or two others, who played these tunes on our arrival at the hotel; and for which they expected and received a fee. The blind man was the owner of the dog which annoyed me so. The Consul and Mr. and Mrs. B. left us, and our first movement was to run to the balcony and survey the street. Miss M. was a great help in explaining things to me. Passing beneath us were several ladies, who appeared to be shopping. I was perfectly delighted with their costumes. Their street dress is a black silk skirt, hooked on over their other garments, which hangs in thick and graceful folds about them, and conceals every thing but their light gaiters. Over their heads a black mantilla is thrown, of the same material as the skirt, and it appears something like a hood. It is held on with one hand, and with the other hand they gracefully dispose the remaining part about their persons. The effect is beautiful, and I was exceedingly interested in watching the movements of the younger ladies, as they followed their mammas around. The custom is for the young unmarried ladies not to appear in the streets without their mothers or nurses. Their gait is slow and dignified, and they look modestly out from under their mantillas. Their hair is parted like our ladies, with two curls hanging each side, and they all have olive complexions, and black eyes and hair.

Our breakfast was brought up and placed on the centre table, and three waiters did their work very quietly. Every thing about breakfast was homelike and very nice. The beef steak, for instance, nice as at home.

Mr. and Mrs. B. returned to go with us round the town, but we had only time to pass into St. John's Church, before the Maltese boatmen came hastily in, telling us the captain was waiting. We could only glance around. It was a gorgeous Catholic church, such as we see in pictures. Many were kneeling at their prayers; but what interested us most, were the tablets, in Mosaic, upon which we were treading, and beneath which the old knights lay buried.

As we hurried down the steep streets to the shore, our boatmen ran behind and before us, jabbering now Maltese, and now broken English, and anxious to put in, each his plea why we should go with him. It was a strange scene, down by the wharf; I verily thought we should be bereft of our reason among their clamors. I stood close to father, till H. and the rest decided which boat to take, and then we gave a hurried good-bye, and rowed off. The Maltese boats are excellent. The boatmen row standing up.

When I reached the ship, I found the excitement I had been in, together with getting much heated, had fatigued me more than I was aware, and I immediately took my berth, and did not leave it during the remainder of the day. We were sailing before a fair wind, and rejoicing in being so near the end of our voyage.

Our ship's company is considerably reduced; but our hearts are so full of Smyrna, we do not mind it much, though to be alone without father, makes me feel I am indeed away from all my early friends and protectors. Saturday we had still a fine wind, but so much motion that I was more sick than I had been for a long time, and I was obliged to keep my berth during most of the day. On Sabbath morning I was able to sit up in my berth, and rest my weary limbs. On Sabbath afternoon, we passed Cape Matapan, the southern point of Greece, and all the afternoon we sat watching the shore, which rose majestically from the sea. The effect of the lights and shadows was uncommonly fine. There was indeed Greece! Upon one of the tall cliffs stood the ruins of an ancient temple; its columns seemed lonely and sad, as they looked down upon the blue waves beneath them. Several villages appeared on the coast. The general aspect of all these shores and islands is very bold. They rise in barren masses of rock from the sea, with here and there green nooks, where a few trees are scattered among the grass; but there is a grandeur and picturesque loneliness about them, which makes them very interesting, independent of the associations which cluster around every spot.

That evening we had service in the cabin. H. read father's sermon, 'Let us come boldly to a throne of grace,' &c., and I was pleased that the steward stopped to listen. Dear father always tries to do good. He has been talking with one of the sailors, who is considerably interested in religion, and H. wishes, now father has left, to find an opportunity to continue the conversation. We did not pass a very pleasant Sabbath, for we were wearied out, and our thoughts wandered too much; but the evening service was pleasant, and I trust profitable.

Monday morning, the captain called us to see some large water-spouts. They were very singular objects. We found we had gone uncommonly well; the Islands of the Archipelago were all around us. We had thought to have reached Smyrna on Tuesday, and had rejoiced in the prospect; but a head wind came, and our hopes were blasted. Dear mother, I would write more, but I fear to use my eyes, and must rest them. I shall write to-morrow, if possible. Oh, can it be that we shall so soon reach Smyrna? I find it is only eight miles to the entrance of the gulf."

"*Thursday afternoon, Nov. 23d.* We shall not reach Smyrna to-day, dear mother, but as some consolation, our head wind has left us, and we are enjoying the most luxurious day we have had since we commenced our voyage. H. has brought my writing materials on deck, and I am writing here beneath a lovely sky, while a gentle breeze is wafting us along to the entrance of the Gulf, and we have every prospect of reaching Smyrna to-morrow morning. The day reminds me of the lines of Herbert:

'Sweet day, so cool, so calm, so bright,
The bridal of the earth and sky.'

There is an inexpressible calmness about every object. The shores of Asia Minor, and the distant islands, sleep in the sunshine, and there is scarce a cloud upon the sky. It has been mild as a day in latter spring, and I have done little else than sit still all day, and enjoy the luxury of basking beneath this warm southern sky. But now I long to finish my journal.

Monday was a very cold day. Indeed it has been hard to keep warm this week until to-day, for the continued north-east wind made it like an autumn day in America. We were in the midst of the islands of the Archipelago, but it was too cold to remain on deck. At last, in the afternoon, I got into my berth to keep warm. Captain was very sober, and H. very sad. Oh, how hard it was to keep patient, when so near Smyrna. Our head wind was very strong. We tacked all night between the islands, and as the passage was very narrow, I had many thoughts whether I was willing to die on the ocean. I rested very little, and hailed the morning light with joy. Tuesday was a tolerably comfortable day. We made some progress, even with our head wind, for we have an admirable vessel for sailing. We passed very near Tinos, where the town, and an ancient Greek church, one of the two most noted churches of that communion, could be distinctly seen; but for the first time I remained below, when an object of interest was to be seen. After dinner, our captain had the matress laid upon deck, and I sat some hours, even till after sunset, watching our progress. The sky was of a glorious blue, and the clouds swept through it finely, casting their shadows on the islands around.

Samos was near us, but the clouds over it hid Mt. Ida from our view. In the distance lay Scio, and we were endeavoring, in spite of our wind, to gain the channel between that and the main land. How my heart felt, when the captain pointed to Asia, rising faintly in the eastern horizon. I gazed there with many thoughts. On Wednesday morning, we were entering the Straits of Scio, and looking upon the mountains, which can be seen from Smyrna. It was very cold, and I sat and worked in our state-room during the morning, while H. read to me—and in the afternoon, wrapped in my cloak, and seated upon the floor, I wrote to you. I wish I could have written every day since we left Malta, for there are many little nothings which, when I write daily, can be put in, and help you to form a better idea of my life. Dear mother, I long to have you know every thing, as when I lived at home by you. To be detained by head winds, just when our hearts were leaping for joy, has been indeed trying, but it has also been good for us. It has led us to examine our hearts more, and to look to our Heavenly Father more. I have had many thoughts during these days of suspense. Did God see that my heart was not in a right frame, and thus for a little time deny us an entrance to that spot so increasingly dear? I have prayed much during these days; I have thought much of my work, and of my preparation for it. I have tried to be perfectly resigned to my Father in Heaven, and to feel that he knows best, and I hope that I have in some measure succeeded—but to rise these four mornings, and hardly dare to ask how we went, and then to have 'hope deferred,' did indeed make our hearts sick.

This morning we found the wind prevented our entrance to the Gulf, and there was no hope of reaching Smyrna to-day. We all ate breakfast in silence.

After breakfast, I remained in our state-room till the captain came to tell us 'there was no use in freezing below, when it was warm and bright on deck.' Oh, how bright and beautiful it was, and a perfect calm, also. The captain said 'a fair wind would come next;' and in the course of the day it has come creeping along. How much cause we have to be grateful! (God is so much better to us than our fears.) H. is very calm, but full of thought. After writing, I sat and watched the gathering twilight, while he paced the deck. The silver thread of the new moon shone over Cape Karaborna, at the entrance of the Gulf, while we glided along as on a summer sea. We came below at half past five, and commenced putting up our things, and we have arranged all we can to-night. A fine breeze is carrying us along, till now we are very near our desired haven. Captain will anchor a few miles from the city, and go the rest of the way in the morning. We had tea between seven and eight, and have been continually watching the sound of the water to see if we advance. The captain is now sounding, for there is a shoal which makes the passage very narrow, and the anchors are ready to lower. I am glad we shall not enter Smyrna till daylight, for I want to see the city and country around. They are casting anchor now. When M. came to kiss me good night, and said, 'where will you be to-morrow night?' the thought that I might possibly be among those new friends, and the meeting with them past, came over me with new power. Will it indeed be? Oh, for strength to go through all which to-morrow may bring! What changes a few months have wrought we cannot tell. Shall we find 'all things well?' O, these are hours of suspense for us. There goes the anchor! We are fast! Thank God! O, my dear mother, how near we are! H. says fifteen miles from Smyrna.

"*Friday morning.* I am writing you beneath a lovely sky, without a cloud, and we are sailing among scenery far more beautiful than I have ever imagined. Dear mother, this Gulf of Smyrna, with its picturesque mountain peaks, and the verdant slopes which surround it, fill my eye and my heart too. We slept sweetly with the consciousness of being so near to the friends who watch for us, but the first streak of dawn started us, and H. was soon on deck. We have been putting up the things and coming up and down the stairs many times, but now all is ready for shore.

We are now by the sea castle, about seven miles from the city, slowly tacking in,—Smyrna in full sight, and the land castle on the hill behind. These scenes which have occupied so many of my dreams and waking visions, are now here before my eye, but far more beautiful than any thing I have ever imagined. We hear the shepherd's calls among the mountains, and lonely cypress trees are rising amid foliage of every variety of green. Now and then a solitary sea bird flies slowly over the mountains, or rests his wing upon the waters, which are smooth as a lake beneath this quiet sky. Every thing is bathed in sunshine. Dear mother, am I indeed here! The city with its red roofs rises before us. H. is all absorbed. We shall not be in till afternoon, for the wind is very light and against us too, so that we can only tack. Could you but see this land, so unlike all that we ever looked upon, so ——"

Here abruptly ends the journal of the Mediterranean. The next communication to friends announced an illness which confined her one month to her room and her couch. She was carried from the vessel in a state of extreme exhaustion, and in that state passed through the desired yet trying meeting with her husband's friends. Two weeks after her arrival, the journal was closed by another hand. She lay upon her bed and dictated a few lines, her husband being her amanuensis.

"*December 7th*, 1843. I must send you my journal, my dearest mother, without giving you any of my impressions of Smyrna. Of the city itself I have seen nothing, and in my two quiet rooms, there is very little comparatively to remind me that I am five thousand miles from my childhood's home, among the bearded chins and turbaned heads of these oriental nations.

You know how many notes and letters I intended to send by the Stamboul; but I must forego that pleasure, and send only messages to my friends. How little I anticipated this illness! I think I have learned somewhat better, not to form plans for the future. I lie on my bed, and ask, have I been brought thus far to be only a useless encumbrance? I hope I may be resigned to whatever station my Heavenly Father wishes me to fill, whether in sickness or in health.

Give my love to all my friends, and when a ship comes, do send me a large package of letters. I want to hear from all of them. Tell dear aunt, I have constantly some little pleasant thing to remind me of her; and I fancy her going down with her bright face to see you very often. My love to Miss B.; tell her how sorry I am I cannot send her promised letter. And all my little friends; give them a great deal of love. Tell them I think of them in their little prayer meeting, and their Sunday school class continually. I cannot mention *all* my friends, but I have them *all* in my mind, and I lie here and think of them one by one, and long to see them. How sorry I am to be sick while dear father is here.

Now, dear mother, I must say good-bye. I come to America almost every night in my dreams. I wonder if you don't sometimes come to Smyrna. I wish you could know how many comforts I have here, and what kind friends to take care of me. But I think of you a great deal, how can I help it! May God give you every blessing.

Your affectionate daughter,

MARY.

CHAPTER XI.

RESIDENCE IN SMYRNA.

SMYRNA, *December* 26*th*, 1843

MY own dear Mother,—It is a great comfort to me that I am able to commence my writing to you again, for I feel as if indeed separated from you, when I cannot come and tell you all that interests me. O, how sweet your letter was to me! We received it last Saturday, and every time I read it, I feel as if I heard your voice, and pressed you to my heart, and could look into your eyes. Its sweet influence follows me wherever I go and whatever I do.

* * * * * * * * *

Oh, how often I thank God for giving me such parents! Now, while I am coming out into the world, beginning to think and act for myself, I feel continually that the holy influences which blest my childhood and youth, in that home of New England, are the richest of inheritances. And, my mother, when there come painful thoughts about the separation, I look beyond this life, to the time when we shall live together in heaven. How like a mother is every line of your letter; but if you forget the hours of sorrow and care I may have cost you, and remember only the little comfort I may have been, I cannot forget them. How many things I would alter if I lived my life over again. How tenfold more carefully would I consult all your wishes. Those were pleasant hours when we sat together and sewed and talked, and when we walked on the hill together! I have been reminded of them while sitting here with my Smyrna mamma, and threading her needle as I used to do for you. Yes, dear mother, I will 'try to be a comfort to her,' and to *you* also. May God enable me to give you satisfaction in all that I do. I will try to follow all your wishes, all your counsels. Oh, tell me as you ever have, what you wish me to do and be, and may you see, that all your care of me, your faithful tender care and love for so many years, has not been quite lost upon your daughter.

I closed my journal to you the morning we came in sight of Smyrna. That day I never can forget, so brightly shone the sun upon the water and the beautiful shores. Smyrna lay far in the distance, with its red roofed houses. *Then* my meeting with H.'s friends and my Eastern life was all in the future; but a few hours after it began to be present; and *now* Smyrna seems almost another home, and these friends have ceased to be strangers. It was late in the afternoon, perhaps four o'clock, when we spied the boat containing H.'s brothers coming towards us. We were some miles from the city, but they had gained permission to come on board, provided they, too, would go into quarantine, if the Stamboul went. How my heart beat when those six tall young men, all joyous in meeting H., came along side. I staid in the cabin till H. called me, which was as soon as they were fairly on deck, and I went through the meeting very pleasantly, for they were kind, good, frank, and very happy, so we soon became friends. The captain, who went on shore to obtain 'pratique,' by some mistake of the officers did not succeed, and so the whole company remained all night on board. Abram, one of the clerks, came to see what was the matter, but nothing could be done to help it. They heaped on coal to make the fire burn brightly in the parlor at home, and waited in vain for us to appear. Just at dusk, while standing on deck, I was taken suddenly very ill, and my illness increased so during the night, that I thought I never could be moved into the city, and almost concluded I must die in the Stamboul, but as morn approached there was some mitigation of my sufferings. The captain obtained 'pratique' by dawn, and a light breeze took us in amongst the shipping to the place for anchorage. I was so weak and exhausted I feared it would be impossible for me to go on shore, but by H.'s assistance I was placed in the arm-chair, and lowered by the sailors into the little boat. I was as you may well imagine, in a sad, strange state. The boat glided on as over a summer sea, and the cool morning air revived me. I was so weak that I scarcely know how we met on shore; but sick as I was, I shall never forget the beautiful sight they all made coming along the court to meet us. At length I was placed quietly upon the sofa in mamma's room, and then I was at rest.

"*December 27th.* My dear Mother,—I am writing to you in my own house, and in a very pleasant parlor. A beautiful clear morning is shining, but it is very cold, and it is strange that I feel the cold here more than I ever did in America. Our house is quite a warm one for this place, and the little parlor in which I am writing is heated by a cheerful grate. The two little tables on either side the fire-place are ornamented by the gifts of my friends. The work-box which Mrs. E. gave me is a treasure. One large window lights the room, looking on the street, and white muslin curtains, with a pretty green and purple fringe, hang very gracefully over it. Our little room I am sure you would call quite cheerful. It has an American look. Our desire is to have things neat, plain and in taste, so that we can be comfortable, and have it pleasant for our friends.

Dear father left for Constantinople the very day we came to our house, which was last Friday, and will return in a few weeks and stay with us. Our house is so comfortable and the prospect from it so beautiful, that I fear we shall become too much attached to it. Could you but have one look from our terrace, of the gulf and the noble amphitheatre of mountains rising in a sky of cloudless blue, you would understand why H. loves his country so well. But I trust we are willing to leave this place whenever duty calls. We have given ourselves to the work of missions, and if it will best promote that cause for us to labor elsewhere, would not you, dear mother, trust us in God's hands, and be willing for us to leave Smyrna? It may be, and perhaps will be best for us to remove to Constantinople. The thing will not be done hastily. Mrs. V. L. appears very sweetly about it, and in the trial of giving up H., knows better how to sympathize with you, dear mother. God will direct. The situation at C. is one which H. is well calculated to fill. It is very interesting, too, to become the guide of young Armenians; for if he goes he is to be connected with the seminary. Here I am in the midst of a pleasant circle of friends, but I am willing to go with dear H. cheerfully amongst strangers. At first, the thought was very painful. All my sympathies are in Smyrna. You know I have loved it for years."

TO HER FATHER ON HIS BIRTH-DAY.

"My own dear Father,—How little we thought, last December, that when next your birth-day morning should shine, it would find you on the shores of the Mediterranean, in the land where prophets and apostles have lived and labored. So strange is our life! so little we know what even a day, much less a year, will bring! And yet, dear father, have we not as our years roll away, increasing cause for trust in God, and for gratitude to Him, who fills our cup with so many blessings?

We have come, dear father, your two children, here in this Eastern land, to offer our earnest wishes, that the life which God has so graciously preserved these many years, may still be blessed with his favor and love; and that your labors in his cause, which in times past have been so richly crowned with his favor, may still enjoy the smiles of his approbation.

Do you wish to know how my heart feels about our removal to Constantinople? I think that as a missionary I can say I am ready to go cheerfully, wherever Christ's cause can be best promoted by our feeble labors; and I hope that this plan is from him, and one which he will own and bless. I know that I need not ask your prayers. I am persuaded that you continually remember us in our work, and that when you return to your sphere of usefulness, you will rejoice in the thought that we are endeavoring to diffuse among those who do not know our Saviour, the light of truth which he has in love granted us. Mrs. Van Lennep has indeed a hard struggle in giving up Henry. She knows now how to sympathize with you and my dear mother, but her Christian feelings rise over every other; and she said to me, while the tears were in her eyes, after Dr. Anderson left, "I have comfort in this promise, 'They that water shall be watered.'"

And now, my dear father, though we are called to endure separations and trials in this life, yet let us look forward to that higher and holier existence which the gospel reveals. There may we all at last be gathered, with many of those for whom we are laboring.

Ever your affectionate daughter,

MARY E. VAN LENNEP.

SMYRNA, *December* 22*d*, 1843."

The winter that Mary spent in Smyrna, there was to some extent a re-organization of our missions in the East. An important change was made in the Smyrna mission. Some of its laborers returned home, and some were removed to other fields. Among the latter was the husband of Mary. It was thought that his usefulness would be greatly increased by removing him to another and a wider sphere of action. This was a great and an unexpected trial to both of them, and particularly to Mary. When she gave herself to the work of missions, it was with the expectation of being located in Smyrna, at least for a considerable time, as that was, and had ever been, the field of her husband's labors. All her preparations had been made with reference to that place, and she expected to remain there, until she should become acclimated, and accustomed to Eastern life. She hoped also to have remained in her Smyrna home, as she had for some time regarded it, until she should have qualified herself by a study of the languages, to take her place among the missionaries of the East. Added to all, she had friends there, with whom she had corresponded from her childhood, and for two years she had looked to it as her future home. A guiding and overruling Providence had led her steps thither, and to human view she was well qualified for the state of society which existed there.

It is not surprising, therefore, that it should have cost her something of a struggle to bring herself with cheerfulness to leave the place; nor that it should have been an additional source of perplexity to her mind, when at length, a new and very important field was assigned as the scene of their future labors, the main burden of which was to rest upon herself, and which would require the united energies both of experience and of physical strength.

During all this winter they were kept in a continual state of agitation and suspense, uncertain where they were to be stationed, and what would be their particular sphere of labor. In the mean time they devoted themselves to the languages, and also to what of Christian influence they could exert over the large and interesting field where Providence had placed them, among whom, as Mary said, there were many "they were longing to win to Christ."

In consequence of this unsettled state of things, they could form no plan of effort which they could pursue for any certain time; and as a consequence of this, there was no account of labor that could be placed in the annals of missions; but it is believed that another day will show that some few names at least have found their way into the Lamb's Book of Life, as the result of her brief residence there.

EXTRACTS FROM HER FIRST S. JOURNAL.

Friday afternoon, Jan. 12th, 1844.

"My dearest Mother,—I have been wishing these many days to commence my journal to you, yet I have so many things to say, I scarcely know where to commence; and if I were not determined you should have a good idea how my life passes, I should be discouraged from attempting it. But, my dear mother, there is coming an hour, a joyful hour, when in heaven and at rest, H. and you and I can talk over all the dealings of our Father, and 'remember all the way that God has led us.'

I have told you of the meeting with H.'s friends, and to the time when I entered his mother's room, all bewildered and weak, and found a resting place on the sofa. That first day of my Smyrna life was full of thought. The physician was immediately called in, and then all left me but mamma, (my Smyrna mamma.) In the course of the morning, Crusula, the Greek woman, appeared with some rice gruel for me. H. shall draw you the picture of a Greek woman, sometime. During the afternoon I slept, and when waking, heard the clock, which stands in the corridor, striking five, and I had the half bewildered feeling which one has on waking in a strange place, after strange events. Mamma and H. sat in the room with me, and other members of the family came in for a few moments. It was soon dark, and they all left me for supper, and my Greek woman came with something for me. Then I lay alone on the sofa, and while dozing, heard the family singing their evening hymn after prayers. The voices all blended so perfectly, and the music came in such a deep, rich strain, in half chanting style, that I lay spell bound, my whole frame thrilled. The words were 'Our days are as the grass,' and though I could not distinguish them, they sang with so much expression I could almost tell the sentiments.

The next morning I had my coffee in bed. Don't be startled, dear mother, it was barley coffee, the family take it for health's sake. Coffee, with a piece of delicious bread, was my only breakfast during my illness there, or instead of bread, I sometimes had a kind of French crust, which comes from France, and is better for invalids. Crusula, or else Adonia, would bring my coffee along the corridor as soon as H. went out to breakfast, and then mamma would come immediately after and see how I did. I used to watch for her sweet smile and cheerful voice. Then after prayers she would come and help me dress and take my place on the sofa. The women here are great enemies to cold water in sickness. I quite laughed at Crusula's idea of heating the water I drank, but I did have to drink boiled water half cooled, some of the time, for I made up my mind to do just as the ladies in this country do.

The day after my arrival was the Sabbath, you know. The Sabbaths at Mrs. V. L.'s are very still. All go to the Dutch chapel at ten in the morning, and in the afternoon, mamma and several of the family attend the missionary service, which is also in the chapel. From my room I heard no street sounds, for the house is in a court; occasionally a camel bell, and the bells of the churches, which ring at eight, twelve, and four, during the week, and every half hour on the Sabbath. These were almost all the sounds that came to my room. The bright blue sky looked in at the window, the evening gun sounded at half past seven, the partridges made their voices heard on the terrace, for E. was taming some, and the favorite cat would jump on the window and mew to be admitted. Thus I had few sounds to remind me I was in Asia. Yet many strange things would come under my observation, and even in my room I gradually became acquainted with Smyrna life, and Smyrna beings. As I was able to bear it, the relatives of the family would come one at a time and have a little pleasant chat with me. On Monday afternoon the Consul called. He had called before, but I had not been able to see him, and when he came the second time, mamma thought I had better receive him. I dreaded the meeting, yet he was so kind, and his blessing was so patriarchal, that I quickly felt easy.

The first part of the time I was at Mrs. V. L.'s my mind was occupied very much with my illness. My state seemed rather peculiar, and puzzled them all—of course it puzzled me, and sometimes I thought I should never be well again. I was indeed sick, and suffered much from pain; but they were all so kind to me, and mamma was so careful, just as you are, that I felt I was indeed amongst friends

The first week we were there, H. was occupied with our things, getting them from the ship, and unpacking.

It was on Monday evening after our arrival that my piano was unpacked, and set up in the large parlor. I was delighted to find how much all were pleased, particularly R., whose taste and judgment are so exquisite in music. How thrillingly the tones first sounded! How they carried me back to the window beneath the cherry trees in my own dear home. The following days my bureau was unpacked, and the things all taken out to see if they were hurt. I lay on the sofa while one drawer after another was opened and brought into the room, and L—y undid the things. There were the beautiful gifts of my dear friends. How precious every thing was to me, even the very papers they were wrapped in. Oh, mamma, if friendship is so sweet on earth, what must it be in heaven, where there are no separations, no regrets, to mingle with our love!

On the second Sabbath after our arrival, dear father came from Athens. All day on Saturday we watched for the steamer, but not until Sunday morning did it appear. Before breakfast, one of the brothers knocked at our door to say that the steamer was in sight, and would be in, in half an hour. So H. took coffee and went with Augustus on board. Meantime mamma came to get me ready to see father, but there were so many things for him to do, that he did not come to us till after the family had returned from the chapel. Then he came, and I was so glad. It seemed so strange to him that he was really in Smyrna. Mamma came and saw him and then he prayed with us.

The Tuesday after his arrival, I began to be much worse and on Wednesday morning I was unable to leave my bed. I was weak and full of pain. Those were weary days in bed. I counted the hours, and tried every way to beguile the time; sometimes by repeating poetry I had long forgotten; sometimes by thinking of home friends; but that, in my state, made the tears come, and then dear H. felt badly, and I could not bear to pain him. He watched every symptom I had, and for his sake I tried to be cheerful and patient. During my confinement to my bed, dear father would come and sit by me a few moments each day. I was very sad at not being able to see him more, and I saw he was sad and worried. How sorry I felt to be sick while he was in Smyrna."

It was during this illness that the proposed plan of her husband's removal was made known to her. Her own account of the matter is so simple and touching that it may not be uninteresting if it is inserted here. "At first, my heart died within me; but I prayed much over it. You know how all my interests were in Smyrna, and then I had got the idea that H.'s influence was necessary to his family. The plan seemed pleasant to H., though the idea of leaving his home was trying to him. He felt that the station in the high school was the place for him, and just suited his tastes; and that so long as he was a missionary, his great work must be on unevangelized ground, and that however badly he and his family felt about separating, yet, if he could do more good in any other field, he must go. I tried to feel just as he did, and became more and more reconciled to it. Sabbath was a precious day indeed; we talked and prayed over all our affairs, and felt comforted that God would order all things right. It was a great trial to mamma. She could not speak of it. Her eyes were filled with tears often, and yet she very sweetly gave up H. to the call of duty. Still she clung to the hope of our remaining, for it was not decided. When every body was rejoicing in our pleasant new house, *we felt* it was not our home; and I tried to look only to heaven, for we felt *there indeed* is our only resting place. Every Constantinople steamer we watched for anxiously; and last week letters told us that the plan could not be effected. Still we remained unsettled, for Dr. A. has the opinion that we had better remove. But we are in God's hands. These trials have been blessed to our hearts, in many ways. It has interested me more in my missionary work, and taught me to look to heaven more. At present H. is occupied with the Turkish language, and perhaps we may live and die in Smyrna. Our greatest desire is to be where we can do the most good, and God will direct us."

On the day Mary entered her own house, her father left for Constantinople. Just before embarking he had "the pleasure of stepping in, and giving H. and herself his blessing," in their new residence. She had hoped to have the satisfaction of his society on entering it, but she consoled herself with the expectation of a long visit when the business which called him to Constantinople should be accomplished. But she was destined to experience another disappointment. Instead of returning and spending the remainder of the winter with her as was expected, it was thought necessary for him to go to Trebizond. Of course he must make the voyage of the Black Sea; and she felt considerable solicitude for his safety during this somewhat hazardous undertaking. And then his stay must be very brief, after his return. He must soon leave those shores for his far off home, and she would look upon him in this world again—never.

SMYRNA, *Jan.* 19*th*, 1844.

"My dear Mrs. F. Those quiet hours when I used to talk with you of Eastern life, come often to my memory, now that I am mingling with scenes which then dwelt in the dim future. H. and I very often talk of you, and I tell him so much about the pleasant times I have had in your family, that New Haven scenes and New Haven friends have become quite familiar. I have brought you all to Smyrna with me in my heart. Oh my dear, dear friends, we are not separated, even by this great ocean; for if warm affection and continual interest in all that concerns you, can make you feel near to me, though absent, then I shall have you close by my side while I mingle in this new life, so strange and new, that I almost doubt, if I ever were 'M. H.' And yet I have too many recollections connected with *her life*, and think too much, and too warmly, of the friends she knew, to doubt my personal identity long. The great trial in my intercourse with my dear home is, that it must be so long before I can know what happens there. But we try to trust you all in the hands of our Heavenly Father, while we hope we are preparing our hearts with you, for a happy meeting, when the sins, the sicknesses, and the separations of this life are forever over.

The talks I have had so many times with you, I find many occasions to remember. Your experience in many things I try to profit by, and something in our household arrangements is continually reminding me of your ways, and I think how aunt Susan did such and such things. I have many scenes which I could describe to you, of our life here. In my journal to mamma, I try to keep her informed of all that passes, and to let her know how Oriental life appears to me. But you will want to know whether my anticipations agreed with the reality. You know I always feared to anticipate much, and so I was not likely to be disappointed; but if I had anticipated much more, there would have been no danger of disappointment. I find myself in the midst of a warm hearted, affectionate, sincere circle, who treat me as one of them. I have every thing I could wish so far as their intercourse with me is concerned. Mrs. V. L. is a very lovely lady, and it is a pleasure to call her 'mamma,' and to look up to her for counsel and guidance. In her I have found one who in a measure supplies the need I feel for my own precious mother.

I like every thing in the manner of living. H. laughs and says I was made to be an 'Oriental.' I believe I have surprised them all, by falling in so readily with the ordinary Eastern mode of life, and they say it must be, because I came prepared to be pleased, and had not the prejudices that Americans generally have.

But why should I write these things. My heart is not now thinking of Smyrna, it has come to your room, and it longs for an assurance that this winter has not made you worse. O, could I know that you were better! God leads us, dear aunt S., by different ways to prepare us for a holier existence. He tries our characters by the discipline they most need. It *will be* blessed to reach at last the heavenly world! The happier I am here, the more I look forward to heaven. I think increasing affection makes our spirits look forward more earnestly, to a higher existence, and we seek in the hopes which the knowledge of that higher existence brings, the pledge of a continued and enduring affection, beyond this fleeting life. The changes through which I have passed these last six months, have introduced me to many new scenes in life's great drama; and I think changing to a life so very unlike what my childhood has been, makes this world seem more what it really is, a *passing shadow;* while all that is connected with the soul and its destinies, assumes a far deeper importance.

I need not tell you, that it is interesting to become acquainted with new modes of thinking, and new forms of character. I find, however, that I am still in the midst of human beings, with human sympathies—but I am continually reminded that I am in the midst of a land where the religion of Jesus does not shed its benign influence. A true Christian is a rare being here; and yet there are such, and their silent influence works slowly but surely.

* * * * * * * *

Our house is most delightful. It stands on the sea-side; and we have a garden filled with roses, and orange and lemon trees, now in bloom, and bearing ripe fruit too. The view from our terrace is the finest I ever looked upon. The gulf reposes in the midst of noble and picturesque mountain scenery, and over all is thrown an exquisite violet and rose coloring, the charm of all these skies. An Austrian frigate is anchored in front of our house, about forty rods from the shore, and when lowering their flag at sunset, the band connected with it play every evening, with exquisite taste, a slow and solemn hymn; which H. says is a prayer of itself.

I thank you very much for your precious lock of hair and for the kind words I received from you both, just before our departure. That was a sad parting in Boston. You, my dear aunt S., I know will remember us, and pray for us. We shall meet again, to 'talk of all the way our God has led us.' It will not be here—but through grace it may be in heaven."

SMYRNA, *Jan. 24th*, 1844.

"My own precious Mother. Your welcome letter of Nov. 30th, came yesterday. As I was passing the glass door, which opens on the terrace, I caught a glimpse of the French steamer off at some distance, and I hoped some news would reach us from you. We have a fine view of every vessel that comes along the Gulf, and my heart palpitates between hope and fear, every time I see the thin cloud of smoke rising over a dark hulled boat. O, my dearest mother, my thoughts of you turn into prayers continually. Only can I keep quiet by prayer, when I remember the distance which separates us. When each evening we remember before our Father's throne, our dear absent ones, it is a comfort to think that God loves you with an everlasting love, and can do for you far more than our most ardent wishes could desire. Dear mother, God is our best friend. He knows just what we need. O, how sweet to trust him, and to trust each other with him, during our separation.

I have always so much to say, that now I have begun to limit myself to so much time a day for writing, I do not love to know any thing which you do not know. But I think there is coming a time, when in peace and at rest, we can talk over all the way our God has led us. Oh, my dear mother, for that blessed hour I do try to prepare, and my thoughts look forward more and more to that world, where we can all be together with our Father, and where there is no more sin. Pray for me, that my heart may be kept. I am in danger continually, I deeply feel, of growing neglectful of the only important things—and yet, the danger is more from my own evil heart, than from outside circumstances. You know my not being well, or able to mix in general society, has permitted me to have much time for quiet reflection; and I do thank God for it. It is just what I have needed, and I have had some heart-searching times, when I have felt that none but my Saviour could help me. It is a comfort to talk with H., for he has gone down very deep into the heart, and he understands the manner of spirit which we ought to cherish; and when we have our quiet talks about Christ and heaven, my own soul feels encouraged and refreshed. The missionary work grows in importance too, and I long to be doing something that will lead these dark minds to the light of the gospel.

I am keeping a journal in which I write every few days. I have already sent you one from this place, and I want it should go home very fast, for I am anxious you should know all about our life—all that interests us. I think that I do not feel very far separated from you. I look off on the blue waters, which shine beneath the bold cape Karaborna, which bear on their bosom the good ships, by means of which we can talk together, though separated, and it does not seem a very immense way to America. And then, I know that we continually meet in prayer at our Father's throne, and that he looks upon us and watches us, as if we were still together, and if daily communion can ever bring friends near, then we are *very near.* Only when I know that you have been sick, I feel troubled that I was not by to lighten a little your daily cares. I picture you moving about in the rooms at home, and each parlor with its open doors, and the table in the centre, and your rocking-chair and the stools, and the thermometer, and all the various articles come up with a distinctness which makes me forget I am five thousand miles from you. Oh, mamma, it would be very hard, if it were not for the hopes of heaven. But are not those sweet and very glorious hopes? And cannot we bear the separation, dearest mother, when we think too that every step was ordered by God; and that H. and I are in the midst of a dark land, striving, though with feeble means, to give to those around us the light which we enjoy? Oh, yes, I am sure you would not call us home.

Mamma leans on H., and I fear it will be a sad trial should we go away. She is so kind to us, and watchful for our comfort, that it will be to me like leaving home a second time, should we go. Yet H. longs to have a larger field of usefulness, and though it is a great trial to think of leaving this circle whom we are longing to win to Christ, yet I hope we are willing to go. I do not know what the younger members of the family would say, if they thought there was a possibility of our going away. We have sweet talks together, while I love to watch their opening minds, and the unfolding of their Christian character. All four are here at our Bible class on Sunday evenings, and they stay afterwards and read D'Aubigne in French. Mr. Adger is translating it into Armenian. How interesting it will be to that people, for their circumstances are similar to Luther's times.

29*th.* Yesterday I attended church for the first time since that rainy Sabbath in October, when we rode to Park-street church together. The chapel is in the court of the Dutch Consul, and much more like a church than I supposed. It is very small, but has an aisle and slips and pulpit, besides a kind of pulpit in which the Consul sits. It is the custom to pray silently, leaning forward, on first going into church; and, in the French service, the gentlemen stand, when they first enter the slip, with the hat before the face, and pray for a blessing silently. It is an appropriate custom, if their hearts are in it.

Dear mother, I thought a great deal about you on thanksgiving. I lived over and over again the pleasant thanksgiving days we have passed at home, and I hoped **you** would not feel very lonely now we were away."

JOURNAL.

"*Jan. 17th.* Went this afternoon with mamma, to call on Mrs. Adger. In our walk we stopped at the Dutch Hospital, and passed into the grave-yard. I stood by E.'s grave. It is a sweet, quiet place, beneath the trees. It will be pleasant resting there when our work is over, till the resurrection morn."

"*27th.* Dear mamma, I have been thinking for the past few days, what would be the use of attending to these various duties,* if it were not for the discipline they are to us, and for their effect on the character; and how tired those must be of a daily routine, who look only at this world. But things are so pleasant and so important, viewed in relation to a future state."

"*29th.* On Saturday evening, we had a pleasant rehearsal, and practiced 'Let us with a joyful mind,' to sing in church. We took only the air, and not the whole anthem, and found the other verses belonging to the Psalm, and yesterday afternoon it was sung. The boys love to practice with us the anthems and chorusses of the Boston Academy Collection, and 'Night shades no longer,' 'Now elevate the sign of Judah,' and 'Glory be to God,' carry me back to our old organ, and I think I am home again."

"*31st.* I have begun Greek in earnest, and say a lesson every day to H., and write a French conversation also. The Hodja† tells me a Turkish word, and Demetro a Greek

* Some rather monotonous household duties, to which she was in the habit of attending, and of which she had just been speaking.

† Turkish teacher.

one, for both seem inclined to have me speak something besides English. I shall learn by little and little, yet very slowly. When ill at mamma's, Crusula, who only spoke Greek, tried to teach me simple words, such as bread, water, salt, &c., and I was forced to learn, so as to make her understand what I wanted. She was determined to teach me, and persevered in making me pronounce after her as she stood before me with my dish of food.

Demetro took dinner here to-day. When he came in he surprised me with "good morning," in evident satisfaction at being able to say a word to me in English. He and the Hodjah both have learned good morning, and I make out by much thought to say their Turkish and Greek salutations. The Hodjah quite laughed yesterday at my thinking countenance, just before he left, as if I were conning over my lesson.

The Turks have far less of scorn for foreigners than they formerly had. The Protestants they particularly like, and call them *Freemasons*, but the Catholics they detest for their image worship. While I am disgusted with the absurdities of their faith, and with the ways they devise to keep each other's courage up, and also to keep away the truth which is shining more and more as they have intercourse with other nations, still I am very much interested in them as men. If we look upon them as having feelings and sympathies in common with us, we shall be the more interested in their eternal welfare. We shall long to see them brought to the knowledge of the only true religion.

We have received letters which tell us we are candidates for Trebizond. You know that is an increasingly interesting field, but there are weighty reasons why it is best we should not go there.

While we were writing dear father on the subject, Dr.

Smith, bound for Mosul, came in. He gave us a very interesting account of the work at Trebizond, amongst the Armenians. After he was gone I went to pray over my feelings, and walked a little on the terrace. Dear mother, my earnest desire is to feel so deep and abiding an interest in this work, which we feel to be indeed the *best*, and the most worthy of all our efforts, that no personal sacrifices shall cool my ardor. It was over this that I prayed when I walked on the terrace.

H. is writing a sermon on a very interesting topic, "Our life, so little in itself, so important in its consequences," and I am deeply interested in the thoughts it brings. How important all things become, viewed in the light of eternity, and the missionary work especially increases in interest, when thus viewed. Dear mother, we do not know what the gospel is doing for us, until we see the 'darkness and shadow of death' which exists without its blessed light. The more I become acquainted with the East, the more precious does the love of God and his service appear."

"*February* 13*th*. Last Friday was a warm, sunshiny day, so after doing various little things in the morning, and writing to dear father at Constantinople, we took our dinner, and sallied forth for a walk to Caravan bridge, that famous bridge over the Meles, with the tall, dark cypresses on either side, beneath which the Turkish tomb-stones rise, and with its innumerable strings of camels and donkeys, and men of all conditions and all appearances,—that bridge I have seen at last. We went through one narrow, dark street after another, for a long time, where every thing is so foreign that the very idea of a street like home seems strange. I sigh for a clean, open, bright American street. When we passed through the Armenian quarter, we looked in at the courts and saw pleasant fountains and green leaves ; and the bright aspect within, was a strange contrast to the buildings without. That quarter seemed brighter throughout than the Greek quarter, and one street in particular was broad and comfortable, but in general the broken paving stones hurt the feet badly. The bridge is a little out of the city, and before we reached it, we passed some of the gardens, and the aspect was a little country like. I had seen nothing so much like the country since I left home, and it reminded me somewhat of large farm gardens *'like,' but oh, how different.* There was green grass growing beneath trees loaded with fruit. Orange trees they were. The tall, towering Castle hill rose on one side of us, with the old frowning ruins, which seemed almost to touch the clouds, and the gardens were on the other side. We should call that Castle hill a real high mountain. Then we came to the cypress trees, the old solemn trees, growing so thick and dark I almost held my breath with awe. There lay thousands who lived and died followers of the false prophet. Among all those white stones, surmounted with their turbans, there is not one which marks a Christian's grave. There sleep those whom the plague has mown down. It is a crowded city, so full I should think there was no room for another to rest. We sat to rest on some seats, just below the bridge, on one side, and watched the throng of passers. Many people walk there to see and to be seen."

" *15th.* My dear mother, you speak in your last concerning my being injured by the worldly mindedness around me. I try to be careful. If constant prayer and many fears will keep my heart from being drawn from my work, then, dear mother, you may hope I shall not forget the object for which I came to these lands. O, for your sake, for the sake of all who love and pray for us, we long to approve ourselves as true, self-denying missionaries. I cannot trust in myself, my only hope is in Jesus. My temptations are somewhat different here, but they are not much increased. Indeed if you knew the quiet life I lead, you would rejoice. It is sweet to watch the ripening piety of some of the younger members of the family; and then our Bible class warms my heart. And when I am in our church, our quiet little chapel, listening to the prayers and sermons and joining in the sacred songs, my heart feels happy that I am not quite debarred from gospel privileges. I hope we shall have a female prayer-meeting; this will be another help. But I long to engage in something more active, when so many are around me in such sad errors. It does increase a missionary spirit to see the state of things here, and I hope by God's grace I shall be able to deny my self for their good. There are some dear ones here, with whom I can as yet say very little. I long to draw them to me and to whisper about better things. Sometimes I try a little, and I pray for them.

I cannot live without much time spent in the quiet study of my Bible, and in serious thought, but I do not, as I once did, nearly wear myself out in feeling, though sometimes the old spirit creeps over me. And though I feel more deeply than ever my sins, and have earnest longings to be free from every hindrance to a holy life, yet I find the way to grow better is to look to God in humble, fervent prayer, and not to sit brooding over my short comings.

The trials of this winter have called many feelings into exercise, and have been a *new*, but needed discipline, particularly the trials connected with our leaving Smyrna. I have shrunk from going away because I dreaded the trials. This has humbled me, and has led me to look at the missionary work, and to daily ardent prayer, that I might have a right spirit. I have feared to pray that we might stay in Smyrna. I could not utter such a prayer; but I have earnestly sought a spirit which would make me happy wherever duty called me. Sometimes I have succeeded, sometimes not, but I trust I do improve in right feelings. I say to myself 'Our Father in Heaven knows best. We are liable to err, even with the best intentions; we will carry our cause to God, and ask him to bless all these trials, and to give us wisdom for the future, and wherein we have erred, to pardon us for Christ's sake.' And if I can cherish this spirit, dear mother, do not you think our trials will be blest to us?"

"19*th.* Early on Sabbath morning, Nicoli came to tell us the steamer was coming; so H. dressed and went in a boat, while I staid on the terrace till I spied them returning. There was my dear precious father. He has had a pleasant time, but it is good to have him with us again; his influence is so sweet, and his sound, candid advice is worth so much to us. In the afternoon dear father preached a sermon which refreshed us very much: 'The Gospel, the power of God to salvation.' The streets were crowded; masquers every where, for 'tis carnival now, and the sweet atmosphere of our little chapel was in striking contrast with the streets, where were crowds of gay, degraded beings.

In the evening we had our Bible class, and father told me the plan was proposed of our going to Constantinople, H. to be engaged with the Armenians, but chiefly for the reason of establishing a female school. I started at the idea, but father explained to me that the responsibility would not be so great as I feared; for they would have only a few in the commencement, and I should acquire experience as I went along. What they want is the influence of a Christian family to be exerted over those who are to become the wives and mothers of the Armenian nation. What a field! How interesting! How responsible! But am I adequate to the undertaking? I fear the sacrifices I am called to make will influence my judgment, and damp my desire to train those young girls for usefulness. I do not like the idea of becoming the head of a boarding school, and superintending all its concerns. I love a quiet way of living too well to make the idea of becoming a matron very pleasant. This causes me, I fear, to magnify the difficulties; and then, *my heart clings to Smyrna.* The matter is all to be talked over—to be considered in all its lights, and *may God direct.*"

"21*st.* Again I am alone, dear mother, and I come to talk with you. I feel the need of prayer more than ever before. I find that when I am so engaged, my feelings become nearer right than at other times. How I long to lay aside the evil of my heart, and the prejudices I have. You know I have always disliked a school, and a boarding school particularly, and I am distressed that I should feel this still. I mean to put it all down, for I am convinced it is foolish as well as sinful. Besides, it is to be a family, and not an ordinary boarding school. Then it will be the way to become acquainted with Armenian females generally, and thus to preach to them the gospel. The Armenians desire it very much. Their females must be raised. We shall wait the leadings of Providence, and we pray that God will do, not what would spare us sacrifices, but what will be the best for this people.

I am full of sorrow that this pleasant circle must be broken up. This is the last week we can all be together. I pity Mr. and Mrs. Temple. Their hearts bleed to give up the object for which they have so long labored—the poor

Greeks. How I wish Mrs. Temple's mantle of devotedness might fall on me."

"*27th.* Dear mother, I have much to say. When H. returned from the meeting on Wednesday, he said that every thing favored our going to Constantinople, and so we thought that God's hand was in it. After dinner, Dr. A. came over to talk with us, and the matter was decided. Sometimes my heart died within me—to be at the head of a seminary, and to have no home but in a boarding school. But I walked in the garden, and prayed and thought of all sides in the question. True, it would be connected with some disadvantages—but what station of usefulness is without its trials? True, our own home might lose some of its quiet, but then we should be helping to make happy homes for many others. True, I disliked a boarding school, and had some prejudices hard to be overcome—but the idea of a thing being unpleasant, is a very foolish reason for giving up a good work. And then it will never be an American boarding school. What is most needed is, to have a sweet Christian family influence over the training minds of the young females. The number must be small, and the charge, in a merely worldly point of view, will not be great. We have looked very closely at that part, for neither H. nor father would consent to have me in a situation where I should be weighed down with care. And then H. will be in a much more useful sphere in Constantinople, than he can be here. He will have continual opportunities for religious conversation, not only with the pupils and their parents, but with others who will be attracted by the school. Besides, he will open a room in C. for religious conversation, and will commence preaching as soon as he is master of the language. His knowledge of the Turkish will enable him, even now, to commence his labors. Well, mamma, this is the outline of the thoughts I have had, and I have had, beside, many *shades* of thought and feeling, with regard to all these, and my mind is persuaded that it is the work for us to do—and I thank God for permitting us to look forward to such a work, and I pray that he will give us *strength* and *right feelings.*

I have looked at *all* the sacrifices. I shrank from them at first, and then felt deeply grieved that I should be reluctant to bear some burdens, when the work was such a glorious one, and when God had blessed me so. But, my dear mother, I have prayed continually over the subject. I am willing now to endure trials—to engage in a work which is so worthy of a far better and wiser person than I. I have committed myself all to Christ, that he may lead me, and work in me, and by me."

TO M.

SMYRNA, *Feb. 22d*, 1844.

"My dear, precious sister. Your letter, so long and interesting, has this evening reached me, and while H. and my dear father have gone to our weekly meeting, I sit down to have a quiet *long talk.* I am ready to answer every question you ask, and many more beside, and also to tell you every thing which can be comprised in the short space of a letter. I think I know just what you would like to learn. From books only a general idea of these countries can be obtained; but I had become, through H., so well acquainted with Asia Minor, that when I sailed down the Gulf of Smyrna, on the morning of the 24th of November, the mountains, the old sea castle, the red-roofed city, the cypress trees rising solemnly toward the sky, all seemed familiar things, and I greeted them as if they were not strangers.

On landing, we went to Mrs. V. L.'s, the mother of H., where we remained a month in the midst of a most lovely circle of friends. As I was quite an invalid, I was confined to the sofa and bed nearly all the time, but I had every attention and every comfort. Things here, are not essentially different from American ways of living; our houses are very pleasant, and the cooking very nice; and one can live here very well, so far as this world goes. The streets, to be sure, are gloomy, dirty and narrow, but you have only to knock at the heavy barn-like looking doors, and you are at once ushered into courts, often beautifully paved, and pass up into apartments which look as romantic as if they were made for story books. There are many Europeans here, Franks as they are called, and they are mostly Catholics. Indeed, we Protestants are a feeble band, in the midst of Greeks, Catholics, Jews, Turks, Armenians, and people from every part of the earth. Turbaned heads look quite familiar. I have ceased to wonder at any thing, excepting the other day when a carriage passed, I did wonder. It was a great sight. I should love to describe minutely every thing, but that would be impossible.

The latter part of December, we came to our house, situated finely on the sea-side, with a garden and place for bathing, and our winter has passed delightfully. Still we have felt quite unsettled, for it has been decided that Smyrna is not to be our home, but that we are to remove to Constantinople. It is a trial to leave this dear place, which seems indeed like home to me, and which is full of so many delightful associations as the home of my dear H.; and it is a great trial also to leave these precious friends. But the station we are called to fill at C., is a most interesting and important one, and we go cheerfully, trusting that God will prosper us, and give us strength to do much for him.

The steamers bring every place very near, and we have constant communication with Marseilles, Trieste, Greece, Constantinople, and in fact every place around. We are in the midst of the busy world, in the central point between Europe and Asia, so that our minds are kept wide awake. I have so many things to say concerning all subjects, dear M., that I scarcely know how to give you a correct idea of any thing. I believe it is a general fact, that the Orientals are regarded by us Americans as semi-barbarians, or at best as grown up children. Nothing is more erroneous. The more we associate with them, the more we feel that they are entitled to respect and friendship, as much so as any polite, agreeable people in our own land, who are without true religion. With them we must observe the same strict rules of propriety, the same careful attention to win them to the truth without disgusting them. They have the same hopes, fears, affections that we have, but their views of religious truth are dark and cheerless. To pray long prayers, and to observe strictly the fasts, are the great things with them. They know no higher motive from which to act, than self interest, and consequently are not guided by principle.

What the missionary has to do on first coming out, is to hire a house, engage a teacher of the language he wishes to learn, and strive as fast as possible to become acquainted with oriental habits and modes of thinking. By degrees he gets introduced to one and another, as any person in coming into a new place does. He interests those whom he designs to benefit, in various ways, and gradually leads them to converse upon serious subjects. It has been found productive of much evil to attack their religions directly. You must strive to win their confidence, and have familiar talks upon religious subjects with them. In this way you can gradually pour light into their minds, set them to inquiring, and sow some seeds of truth, which by God's blessing may spring up and bear fruit. Patience and perseverance are exceedingly needed by a missionary. You will perhaps be surprized when I tell you, that the greatest trial of a missionary, is the effect upon his own spirit, of mingling with such a mass of worldliness. Especially is this the case here, where there are so many things to interest, and where there are not the helps to a Christian course which are found in a land of Bibles and Sabbaths. Another great trial is to see so many whose minds are full of error, and to know that you can do comparatively little to remove it. Oh, how often my heart has ached, when I have looked upon the crowds that throng these streets, and know that there is scarce one among them all, who knows any thing about true religion. It is sad to look at their crowded burial places, beneath the cypress trees, and think how dark their end has been. These are a missionary's trials here; but personal trials are very few. Many are the comforts and pleasant things about this life in the East. Those who come out here as strangers, always have letters to introduce them to some one, and in every place there is some resident, who can and will assist those who come, to some extent."

"*Feb. 24th.* In reading over the preceding lines, I think I may give you the impression that there are no trials here, about our way of living. Of course this cannot be said. But I find things so much pleasanter than I expected, that I am delighted with the East. I came determined to be pleased, and I find it a very easy matter.

And now to return to your questions, you see that I have had my mind upon them in all that I have been saying, but it is impossible in one letter to answer them all minutely. I have tried to tell you something of our life here, because I think, in general, persons in America look upon the East erroneously. There are many discomforts in the interior of the country, but in the Smyrna mission, the privations are not worth the thought. In a future letter, dear M., I can tell you minutely about the habits here; some of them would, I am sure, please you very much. I feel as if I were reading an interesting book all the time. As to *language*, almost every one on the earth is heard in our streets. Our family friends all speak French among themselves, but unfortunately for my improvement in French, they nearly all speak English too. Greek is the language of the servants, and I begin to pick up a few of the common words, and I make use of signs in a most amusing manner. We shall commence Armenian immediately, for our residence in C. and our work there require a knowledge of it.

We all dress in the European style. The Frank dress is also adopted by many of the Greeks and Armenians. But many Frank ladies, when they grow old, put on the Greek dress. Mrs. V. L., my Smyrna mother, dresses in Greek style.

As to scenery, I wish you could have one view of what I look upon every day from our terrace. The beautiful gulf, the mountains around it, so picturesque, and often bathed in the violet light which is the charm of these countries, the curious old dwellings, the dark cypresses, the Castle hill rising behind the city, so very high it seems to reach the sky, and the gray ruins upon its summit, which have frowned down upon the city ever since the days of our Saviour—all these, and many more things I might mention, awaken deep emotions each day as I gaze upon them. Here Polycarp the martyr died; here the early Christians lived. It would have been sweet, dear M., to have spent our lives in laboring here, but it is thought we can accomplish more good at Constantinople, and so we are going.

The Franks here are mostly Catholics, but all our near relatives are Protestants. At the Consul's there is a chapel fitted up for the use of the Dutch residents, (you know our family are Dutch,) and a service in French is performed there every Sabbath morning. The church is Lutheran, something like the Episcopal, though not much. All of the young people are confirmed before entering society, and partake of the sacrament. On Sabbath afternoon there is an English service which the missionaries attend, and they officiate in turn. Mamma and several of her family go also; and we have the happiness of sweet Christian intercourse with her and four of our brothers. These young men, now growing up, will exert a great influence here for the truth. Every Sabbath evening they come to our house, and with a young Greek, who is also pious, form a Bible class, in which we unite. Our class is deeply interesting, and I wish you could see the earnestness with which they engage in the study of truth. They are lovely youth.* It is a great trial to leave them, yet it is a comfort to know that they are so well established in their Christian principles.

Our mission among the Armenians increases in interest. Dr. A. and father, who have just returned from visiting the various stations, say that 'the half was not told them.' God is doing a great work for them. The whole nation are waking up. Many of their priests are sincere inquirers after truth. There is to be a family female school in Constantinople, where young girls are to be trained in the paths of holiness and knowledge. Think, dear M., what an interesting field, to train the future wives and mothers of the Armenian nation. It is for this that we go to Constantinople. H. will be engaged in preaching,

* One of these four young brothers has since died in the comforts and hope of the Christian faith.—Sept. 17, 1845.

and I shall have the general charge of the housekeeping, and watch over the forming character of the pupils, while a competent teacher is to be obtained to do the regular teaching. What is needed is to have the young girls in the bosom of a Christian family, that they may learn how to make their own homes Christian afterwards. Pray for us, that in this deeply interesting work we may be faithful, and have strength to succeed. We shall leave here perhaps in May, and if our lives shall be spared, I hope I shall have much of interest to tell you.

I think, dear M., I have in the main answered all your questions. I could tell you much more of the state of religion here, but my paper is fast filling up. You know that the Armenian nation are rapidly awaking to the knowledge of the truth. If things go on as they have done, there will soon be pastors settled over pure churches among them. The evangelical party is daily increasing in numbers and in strength; and there is every encouragement to work among them, for the Spirit of God is in their midst.

Our dear father's visit we do enjoy, but to-morrow our pilgrims set their faces towards Jerusalem, and this evening we are to have a farewell meeting at our house. We have had most delightful little meetings during the past week. Last Sabbath evening we met and partook of the Lord's supper together. It was in Mr. Temple's parlor, and we were a little company, but it was sweet to think that Christ was present even with a few. Two Armenians and a Greek, partook of the communion with us, also mamma and our four youngest brothers, and several Christian friends. But that company will never all meet again. To-morrow *seven* will start for Jerusalem, and before they return we may have left for C., and Mr. and Mrs. T. will also have gone. Thus we form friendships, and meet in sweet intercourse for a season, and then partings must come, and new scenes open to us. But it is pleasant to think that we are all engaged in the same work, all going to the same home. May we all meet in that blessed home at last. Pray for me, my dear M., that I may shrink from no trials in this good cause, and that I may not fail of the heavenly rest."

JOURNAL.

"*March 2d.* It has been very pleasant to have dear father with us two Sabbaths. He has been not only a comfort in warming and encouraging our hearts in good things, but his advice has been of great use in regard to our removal. Our last Sabbath was very refreshing. It was our communion, and H. and I hoped we might be so much strengthened by it as to enter upon our new duties with increasing ardor.

On Tuesday evening there was a farewell meeting of the missionaries at our house. N. enlarged and arranged our dining-room table, and set dates, oranges, cakes, &c., with tea and coffee for a collation afterwards. Our meeting was most sweet and soothing. I felt then what an honor and a blessing to be a missionary. Dr. A. made his farewell remarks, and dear father made his, and we sang, and wept, and prayed together, and rejoiced, too, that though we were to be separated in body, yet we were all united in spirit, and were engaged in the same cause. Dear father felt so much at home, that he said, laughingly, as he took his seat at our table, that he did it as if he were at his own house. And indeed he was at home, for he was in our house, and we are his children. I was beginning to feel very sad about father's leaving, for the party were soon to go to Jerusalem.

Thursday was a beautiful day. The company of travelers were to be on board the boat by three o'clock. After dinner we stood talking on the terrace some time, saying last words. Then the boat came and took us to the steamer, and dear father was off at four. He will probably come back and pass quarantine here."

"*Sedecui, Monday afternoon, March 4th.* Yes, dear mamma, I have come to this charming place, at last, to spend the week. This morning we rose early and went in a boat to the opposite side of the city, beyond the barracks, where we found the horses and donkeys waiting for us. The donkey driver, Yorca, said he meant to make a good rider of me, but I confess I had some fear of mounting even the meek little fellow, sure footed and good, which was allotted me. Y. walked by my side, and I gathered courage as I went. The country is beautiful, so wild are the mountains, so lovely are the plains. There is a picturesque air over every thing. We passed many loaded camels. Sometimes we were riding along green hedges, sometimes on the edge of high hills and looking off on plains, over which olives and cypresses and vineyards are scattered. The grass is as green, and the flowers as blooming and fresh, and the sun as warm, as in New England in the month of May. The people are ploughing and planting, and arranging the vineyards. We reached Sedecui about twelve o'clock.

We rested and then went at two o'clock to walk among the mountains. I wish you could have seen our brothers. I laughed till I was tired at their curious hunting gear. The very gipseys themselves could not have looked more romantic, and then their hands and faces quite belied the rest of their appearance. I cannot tell you as fully about Sedecui as I wish, but it is very beautiful. The houses are all near each other, with very pleasant large gardens all around."

"*March* 6*th*. This morning H. took me into the large old house and garden where he and his brothers played when they were children O, mamma, it is a place to dream of the past in. The old trees, now covered with ivy, could tell many a tale of those who have played beneath their shade, and grown old and passed away. We passed along the walks and talked of other days, and thought of the generations who have lived in these spots. Every thing was moss-grown and ivy-covered.

"*Thursday*. This afternoon we all started for the same little valley where we had been on Monday, and leaving most of our party there, E. D. and myself went higher up among the mountains, to see the cascade. A little, stony, mountain path, wound along the steep sides, so narrow that only one could pass at a time. The view was most glorious. As we proceeded we became encircled by the rising peaks. A deep valley, through which gurgled a stream, separated us from the lofty ridge which rose opposite to the one on which we were passing, and there, all alone, we woke the mountain echoes, and heard our voices dying away among those otherwise silent wilds. I thought of the lines,

> "Faint as the echoes of far delight,
> And lovely and sad as the sighing flight
> Of distant waterfalls."

"11*th*. We made a long string of horses and donkeys on our return to the city, being nine in number. We took a boat waiting for us beyond the barracks, and reached home by dinner-time on Saturday the 9th."

"22*d*. A few days since we visited Mrs. Temple's school. I was much interested. She feels very sadly about giving it up. Poor children! They will now be left without any guide; but the seed will not be lost. Yesterday afternoon visited Mrs. T. in their own house. She had given up her school on Monday, and her heart is almost broken. The pupils all wept much. May God keep them. I spent the morning of yesterday in thought about my missionary work; read Eli Smith's 'Trials of Missionaries,' and think it very correct. Dear mother, I could not be any thing else but a missionary. I do feel it to be a privilege to cast in my mite of influence in evangelizing Turkey."

TO J. P. BRACE, ESQ.,

FOR MANY YEARS THE BELOVED AND RESPECTED TEACHER OF MARY.

SMYRNA, *March*, 22*d*, 1844.

My dear Mr. Brace,—I was exceedingly pained upon arriving in Boston, previous to our sailing, to learn from M. that you had never received the note I had sent you on the day of our marriage. You were saved the trouble of reading it, but I should have been willing to have intruded it upon you, for it would have told you that I had not been unmindful of the interest you had shown in my welfare, and that I cherished for my former teacher sentiments of love and gratitude which no time nor distance could efface. I am very sorry it was never delivered to you.

The morning I wrote to you, my thoughts were back in the past, as indeed it was very natural they should be. I recollected all my school days, and especially remembered how you, my dear teacher, had borne with me during all the years when it was my privilege to be under your instruction. I had long wished for an opportunity to tell you how much I thanked you for the interest you showed in checking the ambition of my character. You called it by too soft a name when you said it was *ambition*. I have since found it was vanity, and if I have succeeded at all in overcoming it, it is to you I turn as the friend who first opened my eyes to this defect. How often in my heart I have thanked you! And not only for this, but for all the lessons of wisdom which I have treasured in my mind, and for which I find daily use. Those pleasant hours in the composition class, I love to remember. I have them as vividly before me, as if it were only yesterday that I saw you seated by the side of that crazy old table, with the results of our school girl brains upon it, and H., M., M. and S., sitting with me in our accustomed corner. Though I can recall them with a vividness almost startling, yet they seem far, very far in the past, and I am obliged to think over all that has intervened, to realize that I, who am now writing you beneath this glorious Eastern sky, and surrounded by objects widely at variance with those in America, am the same being who formerly took my daily seat in the composition room of the Hartford Female Seminary. Sagely as we girls wrote then upon the vanity of human life, and the transitoriness of all earthly things, I am sure we should write more from the heart now. Yet there is one thing in which I think our band has not suffered by the lapse of time. We have indeed been separated widely, and have formed other ties, but I do believe we love each other more warmly and truly than we did when our friendship was commenced as school girls. I had a few weeks since a long and beautiful letter from Marion, and she is the same warm-hearted being as ever. I need not tell you that it is a great comfort to have one of my school companions so near me as Isabella Bliss is. We often send little notes back and forth between Trebizond and Smyrna, and we shall be nearer each other when we remove to Constantinople. You probably will have heard before this reaches you, that we remove to Constantinople to take the oversight of a family school for Armenian females. The regular instruction will be given by a competent teacher obtained for that purpose. What is desired in our taking the charge of the school is, that a Christian home influence should be exerted over those who will be in a process of education. I shall have the general care of the housekeeping, but as our family will be small, this will not be much. Henry will be occupied in preaching, and in active labors among the Armenians, and our situation will, of course, open the way for a more extended enlightening of the females. The Armenian gentlemen feel that a thorough reformation cannot take place in their nation, until those who will be the wives and mothers, shall come under Christian influence. And they take a deep interest in this enterprise. It is a deeply interesting, as well as a deeply important undertaking, and I fear I have not the suitable qualifications. But we go trusting in God that he will direct our steps and give us all the wisdom we need. When I see around me the sad want of principle which exists, the darkness which shrouds the minds of this people, over which no star of hope shines, the missionary work assumes an interest and importance which it never wore to me in America. These are beautiful countries. There is very much to interest one who loves the past, and who is engaged in the study of human nature, under its various phases. There are constant subjects of excitement, and indeed in these central points of the world, we have all our faculties and all our feelings called into exercise. I have said often that I seem to be reading a story book, I had almost said a novel, since I have been here, and yet while I am deeply interested, I can look upon these things, and move among these scenes with far more calmness than when in other days I used to dream of the far off East, with its old ruins, its cypress and orange groves, and the turbaned beings who dwelt among them. To be surrounded by followers of the false prophet, who believe as firmly in the inspiration of the Koran, as we do in that of the Bible, and to know some of the opinions which they delight in, makes what has before only existed to me in my mind, seem like a strange reality. But we, as Franks, feel more sensibly Catholic influence than we do Mohammedan. We are surrounded by Catholics, and are daily brought into contact with their errors, in some form or other. To-day our cook tried in vain to obtain some meat, it being *Friday*, and more than all, Lent.

Ought I, my dear teacher, to make an apology for intruding so long upon your time? I could not help writing to you, and so I have followed my inclinations. If you ever have a moment that you could spend in sending your old pupil a word of remembrance, I need not tell you how overjoyed I should be to receive a letter from you.

With much affection and respect,

I remain your sincerely attached pupil,

MARY E. VAN LENNEP.

JOURNAL.

"*March* 30*th*. It is a beautiful day, but necessary family engagements have prevented us from taking our walk, as we do each day, for exercise; and as a substitute, I have been walking for a little time in the garden. How much we shall miss this lovely little garden. It supplies us with fresh flowers every day; and when I am binding together beautiful wall flowers, which are in great profusion, with roses, sweet-scented violets, an orange flower or two by way of variety, geranium leaves and lavender, I think, Oh, how mamma would prize such a boquet! And I wish I had you to arrange my vase for me. I have a little mignonette, and it touchingly reminds me of my home in Hartford."

"*April 4th.* Yesterday, had a letter from dear father. He was in Beiroot, but was to start on Monday, 25th of March, in company with Mr. Smith and Dr. A., for Jerusalem. The rest of their company had left the day that he wrote, to spend the Sabbath in Sidon, and tarry for them in Tyre, where they expected to reach them on Tuesday night, the 26th. It really seems like old Bible times. Father had been up Mount Lebanon, and said it was infinitely the worst road he ever traveled. In America, it would not be thought possible for a goat to go where their horses carried them.

We have every reason to rejoice in our contemplated removal to Constantinople. It is a most interesting field, in the midst of most interesting scenes. As regards my health, it is thought that it will be more favorable to my New England constitution; at least, Dr. A. and father think so; for though I am in much better health now than I ever was in America, yet the summers might be trying, and in Constantinople it is much cooler than here. Then the work will be very useful, and also pleasant, and I hope it will not be too much for my strength. I do believe it is the place for us. God seems plainly to indicate that it is to be our work. H. is busy with his Armenian. Oh, if it were not for the language, I do believe all my fears would go now."

"*Thursday evening.* This is the great week in Smyrna. Passion-week is devoted to being very religious. To-day the yards of the Catholic vessels are all crossed, and flags at half-mast; no music from the frigate, and to-morrow will be the same. Every body is preparing for Easter, making Easter cakes, &c. The custom is, to have particular cakes for each great occasion. Eggs stained red are also used. They are cooked, and then the play is to break them. Each one takes an egg at dinner, during the Easter holy-days, and tries its strength by knocking it against another egg. The streets are full of flocks of lambs, (for every family must have a lamb at Easter) and the bakeries are full of cakes, and every body busy with preparations for the festivities. But do not think they have commenced now. O, no, this is the solemn passion-week, when the world is to be given up and forgotten. To-morrow is the great fast. On Sunday, Lent is over, and then the people give themselves up to rejoicings."

"*Saturday, April 6th.* This morning, at 11 o'clock, the flags of the Consuls, and of the vessels which have been at half-mast, were raised, and the yards which have been crossed were squared, and music again burst forth from the frigate; while the bells, which have been silent for a day or two, commenced a merry ringing. The Greeks and Catholics are wild with frolic; pistols are fired all Easter. It is sad to see the death and resurrection of our Saviour, observed in such a way as to call up feelings any thing but Christian.

Last Monday, I went with mamma and a few ladies, to see a Turkish school. The Hodja (teacher) is a female of unusual enterprise, for a Turkish female. Fatemah took us through the bazaars to Turk Town, which is built on the highest part of the city, rising to the castle. The view is very fine. It overlooks the city, the harbor, the mountains, and the house must be very cool in summer. The streets are painfully steep in some places. We passed through the part burned by the great fire, and saw many remains of its devastation; cypress trees blackened and dead, old walls smoked; but what interested me most was, the old stone posts, which mark the gateway of the ancient entrance to the city. We passed the Jewish houses, and it being their passover week, they were very busy in making their preparations. The Jews here are most of them poor, and the fear in which they continually live, strikingly verifies prophecy. They are almost afraid of their own shadows. They dare not be out after seven in the evening, and a child can alarm them. When we came to the house of Fatemah, we saw the bench where the children sat, and the bag hung up on the wall, where their books in manuscript are kept. She teaches them to read and write. I was much amused at her device to keep the books from being torn. She sews the pages together, and when one page is learned, she turns the leaf over, and sews the remainder together. Fatemah sat nuts, &c., before us, and then took us round to see some Turkish houses. The last one we entered was quite pleasant. A fountain was playing in the centre of the receiving room, and black slaves were holding the children. The lady was pretty, and looked good-natured, but Oh, so vacant their minds all seem. We saw the ladies of an adjoining harem peeping at us, and they sent to have us come in and see them, but it was too late. The Turkish ladies are very glad to see Frank ladies. Fatemah not only teaches school, but she teaches young women to sew, and she passes for quite learned among the Turkish ladies. There are a few female Hodjas, and on the days when the men frequent the mosques, the ladies go to the Hodjas, to hear the Koran read."

"*Wednesday, April* 17*th.* I know, dear mother, that your heart was near to mine yesterday, and that you were praying that my new year might be blessed by God's presence. Last year when my birth-day came, I was in the home of my childhood. What changes a year has brought No other year can ever be so full of changes, or so important to me, as this last one. My change of country, and all the circumstances connected with it, were then in the dreamy future, and no effort of mine could make them seem real. Now I look upon all these as natural and true occurrences. How much God has blessed me. Dear mother, let us thank Him for all his undeserved favors.

On Thursday evening, the prayer meeting was at our house, because every thing was in confusion at Mr. Temple's. They were arranging to leave. I thought much of you that evening, and longed that you should see us thus seated in our large parlor, well lighted. H. at the table, with the Bible; mamma, our brothers, and dear L., with the two Armenians, the Greek youth who comes to our Bible class, and Mr. and Mrs. Temple, around in the room. We had a lovely meeting. H. explained the 103d Psalm very sweetly, and I could not help weeping.

On Friday we made a pleasant excursion to Castle Hill. We took dinner at mamma's, and then went to the place appointed, and found quite a party there. We had a Cavass, a soldier of the Belgian Consul, with us. H. thought it unnecessary, but Mr. D., who remembered what times used to be there, thought best to take one. People sometimes lurked among the ruins for evil deeds. We went in a boat to the end of the city, in a southerly direction, and landing at the barracks, ascended through the Jewish burying ground. The tombs, built in the side of the hill and rising like steps, with Hebrew characters upon them, appeared very curious. It is a long, steep way to the Castle wall. I was deeply interested in walking among so many marks of other days. Our thoughts went back to the time when the early Christians suffered for the truth on those very places where our feet were pressing. The Christian church is no longer standing, the stones having been taken to build the Turkish barracks; but H.

well remembers going once with his father and brother to the hill, when R. took a view of the church. We stood for some time gazing at the immense area of what was once the Circus. There were distinctly visible the tiers of seats in the sides of the hill, capable of seating ten thousand, if not more. Of course, the seats themselves have been removed, but the marks of them remain. In that circus, Polycarp was martyred; but grass grows now in the arena, and there is little to remind us of the scenes once acted there. The castle itself is an interesting place. But it is not possible for me to tell you all the things which make it so. It is massy and high, though very much ruined. Only the thick walls are standing, and the towers are all choked with rubbish. The view is magnificent, and the associations with olden times, make that hill a place where memory speaks even more than the eye sees."

"*Wednesday, May 1st.* During all last week we were looking for our dear father, and still he did not come. We wanted to go to Bournabat, to see our friends there. So, on Thursday, our three young brothers came and went with us. We proceeded in a boat half way, and then took the road through green hedges, and open fields, amidst the twining vines and olives, to the village; the glorious mountains every where bounding the horizon. 'Making a sunshine in a shady place,' aptly expresses the way our hedged road looked. Every little while the boys would strike up some beautiful air, half gay, half solemn, and thus we wound along. It is three miles from the water to the village, and though there were donkeys at the landing, I preferred walking, and was not fatigued. We rested half way, beneath a sycamore tree, and saw from where we sat, patches of snow on Tactalee, the highest mountain seen from Smyrna, which is bleak, even in summer. Ice is brought from there to the city. The boys plucked 'hollow reeds, and made rural' pipes, not 'pens,' and greatly amused us by piping the rest of the way to Bournabat. Mr. Riggs' house is delightful—old ivy grown trees; a basin of water, in which gold and silver fish are swimming; and the children play around like birds, free, simple and joyous. I am sorry they must leave, to come to the city, even though ours is so pleasant a house. The storks have made their nests on the roof of their house, and the swallows build in the hall. We went over to Miss D.'s school, and were delighted with the house and grounds. Such a profusion of roses I have never seen before. We started at four, on our return. Could you only see the prospect which I then enjoyed—the glorious waters, sparkling beneath a bright sky, the mountains and green plains, all bathed in sunshine! The boys sang a mournful and wild air, which sounded strangely sweet, in the midst of so much joyous beauty. The wind was fresh, and our little boat rocked and dashed on, scattering the salt sea foam over us.

The Stamboul had been detained in quarantine, having lost a man overboard, and H. sent to see if the little box for us had come on shore. With what joy did we hail E., who came bringing it to us. I could have gazed a long time at every mark on the outside, but H. hastened to open it, and then I did not want to move the papers and cotton, they looked so like you. But my curiosity soon triumphed, and then the letters and articles were all greeted, and talked over and examined. Thank all my dear friends, and the little girls particularly, for writing. I shall answer them all as soon as I can. O, how good and kind you are. Dear, dear mother, can I ever repay your kindness? How *near* that little box makes us all.

In the evening was our prayer-meeting. It was held at

our house, and Mr. K. presided. On Friday, dear father came."

"*Smyrna, May 4th.* To-morrow H. will go down to the Lazaretto to bring dear father. I hope I may find time to go to Sedecui with him, but we must pack all our things. I feel sad to be so busy the last days in which my dear father is here."

"*Smyrna, May 9th.* O, my precious mother, I shall indeed be separated from you all when to-morrow evening comes. May God keep this dear parent and restore him safely to you; and will not you write me always just as particularly as you can, so that I may feel close to you? Dear mother, think of me as ever with you. Do not call me 'afar off,' for I am with you, and H. is with you more closely than ever, by affection, and by spiritual intercourse.

Yesterday we went to Sedecui. The family were anxious that dear father should see that charming place; so we *made time* and went. We had a lovely ride, and enjoyed it very much.

Dear father's visit in these lands will long be remembered with interest and pleasure. I know he has done good by coming here. We thank God for it. O, my dear mother, when you read this, dear father will be again with you; and you will rejoice and bless God, and so will I, and so will H. Our prayers and our hearts' best wishes follow that dear parent; and we, dear mother, will work here in these lands, and you will pray for us. And shall we not all meet in heaven?"

FROM MR. V. L.

"*Smyrna, May 10th.* We have been enjoying our father's society here exceedingly. Last evening at our little conference meeting he took charge of the exercises, and I have hardly ever enjoyed any words of his as much as I did his remarks on the text, 'I shall be satisfied when I wake up in Thy likeness.' He spoke of the satisfaction of the soul in heaven, in such glowing language, and with so elevated a spirit, that his countenance seemed to put on a brighter hue; and I thought I should not want a better swan's song, not merely for parting with loved ones, but for death itself. I do not know how either Mary or he will bear the hour of separation. I only pray God to strengthen them both. A good many tears have already been shed on both sides. I trust that God will give them resignation and fortitude. But we ought surely to comfort ourselves by remembering, that what is our loss is your gain, and also that of many who love him.

This visit has proved exceedingly beneficial here, as also I trust it has in all the places he has visited. I look forward with great expectation to its bearing on the cause of Christ in America."

TO MRS. C.

SMYRNA, *May* 10*th*, 1844.

"I almost hesitate attempting to write you a note, my dear Mrs. C., it must be written so hastily; but I do not like to permit my dear father to leave without carrying a few notes to my friends in Hartford, and so I have taken my pen to address the beloved parent of my dear Sabbath school teacher. I have found the little books you so kindly sent me to the boat, when I left, a great comfort. I love to look over especially the hymns that are marked, some of which I learnt when I was in the class.

Our dear father leaves to-day. I regard it as a great mercy that he has come to this land; he has made pastoral visits to all the stations here, and his prayers and sweet counsel in our own family can never be forgotten. I would not detain him here, though it is great bitterness to part; he will go home to the dear people, and our hearts follow him, and our prayers go up to God for him, that he may be carried home in peace.

In our meeting last evening, dear father made remarks on the hopes which the Christian has, on the satisfaction which he will feel in the other world. While we were meditating upon these blessed truths, it made the separations of this life seem very little indeed. If our Heavenly Father will only be near us, and give us his gracious presence, we can pass through the trials of this world.

I am more and more glad that I am here in this land, and that I may join my poor feeble efforts to those of others in spreading the light of truth here.

The missionary work, I have said often, increases in importance when these dark lands are seen. We do not fully appreciate the blessings of the Gospel, till we see the misery that exists where error and superstition reign.

You have no doubt heard of our expected removal to Constantinople. My dear father can tell you the reasons for this more at length than I can write them. We go cheerfully, for it seems to be the indication of Providence.

I have written two notes to Miss A. W. It is a great pleasure to be able to communicate with these dear friends on paper, it brings them nearer than I supposed it would, and indeed I do not feel very far off. We are united by stronger ties than time and distance can break. I often think of the remark made by Henry Martyn, 'that time and distance ought not to be much to the Christian.' I hope that you are able to see my dear mother often. She writes me that her friends are very kind to her—and Hartford people are dear kind people. H. and I carry with us a grateful remembrance of their unwearied kindness to us, and our hope is, that God will give us strength to prove ourselves not wholly unworthy of it. May we strive to do here, as our dear friends at home would do, were they in our places, and surrounded, as we are, by multitudes who know not God.

My dear Mrs. C., when I remember the blessings of my life, the dear friends whom God has given me as guides, when I think of that dear teacher, now in heaven, who pointed me to Christ, my heart is filled with gratitude, and I try to become a blessing to others, as they have been blessings to me.

H. unites with me in much love to yourself, and your dear family, and believe me,

Very affectionately, your friend, M. E. V. L."

TO HER FATHER.

Friday Morning.

"My own precious Father,—God will take care of you on the great waters, and will bring you safely to your dear home and people; and we, shall we not pray for you and send our hearts with you; and does time or distance separate us? O no, my dear father, time and distance cannot break the ties which bind our hearts together; for we are united by our Father in Heaven, and it is his love which makes us *one company*, *one family* still. Do not think that H. and I are 'afar off;' it will not be true if you do. We are close to you, and God up in heaven, who sees our hearts, looks upon us as if we were not separated. O, my dear father, it is good to be in his hands, to know no will but his, to work just where he appoints, and just how he appoints. We thank God that he has brought you here. You will never know the good you have done, in this world. It has been a sweet comfort to H. and me, and every word of yours is treasured in our memory. I thank you (*thank* is a poor word,) for every counsel you have ever given me; for every prayer you have prayed for me; for all the sermons I have heard you preach; for all our pleasant talks together.

Dear father, you will not be sorry that we are working on missionary ground, when you get to heaven. How I shall remember and live upon your last words at the meeting. It was a good meeting, and I wish we could keep heaven every moment in our mind. And now go home to dear mother, and comfort her heart, and train up dear E. to be a missionary, and tell all my young friends that there is a great and a blessed work to be done in this world, and that they have but one life to do it in. O, beseech them to be in earnest about doing good. I have never been half earnest enough about it.

Our hearts go with you. Do not you believe it, dear father? Why will you still think we are, after all, separated? What is a mass of water or a piece of earth? It does not keep our hearts apart; it may have power over the body, but never any power over the spirit. May God help us to believe this, and to live in the sweet hope of spending our eternity around his throne. And now, dear father, I embrace you and kiss away all your tears, and I am

Your own affectionate daughter."

FROM MR. V. L.

"Dearest Father: I cannot resist the temptation of writing a few words which the lips refuse to express. I wish to thank you for all the happiness your visit has occasioned us, and for the good you have done us by your presence, your words, your prayers, and your example. How pleasant will be the thought of it when we are separated, perhaps to meet no more on the earth. But God will make us meet again. Or if he does not, it will surely be in love, and why should we repine?

You have seen your Mary's new home, you have lived a short time amid the scenes which will probably surround her till death. Will it not be a comfort to you? And if you must be separated from her on the earth, where would you have her but in such a field, engaged in laboring for a cause, by the side of which all human occupations dwindle into insignificance, a labor, a situation I would not exchange for any on the earth.

You go with our best prayers, our best wishes for your happiness. May God keep you safely on the waters and on the land; may he bring you to your beloved country without accident, rejoicing in all the way he has led you; may you reach home in peace, and meet with joy all your dear ones! Good-bye, dearest father; think of us with comfort and happiness, and know that we love you with truest love.

Your devoted son,

H."

"SMYRNA, *May 24th.* My dearest Mother, it is a great while since I have said a word to you, and now I can only come and tell you, that to-morrow we must again break ties that we have formed, but I mean to try and be cheerful. I have told you nothing of the parting days with dear father. I am glad that scene is over, and that soon he will be with you. It was harder parting with him here than it would have been in America—far more trying for each of us. But I regard his visit as a great blessing. and so we all do. We go and come, meet and part, live together and then separate. Oh, what a strange world!

I have picked flowers for you, dear mother, and you will find them pressed in two little books. A bag, too, I have knit for you. Please carry it for my sake."

CHAPTER XII.

RESIDENCE AT CONSTANTINOPLE.

FROM MR. V. L.

"CONSTANTINOPLE, *May* 28*th*.

"OUR ride here from Smyrna, in the steamer, was as pleasant as possible. The weather was beautiful, and the sea exceedingly smooth. I rejoice that these things have aided in giving Mary good first impressions of Constantinople. We enjoyed a rare sight in the channel of the Dardanelles. As we were going up we saw several vessels anchored on both sides, waiting for a favorable wind. The north wind had prevailed for forty days, and all that can be done in such circumstances is, to anchor and wait for the south wind.

Our steamer anchored before the castle of Asia, and staid there four hours; the captain doing us the favor of waiting, so as to reach the city by daylight. While at anchor a very light breeze sprung up. In a moment every sail was unfurled, and a dense forest of masts, whitened with canvas, came sweeping by, in a channel about a mile broad. The sight was magnificent, and altogether beyond description. After all had gone by we started too, and passing through the whole fleet, many of them within speaking distance, we left the fastest sailers at the entrance of the Marmora.

The evening was charming, the sea smooth as a mirror, the moon pouring her mild rays upon the quiet waters, and a bright star sparkling like a gem in the sky. One of our Armenian friends said with truth, that it was not a night for sleep. At half past three the next morning I was up and on deck. The sea was smooth as glass, and the smoke of our chimney remained where it was thrown out. The faint light of dawn showed the minarets and domes of Constantinople, whose outlines were engraved on the sky. The captain ordered the wheel down, and the steamer went round and round in a circle, until all the passengers were up and dressed, and the rays of the sun had begun to gild the highest buildings of Stamboul. I will not attempt to describe to you the splendor of the scene as we entered. Every eye on board was stretched, and every bench on deck was lined with people standing as high as they could.

We have been received here with the utmost cordiality. Mary and I have talked much together about our work here, and every thing connected with our change of station; and we both come fully determined to be as happy, and to do as much good as is in our power.

We now need God's grace continually to sanctify and to guide us, to imbue us with the spirit of the Gospel, and to give us all the wisdom and the prudence we need. It is a great comfort to me to think that so many dear friends remember us in their prayers, and especially that we are remembered at two altars, where we have knelt—the altars where our two mothers offer their petitions."

JOURNAL.

"*Constantinople, June* 21*st.* Dear Mother,—I closed my last journal and sent by the Cameo, just the day before father came from quarantine. On Sunday morning, May 5th, H. rose early, while I slept, and went off in a boat from our garden wharf to get father. It was a lovely day. I went and walked on the terrace to wait their coming. That beautiful terrace! Then I ran down to the garden wharf and welcomed my dear father, and we walked hand in hand along the court, trying not to think how soon we should part. You know we had packed much of our furniture, but we had a few things in order. Then father dressed, breakfasted, and we had prayers—one of his sweet prayers, and then he prepared to preach. His sermon was refreshing and deeply interesting, 'Behold I lay in Zion,' &c. I remember it now, and his looks and tones distinctly. The people were very attentive.

On Monday we were all packing, and in some confusion. Our friends called during the day, and in the evening came the monthly concert. Tuesday morning I walked on the terrace and committed our interests to God. The confusion increased hourly in our house, or rather I should say the desertion. Our younger brothers were packing, and N. and a Jew were doing the hard heavy work. In the evening our brothers came and sang their beautiful songs, while dear father sat by me on the sofa. Through every scene of those days, was the consciousness of the coming separation, and I could only pray for strength.

On Wednesday we went with dear father and Dr. A. to Sedecui. The next day my heart grew sadder. Dear mamma came to see what she could do. How much she felt for father during those days. In the evening we had our farewell meeting at Mr. A.'s H. has told you about that. The next day we gathered at dinner, and then H. went with father to mamma's. While they were gone I passed my time in writing to some of my young friends, for I knew not how to support my thoughts. We all went in a boat to the steamer. I cannot write about it. We staid only a few moments in our poor deserted house, and then we went down to mamma's. We watched the steamer from the great parlor. I saw the same steamer the other day. That steamer has seen father since I saw him.

On Wednesday, the 15th of May, we made an excursion to the Tchiflick. It is a country full of romantic interest. Wild animals abound there. Recently a panther eat up a little Mytilene poney; and there are robbers around, who make bold attempts to steal the horses. Nature has done every thing she could for the Tchiflick, and R. and C. are doing all they can to make it a beautiful as well as a profitable estate. I have written C. C. an account of it, which you have doubtless seen, so I will not describe it here."

EXCURSION TO THE TCHIFLICK.

TO C. C.

SMYRNA, *May* 22*d*, 1844.

"Wherever I go, my dear C———e, whether alone or in the midst of the friends I have found in these lands, 'I have ever a presence that whispers' of the dear friends I have left. I carry you with me amid every scene of interest through which I pass. I look with more than two eyes, and feel with more than one heart, while the past comes with my present, and I seem to be living two lives, which are not two either.

I went last week to the Tchiflick, or landed estate owned by R. and C., brothers of H., and I enjoyed so much I could not but wish that all my friends were with me. As this could not be, I concluded to make some little collections of flowers, both for you and my dear mother; and although they will lose their fragrance and beauty, and give you but little idea of their exquisite loveliness when I gathered them, yet they will serve, perhaps, to give more distinctness to your thoughts of my eastern home. We went to Sedecui on the 13th, to rest, having become much worn, both in body and mind, by packing for Constantinople, and by parting with our precious father, who left us on the

10th for Trieste. Sedecui is a lovely, quiet spot, and full, painfully full of associations with the past. It is also a place full of present interest and enjoyment. Beneath its ivy-grown trees, and amid its old dwellings, other voices have echoed, and those whose graves are now scattered in different parts of Europe, once lived there, and called it home; and another generation, and still another, have grown up in their places. The same story of youth, life and death, is going on all over the world, and I could not keep from my mind the coming years, when I looked upon the buoyant group which now wake the merry laugh, or breathe the tones of feeling in the social gatherings of Sedecui; and I thought how youth must ripen to manhood, and manhood sink to decay, and all, all must pass away, even as those who once peopled that quiet retreat, and whose fading memory and antiquated pictures alone remain.

It had been previously arranged that we should form a party to the Tchiflick on Wednesday, and so between four and five o'clock we were up, and our donkeys and donkey drivers were brought with the mules for our baggage. Baggage does not mean trunks, but pack-saddles, beds, bedding, &c. We took coffee and were on our way before six o'clock. But I must describe. Did you ever see a donkey in America? I never did. But imagine a little animal something like a mule, only with a meeker and more silly face, so low in stature that when a tall person like father rides him, the feet almost touch the ground. It is a sight worthy the brush of Hogarth. I have had so many donkey frolics that I have almost ceased laughing at donkey parties. Gentlemen generally ride horses, but at this season the horses are put to grass. Ladies look tolerably well upon these animals, but a gentleman looks strangely out of place.

Our party consisted of H. and three of his brothers, all in hunting dresses, some with guns, some with pistols, and all together making quite a picturesque appearance, particularly as a hunting horn was slung over E.'s shoulder. C. alone bestrode a horse, and he rode behind to keep the loiterers with the party. Our two cousins, Emily and Helen, rode on country saddles. A Greek maid servant, in the fashion of the country, rode beside them, and a Greek donkey driver walked by their side. It is useless attempting any such persuasion as influence other animals; donkeys listen only to the voice and stick of their driver. L. and I wore broad straw hats which served in place of parasols, and which are convenient in riding. We all tip'd, tip'd along, waking up the villagers with our merry horn, and they came flocking to their gates, half dressed and half asleep.

We do not meet houses scattered here and there as in America; but ride along narrow paths, such as you would call bye roads, with low trees or brushwood on either side, and sometimes between hedges which are so high above the road, and covered by creeping vines, that they half arch over the way. There are, now and then, groves of olives, and many detached trees, such as the almond, (like our peach,) the willow, the pine, the plantanus, wild pear, &c., and an endless variety of low shrubs and thorn trees; but you would miss, as I do, the tall thick forests of our land. You would look in vain for a rail fence, or a little farmhouse rising among the trees. If you saw any red roofs, there would be a red tiled village with a mosque and cypress trees clustering together. About an hour after starting we reached a caffeney at the end of a miserable village all in ruins, and dismounting, we sat upon the stones by the well and took coffee. Then we entered upon a long, long plain, at the other end of which, just at the base of the mountains, the little cottages of the Tchiflick lie. We saw their red roofs for a long time before reaching them, as they stand upon ground somewhat elevated. Now and then a few black tents of the wandering Turkomans appeared, far to the right and left of our road, and camels which they had turned out to graze, would lift their strange faces occasionally as we passed. The Tchiflick is the great hobby of our family, for besides being full of the most majestic scenery, it is a farm in which American and European improvements in agriculture are being made. Every improvement is so intimately connected with the missionary enterprise, that the Tchiflick cannot but interest the friends of missions. Already the American plough is introduced, and they hope before long to establish a carriage road between Sedecui and the Tchiflick. It is a large estate, being six miles one way and three the other, and it is a most charming spot. There is an immense garden of fruit trees and vegetables; and the forest trees there are larger than any where else. Indeed, among those beautiful mountain trees which shaded the gorge, I did not feel the want of the trees of America. But it is of our excursion to the great gorge I wish to speak. On Thursday, very early, while the mists were rolling up the sides of the mountains, we were winding along a narrow path, at the entrance of the wildest scenery I ever looked upon. Never can I forget that day; it was such a one as Burleigh pictures in his June. It was a day and a place for luxuriating in thought, and I rode slowly along those scenes, generally behind the others. A little river was making its way through the gorge to the sea, and we were winding on its banks, and looking up at heights so bold, so frowning, so majestic, that our hearts were filled both with gladness and awe. Immense ledges of hard limestone, blackened by age, rise abruptly and in perpendicular lines from the bed of the river, which is so wedged in between two mountains, that there is no room for a foot-path on either side. Pine and sycamore trees are there in their glory. We forded the river ten times, and came near getting a wetting at each crossing, but by holding up our dresses, and putting our feet nearly over the donkey's head, we escaped most of the water. But those rocks! those glorious heights! how can I describe them? My heart was full. And there, among those mountains of Asia Minor, I remembered the friends far away, and resolved to send them some of the exquisite flowers which grew in such profusion around our path. How can I enjoy any thing and not wish you all with me? And so, dear C——e, though my flowers will fade long before they reach you, try to imagine the day back again in which they were picked, and wander with me by that stream in the gorge. There were every where scattered tall oliánders, but it was not the season for their flowering. After riding perhaps two hours or more, we stopped to spend the day in a shady place. We were at no loss there for shady places, for the trees grew thick and large, and beautiful vines were twining amongst them. We ladies sat down on a carpet which had been spread for us in a little grove of majestic sycamores, which formed a natural alley on both sides of a road rarely trodden by the traveler, twining their branches over head, and casting a deep shadow underneath. Our gentlemen soon started for the heights, and we heard their voices as they ascended the rocks. Soon came the cry of "the sea, the sea!" and looking up, we found they had reached a lofty summit, and were enjoying a glorious prospect. They fired their guns, and then a thousand echoes answered. But when the horn sounded, all that ever was written of mountain echoes was more than realized, and I have come to the conclusion that no sound can equal that of a horn echoing among the mountains. I can hear it now. I can almost imagine I am back among those rocks, beneath that sky so brightly blue, and sitting where the golden light made a 'sunshine in a shady place.'

We took our dinner in primitive style. The men roasted for us a lamb whole, and with yoourt and pilaff we made quite an eastern dinner. Pistol shots are signals here. In the morning, when Yanee, who came with our dinner, wished to find where we were, he fired, and C. answered him. And whenever any one is in distress, or a fire occurs, pistols are fired.

About four we started to make our way back. That evening, after we had returned to our cottage, we felt an earthquake shake it quite sensibly. There are no houses but those of the men who work on the land, and one little cottage of only two rooms, and hardly large enough to turn round in. It was fitted up to make the young gentlemen comfortable when they go there to superintend operations, and also to hunt the wild boar, &c. It was in this little cottage that we staid. It is very wild and lonely there. We heard the jackals cry in the evening, and sometimes hyenas come into the garden. In the night we heard a terrible barking, and calling of the men, and feared some wolf had entered the fold; but we learned next morning that it was only some of the domestic animals that had got loose. We saw the large, kind, brave, shepherds' dogs; some were at the cottage, but others, and the most of them, probably, were off on the mountains with the flocks. The third day we came back to Sedecui."

JOURNAL.

"Our last Sunday at Sedecui was very lovely. It was so warm and clear that we spent nearly all the day under the trees at the foot of the garden, reading and meditating.

We had service in the parlor in the morning, and in the afternoon, at five o'clock, we had our last Bible class under the ivy at the foot of the garden.

On Tuesday evening we gathered for the last time together in that dear place. The next morning we came to the city. Mamma, L———y, and the brothers with us. They would not separate from us until we left for Constantinople.

Those few remaining days were full of business, doing last things. On Thursday afternoon I took tea with Mrs. Riggs, in the house which had been so recently my own dear home. On Friday evening there was a general gathering of our missionary friends and others at Mr. Calhoun's.

On Saturday we took our dinner for the last time together at dear mamma's. Then, after a little time, H. and I were obliged to say farewell. Dear mamma, it was hard. All our brothers went with us in the boat. They stood in the steamer with us some time. Our missionary friends were there also. Then they all left us. H. and I did feel lonely while we gazed on the fast receding city, and its noble amphitheatre of mountains, and felt it was no longer our home. Just six months before, we had greeted its red roofs, and those dear friends were then unknown by face to me. God only knows when again we shall meet.

And now, dear mother, I will commence my Constantinople life. I will tell you, my dear parents, I shall be contented and quiet here, but it is hard to remove my affections and sympathies from Smyrna. I suppose you do not wonder that that place seems more like home. But I am contented to be here. The Armenians interest us very much. H. says he could sit all day talking with them and not be tired, their minds are so wide awake. I hope I may be useful among the females; they seem a lovely set of beings; and they look upon us with much kindness and with hope too. The men gather around H. and express the deepest interest in our plans. The language does not discourage me. The words are easy to remember, and I am trying on all sides to pick them up. How I shall love to mingle with them when I have the language. Viewed in this light, Constantinople becomes far more interesting than Smyrna.

The warm weather I do not mind at all; it has none of the lassitude and insupportableness of American heat. The thermometer is at this time ninety in the shade, in some of our houses; but I do not mind it at all. Nor do I feel the heat as the others do. But if my life is spared, I shall probably feel it more another summer.

H. has described to you our ride here in the steamer. Early on the morning of the 27th of May, we were on deck, watching the dim minarets of old Stamboul, in the grey light. How magnificent was our entrance! As we came up to the city, the sun had just begun to gild its mosques and towers. Then we passed the green shades of Seraglio Point, and came into the Golden Horn. You can tell mamma all about it, dear father; only imagine it summer, and not winter as when you were here, and imagine the white Seraglio Palace, looking out from its green bosom. The little kaiques glided along, covering the waters. These kaiques are fairy boats for summer seas. Are they not pretty, dear father, with their curious carvings? Mr. H. and G. both came for us, and we climbed up the steep streets of Pera, and found ourselves at Mr. H's., where Mrs. H. waited to receive us. We were treated with great kindness. Soon all the missionaries began to come in. We passed a pleasant time there, getting acquainted with our friends, and searching in vain for a house. It is very difficult to find any thing in the shape of a dwelling, that will accommodate us.

On Saturday I went to a Turkish bath—a *real* Turkish bath; and it was more like Babel than any place I was ever in before—children screaming, women calling, shouting, scolding, and every sound multiplied a thousand times, by the resounding of those vaulted walls, till my brain no longer contained a calm thought. I only knew that I, and all the rest of the yelling community around me, came to be washed. We sent a bundle of clothes, combs, brushes, scrubbing flannels, napkins, &c., on before us. When arrived at the bath, we first entered a large room with a raised platform around the sides. This platform is divided into various compartments by railings, and each party occupies one of these compartments. Here we left our clothes, and wrapped in immense bath towels, we stepped down from the platform on clogs, and walked along to the inner door. Katrina, Mrs. H.'s woman, was in her element, and was greatly amused at my wonder at things and beings around me. The heat was great in the room we entered, and we were immediately in a profuse perspiration. Here the people were yelling and screaming, and the awful din, together with the heat, made my brain swim. But we had engaged a private room, and this was hotter still. The floor was of marble, and the water flowed over it. I ran for the cold water, and held it to my face, as H. had told me to do, and then I was able to bear the heat, which was at first insupportable. The room is perhaps ten feet square, lighted from above, all of marble, and not a particle of wood work any where about it. There are two marble basins raised from the floor, over which are two stop-cocks, one of warm and the other of cold water. These are kept running nearly all the time, so that the basins overflow. Here we were nearly drowned in the hands of the bath woman, while sitting on the floor. I should think we remained in two hours. Then a dry covering was wrapped around us, and we went out gradually into the outer room. Here we remained until quite dry, and sufficiently cool to go home. It makes one quite thirsty, and while waiting to dress, we sent out for some oranges, which we found grateful and refreshing to us. The people of the country enjoy the bath mightily, and would stay in all day if they could.

Our first Sabbath passed very pleasantly. There is a little garden attached to Mr. H.'s residence, at the foot of which, on a little seat, H. and I took our barley coffee, which Nicoli, our man, prepared for us. We read Harris' 'Great Teacher,' till church time, and then went to attend service at Mr. D.'s. The room, though it does not look much like a chapel, answers very well. It has merely seats, and holds about fifty persons. Mr. T., of the Syrian mission, who had come in company with us from Smyrna, preached. H. went at two and a half, to the Turkish service for the Armenians; and we all went at four, to the Bible class, at Mr. G.'s, for old and young. As I looked round upon the children, I thought it would be a good thing to separate them from it, and have them taught by themselves. I had written thus far, when I spoke to Mrs. D. and Mr. C., who were present, about it; and we all agreed that it was best to do so, if practicable—and I, remembering my dear class in America, spoke my thoughts right out, and said I should love to teach them.* The tears came into Mrs. D.'s eyes, and she thanked me as if her heart was too full to speak. I wanted to put my arms round her neck, for I knew then we should sympathize—and so we have been talking about it, and I hope we shall succeed.

* In reference to this desire of hers, to collect the children of the mission families into a Sabbath School class, and also the interest she felt in teaching them after the class was organized, her husband remarks,—"She could not rest without some such means of usefulness. Besides, she would often say she was doing nothing, and though she could do but little, yet that little she must accomplish."

On Friday, the 7th of June, we went to a little village called Belgrade, about two and a half hours from the city. G.* has taken a house there for a short time, and he invited us to go and occupy it. Our friends thought it would be best for us to go; so we took beds, bedding, &c., and Nicoli to cook, and kept house there very well. It is a lovely, quiet retreat, in the midst of a forest, and beautiful sheets of water around. The whole is so like the deep green quiet American scenery, that I almost imagined myself back in my dear home. There is just the same look to the trees, and soft shadows in the water, and the cattle feed quietly in the green meadow land.

Our ride was very fine, in a Frank carriage, but the road would be thought impassable in America. The abrupt declivities are a peculiar feature of these countries. Even where the hills are not high, they are extremely steep. At first, our ride was over a barren road, but the view from it was magnificent. Occasionally a peep at the Bosphorus, with its green banks and villages. We were on high land. Mount Olympus, so shadowy, reared its snowy heights, far away to the south. There is something indescribably beautiful in distant and snowy mountain land. Then before us we caught a glimpse of the stormy Euxine, but its waters stretched far away in the calm sunshine, quiet and blue.

We lived quite rurally at Belgrade. We read, studied Armenian, rambled in the woods, picked wild strawberries, and found pretty sweet-briar roses, while the nightingales sang all night. The notes of these little birds is the most liquid music I ever heard. At first, I thought it not so plaintive as I had imagined, and was surprised to find it had so many merry notes; but it is a most tender and loving sound, increasing in meaning the more it is heard,

*The brother of Mr. V. L.

and one beauty of their song is, they choose the most quiet and shady places to pour forth their warblings. That little village is full of them; and among the dark cypresses in the large burying ground at Pera, they sing.

Our Sabbaths at Belgrade, were not as pleasant as other days, for that was a day of frolic, and there were many gay people there. But we were very quiet. It was a sweet place for thought, and we improved it.

Our last Saturday at Belgrade, we rose early, and went on horseback to the Black Sea, about an hour and a half distant. I should never think of going over such a road in America. We went down places so steep, that I nearly tipped off, but the others took it so quietly, I found it was nothing uncommon. We rode to a lonely village, where it seems a Frank lady is a rare sight, and then we went on to the sea, where there is a small Turkish hamlet. The village is built of the pieces of wrecked vessels, for the sudden storms and the fogs are fatal to many vessels every year. There is what is called a false entrance to the Bosphorus, by which many are wrecked. The Black Sea looked very finely beneath a glorious sky. We gathered shells on its yellow beach. When we returned, we rode just beyond the village, and dismounted, to eat our bread and cheese. While there, I almost doubted my personal identity—so recently a school girl, rambling amidst the quiet groves and valleys of dear New England, now gathering shells, and eating bread and cheese on the shores of the Black Sea."

EXTRACTS FROM A LETTER TO HER FATHER.

BELGRADE, *near* CONSTANTINOPLE, *June 17th.*

"My dear, beloved Father.—You will have been in our own home some weeks, I presume, before this reaches you. I wish I could have sent a letter to welcome you on your arrival; but our removal here has made it impossible for me to write sooner, and now I have so much to say, I hardly know where to begin.

Your ardently expected letter from Trieste, reached us on the third of this month, and it did make me very sad. Dear father, will not Christ be your comforter? Will not *He* be more to you than any thing else? Will He not comfort us all in this separation, and give us the joy of knowing that it is all for His glory? I ask myself, why, my dear father, why should you love me so! If I were better, if I had really been the child that I ought to have been, then I should not wonder as I now do. But it makes me very humble to know that my dear parents do love me so, even with all my faults, and I continually pray God to make me worthy of your love.

And now you are once more to see your home, and before my letter comes, you will have seen our house beneath the cherry trees, and the good old church; and the organ, and the bell will have sounded—oh, how many thoughts come crowding into my mind. I, too, almost feel as if I were seeing them again. My heart leaps to think you will be *there*. I can see them *all*.

That sad afternoon when you left, mamma and Adeline came to our house, and we went home with them immediately, and H. and I sat alone in the large parlor, watching the steamer. The tears come so fast while I think about it, it almost stops my writing. But your letter, dear father, tells me you are not sorry I have come to dwell on missionary ground.

The day we left Smyrna, we did feel sad; but we had a fine voyage, and enjoyed the glorious view exceedingly. And now H. and I are separated from both our homes, and from the dear friends and companions of our early years, but God is with us, and he will be our Father, and will be the Father of all our dear circle. We have appointed separate evenings to pray for our friends—Monday for missions, and our missionary friends—Tuesday, for our Smyrna friends—Wednesday, for our American friends, and Thursday evening for our American relatives—you, and dear mamma, E. and aunt M.'s family; Friday is for our own work. We have Thursday for you, because it is the evening of your lecture. These are our stated times; but besides these, do not our hearts *daily* and *continually* ascend to God for you? It is a great comfort to me that I remember with such minute distinctness, every thing about my home. There is a freshness about every thing in the past, a vividness at times overwhelming. I can call up day after day, hour after hour, with all its attending events, conversations, looks and emotions. Almost every time I lie down, some scene in Hartford rises to memory—either the chaise is just ready, and I ride down by the South church with you; or I am sitting with my dear mother in her own room, talking of the future, which is now present. Often, often, when you will think of me as being interested in some scene in my new home, if you could see our spirits, you would find that both H. and I had come to visit you."

JOURNAL.

"On Tuesday, the 18th of June, we returned to the city, and H. commenced looking for a house. In a few days he obtained a very nice stone house, and the keys were given us. While our house was being prepared for us, we went to Bebec, where we had been invited to spend a few days. The usual way to Bebec is by water, and I wish my dear mother could for once enjoy the magnificent Bosphorus. You must imagine it in all its summer robing,—the fairy palaces in the midst of green trees. We sailed slowly up those smooth summer waters, while the boats of many Pachas were gliding swiftly by us; for it was just the hour that they return to their palaces. I admire these little kaiques; and the dress of the boatmen, which is quite picturesque. They wear only full trowsers, and shirts of white raw silk, with very large straight sleeves. But we must sit quite still to keep them from tipping over. I found it difficult to do this at first. We were about an hour in our sail, and then landed under the shade of some magnificent trees, near the Sultan's kiosque. These kiosques, which are found in every pretty place, and wherever there is a fine view, add much to the scenery of the Bosphorus.

We climbed up the hill till we reached the house, where Mrs. H.'s two sweet little girls met us at the gate, with their nurse. The house is quite romantic—large, airy rooms, and marble basins with curiously carved stoppers; and though a gloomy looking building outside, it is magnificent within. The Greeks build their houses gloomily outside so as not to attract the notice of the Turks.

On Friday evening we were informed that we had lost our house. There had been some fraud practiced. It had been previously rented for three years, but the owner, fearing he should lose the rent, had stealthily obtained the keys and determined to rent it again. These instances of deceit are very common here. H. went early on Saturday to the city, to see about our house. It was indeed gone. We felt very sorry to lose it, but when the keys were demanded we of course gave them up.

On Saturday a flock of Armenian ladies and gentlemen called on us, many of whom were deeply interested in religion. Mr. H. conversed, and read, and prayed with them. Our Sabbath at Bebec was quite pleasant. We had service in the afternoon. Monday evening was spent in returning the call of the Armenians, and H., who could understand them, was delighted with their conversation. On Tuesday evening we had a beautiful walk to the hill above Mr. H.'s house. The view was indescribably fine—the castles of Europe and Asia, on the Bosphorus, in full sight. Our thoughts were back in other days. This is indeed the land where the past speaks. We found that Mr. C., American Minister at Constantinople, intended celebrating the Fourth of July, and that we were to unite in it.

On Wednesday, when we returned to the city, we found our friends busily engaged, preparing for the celebration. An American steamer, in the Turkish service, had been engaged to take us up to the Black Sea. The Fourth of July was a glorious day and very warm. We ladies and the children rode to the steamer in a Turkish arabar, or carriage, all the dogs in the street making a terrible din at us, while we were shaken nearly to pieces by the rough pavements. Our party consisted of Mr. C. and his household, the mission families, and a few others under American protection. A fine band had been engaged, and with our American flag we made something of a sensation as we sailed up the Bosphorus. My heart was back in my native country, and many silent prayers went up, by many wanderers that day. Our view of the Bosphorus from the steamer is far better than from a small kaique. How like fairy land seemed those glistening palaces and green trees! We were all animation on board. The company at Bebec waited for us, and came off in boats to the steamer.

As we began to go into the Black Sea, some of the ladies felt a little sick; so they immediately put back and anchored in the Bosphorus, just under the ruins of an old Genoese castle, covered with creeping vines, where we dined. The Declaration of Independence was read by Mr.

D., then we sang 'America,' and Mr. G. offered a prayer. Our music was very fine—a band of Hungarians ; our dinner, too, was nice, and when we toasted the *American Minister* at Constantinople, Mr. C. immediately rose and proposed the *American Ministers* at Constantinople. Every thing went off pleasantly. We saluted the French Ambassador, as we passed his palace, by playing the Marseilles Hymn, and he returned the salute by lowering his flag and raising it three times. We came home in fine spirits just at dark.

On the evening of the 10th of July, G—s came to tell us there was an opportunity for us to visit the mosques, &c., if we liked. The great things of the city cannot be seen without a firman, and then every one in the employment of the government, and keeping these places, must be paid, so it is too expensive ; and the way people go who reside here is, under the wing of some wealthy traveller. Every one does so, though it seemed to me at first half mean, and yet as a gentleman would not like to go alone, and invites whom he pleases, it is not considered so by any one. A Dutch traveler was to go on Thursday, (the 11th of July,) and G. brought us an invitation.

In the morning we assembled at the Dutch embassy, and a large party started to walk across the bridge to the city. The other side we found carriages, and all started en masse for sight seeing. At the first mosque where we stopped we bought slippers to put on over our shoes, for that is the custom, and whenever we entered the sacred place of the Moslems, we stooped to put them on.

The mosques, the large ones, are surrounded by a paved court, and we entered always this immense court first, and then on one side the door of the mosque opened. Outside, the mosques look exactly as in pictures, and their myriad lamps are also very well pictured. They are immense structures, and the dome rises like the vault of heaven above the head. There are curious stained windows, exceedingly beautiful, and fine work, I think in arabesque style, adorns the walls. I saw so many things that day, that I cannot describe them so distinctly as if I had seen only one. We visited three, beside St. Sophia. All of them were very beautiful, and one had been a church. The mausoleum and fountain of the late Sultan are exceedingly beautiful. It is a building perhaps fifty feet in length, and the tomb of the Sultan is there, and a large, coffin shaped structure rises over, with nodding plumes and the Sultan's cap, while its diamonds and herons' feathers told of its royal owner. (You know the heron's feather is worn only by kings.) A large Koran on a silver stand lay near by, and a holy relic (a single hair of Mahomet,) of the Prophet, was shrined in a silver case by its side. A garden adorned with carnations and roses threw its fragrance around the building, and a light breeze lifted the long curtains of the windows, and brought fresh air into this incensed room of the dead. His children's tombs lying around him, were recognized by the shortness of the sable structure above them. Other relatives were also buried there. Oh, it was a sad room, though wreaths of snowy flowers were worked around the walls and on the ceiling above. There was no gleam of religion to brighten its gloom. But I am hastening to take you to the spot which interested me most. We stopped a short time in a coffee-house, and then entered the old and massive structure of St. Sophia. It is impossible to describe it. It is unlike any thing I had ever seen or imagined, and its effect is also peculiar. How I wish I could transport you to its ancient galleries, deserted now to the doves and swallows. How I wish you could have sat with me far above the kneeling company of turbaned heads, from whose midst came up to my lonely seat a confused murmuring, as they repeated their prayers. It is a place where the mind wanders far back to the early days of the church, when even then, the light of pure religion was becoming extinct amidst the gloom of cloistered piles, and the drapery of its thousand vain and sinful rites. The mind wanders through the days of the Greek empire, and follows its decline to the hour when the turban and scimitar gained admission into this consecrated pile, before whom the priest and the Host forever fled, and gave place to the worship of the false prophet, perhaps less insulting to the Majesty of Heaven, than that which preceded it.

Pictures and images are forbidden by the Koran, and those which could not be taken down were covered by large cloths which bore the name of God, or a sentence from the holy book of the Moslems. But some cherubim still remain, being too high to be reached. The dome is a dizzy height above the marble pavement, and its height seemed hardly diminished, when we had ascended to the first gallery, which is itself higher than the centre of our church ceiling. There are two smaller galleries above which we did not ascend. As I said before, these galleries are deserted, being visited only by the curious, and the birds have liberty to roam freely through the wide and lonely spaces, finding an easy egress through the deep, but broken and ivy-covered windows. While our company lingered on one side, H. and I passed around to another part of the gallery, where there is a curious old doorway, now filled up with stone and mortar. It is said that when the Turks rushed into the church, the last priest escaped through this door with the Host, and that one of the first signs of the fall of the Turkish empire, and the overthrow of Constantinople, will be the returning of this very priest through this doorway. The Turks tell this, and say that after his escape the door was supernaturally closed. By the time our party came round we were ready to return, and then we enjoyed a long time of silent sitting, looking down on groups of worshippers beneath, to whom some readers were delivering instruction. Immense pillars support the building, of curious and beautiful marble, I think principally porphyry. The galleries themselves are large enough for a church on each side, and the idea of *immensity*, and *massiveness*, and *antiquity*, fill the mind at every glance. Just before descending, I espied an ivy branch I could reach, and hastily gathering a few leaves, we prepared to go down. This descent is a very curious one. Perhaps other churches which father may have seen, are arranged in like manner. We did not go down by stairs, but by solid mason work, winding round and round till we reached the bottom, and seeming like the pathway of a cavern, lighted occasionally by small windows in the deep walls.

We then visited the Turkish mint, and an old church which has been converted into an armory, and where ancient armor is exhibited; and then spent the remainder of the day amongst the buildings and grounds of Seraglio Point. Here, every spot is associated in the mind with assassination, murder, and treachery. You know, perhaps, the Sultans avoid this place now, so many have been killed there, and consequently many parts go to decay. The gardens are in European style, and the rooms are furnished in half European, half Turkish style; and to my eye, which has seen nothing of royalty before, it all seemed very fine and full of luxury. There were beautiful baths and lovely kiosques. These latter are little buildings with light summer rooms, beautifully furnished, standing on a place which commands a fine view. They are erected all along the Bosphorus, and wherever there is a good view in the country, and the Sultan visits one and another, as suits his fancy. They are little palaces. We were shown one lovely room, and as it was a very warm day, we could appreciate the luxury which the Sultan enjoyed. It was in a part of the buildings which have been recently erected, and which are quite new compared with the rest. We entered a room, the centre of which was occupied by a marble basin, filled with water, and surrounding a fountain which threw out lovely jets. A profusion of beautiful flowers were placed in bunches in the basin, and by the sides of the room, and it was arranged so that jets of water spouted from marble fountains from the sides of the wall, and fell into the basin where the flowers stood, keeping them fresh and fragrant. Gold fish were swimming in the waters, and imprisoned birds warbled sweet music, and we, overcome by fatigue, sank down on the softly cushioned chairs, and low carpets, which covered a raised floor on one side. It was a fairy room. Our cavass, (Turkish soldier or guide,) picked some of the carnations and distributed them. Mine are pressed for you; and on coming out, he told us to pluck some laurel which grew in the garden.

We passed through many long corridors, and room after room of the harem, and saw where the poor prisoners lived. Every window was closely latticed, and the outer world is only seen through their prison bars. But they are said to be happy, because they know nothing else, and they would be frightened to be let loose into the world.

When we were going through these rooms, we had become so fatigued that we sank down any where, and you would have been amused to have seen how worn out we were. It is my only day at sight seeing, and I think it enough to go once in one's life on such a pilgrimage as we went."

CONSTANTINOPLE, *August 1st.*

"My dear precious Parents,—H. and I are living over the events of the past year. Reckoning by the days of the week, to-day was H.'s last day on the water. Just a year ago to-night he stepped on shore at Boston. Oh, with what vividness those scenes come up to me now. We linger with delight and regret over those few lovely days into which so much of *deep*, *deep* interest was crowded. Our hearts are celebrating them now, and thinking of all God's mercies. Do not you, too, think of them, my dear parents, and are you not glad that we were permitted to come and work here together for our Father in Heaven? We have been thinking which of us will die first, and for H.'s sake I could hope it might be he, but oh, it would be hard. I wish we might die together. But God knows best. Yes, God does know best; and pray that we may be ready for his holy will. Dear father, dear mother, we shall all meet in Heaven. H. has been sweetly comforting me now, for he says Christ will reward you for your sacrifice in his cause, even in this life. He will make it up to you. O, will he not? It grows dark, and at eight o'clock we go to meeting; and by and by, when we are asleep, dear father will go to the *Lecture room* and preach one of his sweet sermons."

LETTER FROM MRS. V. L.

MAKRY KEUY, *near* CONSTANTINOPLE, *August 6th.*

"I received dear mamma's letter, dated June 29th, yesterday, and she says 'I shall not write again till your father comes,' and perhaps only three or four days after she said that, dear father did reach home; and now are your four eyes looking together on this page. Imagine my face above it, with my blue muslin dress on, (the same I wore this very day last year, counting by the days of the week,) and my black velvet ribbon around my neck, confined by my pin, my pretty wedding pin, the dearest part of which to me is the hair of my dear brothers and sisters within it, and the date on its back; yes, infinitely more precious than gold or pearls are these. And now father don't put on a long face because I speak of my dress. I want you should know that I look just as I used to; only I do believe in much better health than last summer at home. So far, the climate suits me admirably. I am telling you the truth when I say I have not minded the heat at all.

The sun has set, and the twilight shadows are gathering over the Marmora, but I must tell you we have come to a little village on the sea, a short distance below the city walls, and are enjoying ourselves very much. Most of the families leave the city in the warm weather. This is a fine place for sea bathing, and has the advantage of being unfashionable, there being scarcely any Frank families here. There is one English Methodist family, and some evangelical Armenians; so we can be useful. We have hired a small house for a short time, and have brought a little furniture with us, and live very pleasantly, though in very rural style. There are only open gardens, or rather cultivated grounds, filled with fig-trees, between us and the sea. The blue waters of the Marmora roll beyond the gardens, and the Princes Islands, in their beautiful rose and violet light, sleep in the sea beneath this glorious summer sky. Then beyond, rise the heights of Asia, blue and dim, and farther still, the snowy summits of beautiful, shadowy Olympus. Dear father, you know just how it looks, only imagine it summer. A lonely owl is uttering his night cry, and I must wait till the lights are brought. I think we will step over and see Mrs. Hague. We have just been in, and while there, H. prayed with the family.

Mr. Hague has had a stroke of the sun, but is better this evening. I hope he will soon be well. He is an intelligent man, an engineer, and occupies quite an important place over all the Sultan's factories. It is pleasant to have him a Christian. Father, you know the pious families who were brought from England to establish themselves in Nicomedia. It is over this company that Mr. H. is placed.

The Saturday after our visit to the mosques, July 13th, we went to our house and arranged our things, and then went back to Mr. Dwight's and passed the Sabbath. My little class met the first time that morning, but we only organized it, William, Bell, and Mary Goodell, and James, William and Charles Dwight. I explained to them how I wished them to study. The Monday following, we went into our new house to reside, and there at first we did feel lonely, with our *tall* house, and nothing of nature, and no near friend to consult about any thing."

JOURNAL.

"*August* 9*th*. These are our happiest days since we left Smyrna, for we are quiet in the midst of nature, away from fashion, and not away from usefulness. It is hard to live shut out from nature, but we must become willing, for our house in Pera is sadly in want of natural scenery. I am sure this is one great reason we have been homesick for Smyrna. Oh, we have pined for the blue sea, and the violet-colored mountains; but now we rejoice in a little season for communion with nature, and our hearts are all the better for it.

"*Tuesday evening*, 13*th*. While I am writing, three Armenian youths sit round our table, reading the Scriptures with H. It is delightful to be engaged for these interesting people. A few days since, one of the Armenian brethren from Constantinople came to call on us, and we had a delightful Christian interview. After reading a chapter in the Armeno Turkish Testament, H. prayed in English, and the Armenian in Turkish. After these young men have been here reading and conversing with H., it makes us happy to know that it has been of use to them.

"14*th*. It is nearly twelve o'clock, and the sunshine covers every thing around; trees, water, islands, and faint snowy clouds, all sleep in the flood of light. Noon is very still in these climates. The 'stilly noon' is expressive here. I have had a grand study over my Armenian all the morning, and now I have come to have a little talk with my dear parents. I am sitting on our low sofa against the window, and am refreshed every moment by the lovely prospect. A faint breeze is stirring, and the sails on the water glide almost imperceptibly on their course. In the chimney of an adjacent house is a hawk's nest, and immense, vulture-like hawks are coming occasionally and lighting there for a moment, uttering a peculiar kind of cry, something like a querulous complaint. So far, the Armenian is very simple. Strange to say, we do not find its grammar hard. It is by no means a complicated language. The only real difficulty is in its long words. But it is amusingly uncouth. When I took up the Greek grammar, it troubled me very much, and I have not yet mastered its everlasting declensions: but the Armenian are very simple, and easily learned, and there is a uniformity which renders them easily remembered also. Mr. Riggs has printed a few notes on modern Armenian, and it is these I am studying. To-day I have been learning the pronouns, and I have them all ready to recite. Heleni makes me learn Greek, and I am happy to say I learn something of it daily. She wants to learn to read, and it will be a fine thing for me to teach her. H. will bring me a Greek spelling book the first time he goes to the city. The women and children here are very kind and sociable. If I only knew how to speak Greek, or Armenian, or Turkish, I should have a fine opportunity of studying native character.

In my last journal, which I sent on the 10th of July, I did not tell you how worried I felt about my piano. It had been shipped at Smyrna, and we were surprised at the delay of the vessel, especially as it had been south wind. I prayed that I might be willing to part with it, for I feared we loved it too well. We were about having it insured, but that very afternoon, Nicoli came to announce its arrival. It was brought up and unpacked, and found to be in fine order. How sweetly its tones sounded when I played on it with H. I felt that it was a blessing restored to me by God, and I prayed that it might be all consecrated to him, and never used for any wrong purpose. I find its size and appearance surprise, as well as please every one here, for they are not accustomed to this heavy style of making pianos."

CHAPTER XIII.

SICKNESS AND DEATH.

"*August* 19*th.* H. has gone to the city. As I am slightly ill, I could not go with him, and I have been lying on the sofa all day, doing a little sewing, and a little reading, and finishing a note for dear Mrs. Fitch. Heleni came to tell me as soon as H. went this morning, that 'Chelebee told her to take good care of Cocona,'* and she has been most of the time sitting by me, and while sewing on the coverings for our sofa, she has been teaching me Greek words, and telling me a variety of things. She talks about my father and mother, and wonders how we can be separated; and she says often, 'by and by we will go to America.' Last evening I had many thoughts of absent friends, and of those who have died. I read the hymns in the little book which Mrs. Chester gave me, and which belonged to Mrs. Hovey, particularly those which were marked by her own hand. You remember the morning that I left Hartford, Mrs. K. brought it to me, and put it into my hand at the boat. I thought much of the past; and of the lovely circles of which Mrs. Hooker and Mrs. Hovey were the bright stars. And I thought how broken and dispersed they are now! And so it must be with every dear circle of affectionate friends. And were this world *all*, what should we do? I pray God we may be prepared for

* Father has heard these names before, and he must tell mamma that they mean gentleman and lady, or master and mistress.

that heavenly world. Oh, how little will the sorrows and the joys of this life appear when we reach the other world. How much we need faith to bring near eternal things. May God bless us all by his sweet presence, and prepare us to enjoy Him forever."

TO MRS. FITCH.

August 15*th.*

"My dear aunt Susan,—My heart has gone back to this day last year, when I was at your house with H., and we have been speaking to day of commencement exercises, and wondering what now is going on in New Haven. It is now ten o'clock in the evening here, and the exercises in the church must have drawn near the interesting part. I can bring it all before my eyes, but I shall not go to the church and the crowd, but remain with you in your own room, and take my chair beside yours, as in good old times. Oh, how sweetly can our thoughts commune with the dear friends from whom we are separated. Do not for a moment imagine that the things at home, or in your house, which is another home to me, fade upon my memory, now I am so far from them. I cannot bear to be thought a stranger to one thing in New England, among those dear scenes where my youth was passed. But I am sitting to talk with you, and I want you to know just as much about my concerns and my dear friends as you would like to know. To my dear mamma I tell *all*, and it is a sweet comfort. She may read you my journal, all that she thinks best, and then you will know our pleasures and our troubles, and you will understand about our leaving Smyrna. We are very sorry to be separated from our dear friends there; and although we hold constant and sweet intercourse with them by writing, yet we miss their pleasant society more than I can tell you. There is a home feeling about Smyrna that there cannot be here."

"*August* 19*th.* I wanted to finish my note on Thursday evening, but it was too late. To-day I am writing you by my window, where my eye is continually feasted by a most magnificent scene. Distant views in this country surpass those in America, but near views in America are the finest, because the verdure is richer than here. From our windows we enjoy a delightful view of the Marmora, amid whose waters the Princess Islands are sleeping. They are bathed now in golden sunshine, but as the sun descends they give forth the most exquisite violet and rosy hues, which are the charm of these lands. The mountains of Asia rise dimly in the southern horizon, and far beyond, tower the summits of Olympus, white and dazzling as if even now its crests were still frozen. If I had finished my note on Thursday evening I should have told you that notwithstanding our love for Smyrna, we are happy here, for our work with the Armenians interests us more and more. It is delightful to see their inquiring minds, and when H. has spent some hours in conversing with them, he feels very happy, for he says their minds are awake on every subject. The evening I was writing you, three young men sat round our table; but as they talk with H. in Turkish, I could not understand them. There is an excellent translation of Young's Night Thoughts into the Turkish, but with the Armenian letters. This interests the Eastern mind very much, and it was this about which these young men talked with great earnestness and great delight on that evening. I want to have my friends at home regard the people here as real human beings, with feelings like their own. I am striving to learn their language, and I do not find it very hard. H., too, is studying it, but he has the advantage of me, for he speaks Turkish; and though the Armenians prefer their own tongue, yet they all use the Turkish."

JOURNAL.

"*Wednesday evening*, 21*st*. When H. returned from the city, on Monday evening, he brought me the good news of the arrival of my own dear father in Boston. My heart is very grateful to God. Oh, that meeting! I can imagine it all—and *we* are happy, and rejoice too. I have not been well for a day or two, but I hope I may soon be better. I want to trust myself, and all I love, in the hands of our blessed Saviour. He can bless us with far more than earth can give; but how slow we are to believe it."

"*Thursday evening*, 22*d*. When we have been only slightly indisposed, and have become well again, how much it makes us value the time which our Father grants to us. And this is the way I feel to-day. For the past three days I have not felt like doing much, and have lain upon the sofa; but to-day I feel like myself again; and I do think it is good to be reminded of my frailty, that I may learn to prize every moment more. How thankful we ought to be, my dear parents, that my health has been so good since I came to these climates. I have not for many years, felt so well as I have during the past year. But the climate of Constantinople is almost too changeable; it is too much like America in this respect. Were it not for this, it would be a fine climate, for it is very far from being oppressively warm. I have luxuriated in the warm weather, and have not suffered at all from it. During our first week in our house at Pera, we went to the Bazars in Constantinople, to get some calico for covering our sofas. The weather was cloudy and warm, and we became much heated in going to the water, but on reaching the cold, damp, dark places near the water's edge, where the sun never shines, an almost death-like chill came over us, which crossing the Horn only increased. These sudden transitions from heat and profuse perspiration, to cold, are very bad for the health. But we have not to suffer them often.

And now, my own dear parents, I must close my journal for H. to take to town. My heart comes to you. Think I am talking these very words. May our Heavenly Father bless us, and all whom we love. May he give you joy and comfort. Love to all. My dear parents, *I am ever, both now and forever,*

Your own affectionate daughter."

FROM MR. V. L.,
INFORMING HER PARENTS OF HER ILLNESS.

MAKRY KEUY, *near* CONSTANTINOPLE,
August 28*th*, 1844.

"My dear Parents,—Both Mary and myself thought, that as the Vienna post leaves to-day, I had better write by it, and inform you that she is sick. She has a dysentery, which came on about a fortnight since. She has at times improved by the medicine given her, but last night it came on with redoubled violence, and some of the symptoms are alarming. I have sent this morning for Dr. S., and am sorry to be obliged to send this to the post, before he can have seen M., that I might give you his opinion of her case.

M. has many apprehensions that it may end badly; but she appears beautifully in it all; no one would suspect that she was at all sick. She appears as calm and quiet as in the happiest moment of her life, and I believe she is happy. I believe I have less fears respecting the issue, yet I confess I feel quite alarmed by some things. But I bear it very differently from her. The only way I can be at all quiet in my mind, is to be very busy, especially in things that concern her welfare. I cannot for a moment bear the thought of separation; but this may be the very reason why I need to be chastised. Oh, that my heart might feel perfectly at rest in God's hand, and willing to have him do whatever he pleases. I approve all he does, I love his character, but the flesh is weak.

M. says to you, that you must trust her in God's hands, for he will do *all* which is best."

EXTRACT OF A LETTER

COMMENCED BY MARY HERSELF, BUT WHICH SHE NEVER FINISHED.

MAKRY KEUY, *Sept.* 6*th*, 1844.

My dear Parents,—I fear we distressed you too much, by writing you last week concerning my illness; but it is my desire that you should know all about your children here, both in sickness and in health. I am better now, you see, and amuse myself in reading and writing; but I am not yet well. I know you are thinking much of us these days. Oh, how vividly they pass before our minds; and yet I have refrained from thinking much of them, for I am too weak. Dear mamma's letter, dated July 15th, came on our wedding day—oh, what a comfort it was to me! I think it is among the best. One thing made me sad, and that is, the fear she expresses that I shall lose my vivid impression of home and home faces. Oh, *no*, *no*, this never can be. You do not know how my heart twines around the slightest thing of home; how distinctly I remember each minute thing, each minute circumstance. You know that God has blessed me with a good memory, and now I find what a rich blessing it is. Do not imagine that any thing new or strange, can efface in the slightest degree my beloved home from my mind. It is too deeply engraven. My heart itself would die if the picture faded.

During this sickness, I have had many thoughts of Christ and of heaven, and I shall know why God afflicted me, if I ever recover. It is very hard to be sick, but I do try to be patient. H. is a sweet nurse—I hope he will not be worn out. Heleni, too, is very kind and affectionate, and I have every thing to be thankful for. As soon as I have strength, we shall return to Pera, for there are many more comforts there, than can be obtained here. I have suffered so little during my life, that I cannot bear sickness with patience; but I hope I shall learn.

O, my dear parents, do we not pray for you every day? Half my thoughts turn to prayers for you. Let us prepare for that blessed world, where our Saviour makes all happy with the light of his countenance. I have not known till this sickness, how happy Christ can make our hearts. He *can satisfy the heart.*

I sometimes fear that this sickness is a judgment upon me for improving so little my great blessings. I try to pray that God may make me suffer till I feel right. But it is hard to pray this, and I stop short with the prayer that I may be *willing* to suffer. God will do all which is best; and in heaven we shall rejoice in every dispensation.

It is a great comfort to sit here on the sofa, and write you just as I feel. I feel as if I were talking to you. And are you not thankful, my dear father, now that I cannot talk as fully with you as I once did, that H. has such a deep experience in spiritual things? H. comes to say, 'What would you like to eat?' and I think of mamma's good beef steak and bread. The bread here is almost always sour; but Andrico is going to hunt in Pera to-morrow, till he can find some sweet. New England bread and butter and milk, are the things I most feel the want of, and New England cleanliness.

Good-bye, my dear parents; this letter will not go till next Wednesday, and before that time, I trust we shall have something new to say."

TO THE FRIEND
DESIGNATED BY ———, IN THE FORMER PAGES OF THIS MEMOIR.

MAKRY KEUY, *Sept. 7th*, 1844.

"My dear H.—I believe, that just at present, I am becoming acclimated. Something is making rather uncomfortable work with my health, which you know has been uncommonly good since I came to the East. Whether it be H.'s love for Smyrna, or whether it be in reality the case, he is tempted to believe that the climate of Constantinople is not as good for me as Smyrna. The changes here are too great. When the north wind blows, as it comes from the Black Sea, it is too cool, and when the south wind blows, it is very hot. The heat I do not mind at all—indeed it is very pleasant, and there is a luxury about it very delightful. I hope I may soon be better. At present I am unable to do any thing, except occasionally to write a little, as it is a recreation. It is three weeks since I became ill—part of the time have been in bed, and now I can with much difficulty walk from one room to the other. Before my illness, I had commenced studying Armenian in earnest, and shall resume it as soon as I can. Constantinople life has nothing of the charm which Smyrna life has, but we content ourselves with the hope of doing good among these dear Armenians. Their minds are wide awake.

Did you think of us this week? our wedding week? Last year this day, we were at 'the Falls'—those glorious falls! How much has happened since then. How tender the recollection of those days in Hartford—our school days—our days when we met to read together, and afterwards those quiet walks when the sun was setting, and the evening star beginning to look quietly down, and we were communing of holy things. Our Saturday evenings—oh, they were the sweetest. Do we not remember each scene in the beautiful past as vividly as if we were again treading those very spots? We have a great deal to talk about—and if we do not in this world meet, I know we shall remember them all in heaven. And do not you believe, that our memories will be far more vivid there, than they ever can be here?"

TO ONE OF HER YOUNG FRIENDS IN HARTFORD.

MAKRY KEUY, *Sept. 9th.*

My dear S,—I have thought of you, and prayed for you many times, and particularly since I have heard of the deep affliction* which our Heavenly Father has sent into your family. You have learned very early in life, that this is a world full of sorrow, and that if this were our only state of existence, it would be hardly worth while to live. But let us thank our Father, who gives us the promise of a glorious home beyond the grave; a home where no pain can enter—a home where existence is perfect happiness. While we are in health we are apt to forget that other world, but in sickness the mind returns to it with new feelings. This is the case with me. I have been prone to forget heaven; while I have been in health it has seemed far off, and I have not tried to fix my affections there, as I now feel that I ought. But for some weeks my health has been very feeble, and the world has grown dim, and I bless God who has in mercy afflicted me, so that I might look up to that better world, which should occupy our

* This young friend had lost a brother who was very dear to all.

chief attention. Dear S., this world is not to be our home. Let us rejoice in this. A few days of care will soon pass, and then we, and those we love, will begin a blessed existence in the presence of our Saviour, who will make all our hearts happy, through all eternity. But how little we think of heaven, and how we start at the thought of dying. Yes, dying is a solemn thing. I shrink when I think of the hour of death. But then I say, 'will Jesus leave those who put their trust in him?' Oh, no, we may safely confide in him, and he will take away all fear of death, and he will put such sweet thoughts of heaven into our minds, and of the lovely company of redeemed ones who are gathered there, that we shall no longer look upon this life as desirable, but shall joyfully meet death as a messenger sent to carry us to our beautiful, our glorious home. I think our views of heaven will depend very much upon the manner in which we view Christ. He is the chief attraction in heaven, and he must have our highest love, if we would hope to have heaven attractive. If we meditate much upon the perfect character of our Almighty Saviour, we shall see how adapted he is to satisfy our hearts. Yes, dear S., he can satisfy as no other being can; and I trust you have long ere this found it out. But if you are troubled at finding that Christ is not all to you that you wish him to be, though you do sincerely put your trust in him, the best way to remedy this is to think very much of him, to strive to have your thoughts go up often to him, and also to pray earnestly that he will show you how lovely he is. Christ has sources of comfort and happiness in himself, which he is ready to impart to us, and of which we now little dream. Our minds are too dark to see his loveliness. Oh, when will these clouds be rolled away? Dear S., let us no longer think of him as a being far away, but as a kind and faithful friend, who loves us with so tender a love, that he longs to draw us to his bosom, and make us forever happy. But you may think, dear S., that I intend writing a sermon instead of a letter, and I will tell you frankly, that these thoughts have dwelt so much in my mind of late, that I could not refrain from writing them.

I have had such good health almost ever since I came to the East, that it is hard now to think of being an invalid; but I must trust in God, and have patience. Oh, it is very sweet to know we are in the hands of a kind Heavenly Father, who knows just what is best for us.

Dear S., how much I would give to see you once again! but let us strive so to live, that we shall meet in heaven."

FROM MR. V. L.

CONSTANTINOPLE, *Sept.* 18*th*, 1844.

"My beloved Parents,—I have so long delayed writing again, in the hopes of being able to give you a more satisfactory account of Mary's health. I am rejoiced to say that she is better, and that her fever has left her. But she has been very much reduced by this sickness. She is weak and emaciated, so that you would hardly know her.

M. sends you her very best love, and wishes you to trust her entirely in God's hands, fully believing that he will take care of her, and do all that is best for her. Miss W. has been very kind to us in M.'s sickness, being the only one who has been able to afford me any assistance in taking care of her."

FROM THE SAME.

CONSTANTINOPLE, *Sept.* 25*th*, 1844.

"Mary has had some clouds, but generally she is in a happy, contented state of mind, trusting in Christ as able to do all things for her, and alone able to wash away her sins, and to save her at last. I have just asked her whether she had any message for you. She says, 'give my love, my very best love; tell them I have a great many things to say to them, but I can't now. Tell them it will be very, very sweet, when all the redeemed meet together in heaven.'"

FROM THE SAME.

CONSTANTINOPLE, *Sept.* 27*th*, 1844.

"My dearest Parents,—I wrote you the day before yesterday, about M.'s state, but as the letter is to go by ship, and it may be long before you can receive it, I now write you by post, especially as the disease has made great progress since that time. Yesterday morning the doctor told me that her disease was typhus fever, and that he had very strongly suspected its nature from the beginning. In the afternoon a consultation was held, in which the physicians agreed perfectly.

Mental aberration had slightly commenced the day before. Yesterday it gradually increased, with a pulse at one hundred and forty. During the last night she did not close her eyes, and has constantly been seeing a variety of imaginary sights, and talking with many of her friends. Once in a while she has had a lucid moment; but it has been short, and apparently given her to express her entire confidence in Christ, and her full committal of all her friends into his hands.

In the midst of all her delirium and agitation, she shows in a touching manner her love for her friends. She has often called you to her, and been conversing with you. Last night she called me to her, to catch three letters which her father had thrown her, and which were fallen into her bosom. She was also certain he had passed in the street, and asked why he had not called to see her now he was in town. At one moment she begged me most touchingly, to let her go and see her father and mother. She has several times called M. M., and spoken to her, and has also spoken of several of my relatives.

I have done all I could to find out her state of mind, as well as to help her to fix her hopes on the sure foundation. Before the critical turn which the disease took, we talked a great deal together on experimental religion. She often expressed doubts as to her state; they came from her deep sense of unworthiness and short coming. She always called herself an unprofitable servant, and deeply mourned on account of it. But her mind was stayed on Christ as her only hope; and she looked for no other Saviour—wished for no other. From the first of her illness, she has believed that she should not recover, and all our reasonings upon the subject have proved of no avail. This impression has led her to make her preparation thorough. She has conversed about it with whoever could give her any information. But now all doubts seem dispelled. Whenever she has been lucid, and before she lost her mind, her hope was strong, believing that *Christ* could and would save her.

A few hours later. The doctor has been in, and finds that the disease has made alarming progress during the night. He thinks her in a very critical situation. Her limbs have become cold, and all the hot applications fail to draw the heat towards them."

" *Sept. 27th. 1 o'clock.* Thus far your son-in-law had written,—and now, at his request, I enter upon the painful duty of announcing to you, that your beloved daughter's race in this world is run. She *has fought the good fight;' she 'has finished her course;' she 'has kept the faith.'*

I have just come from the bedside where her lifeless body still lies, and it is only fifteen minutes since she drew her last breath. But her soul is not there; it is not any where in this world; but we doubt not it has gone to dwell with that glorious and faithful Saviour, to whom she had dedicated her life. She loved much, and would have done much for her Lord in this dark world, and he accepted her offering of herself—but has removed her to a higher service in his own bright world of glory.

Would that I could speak a word of comfort to both your hearts. But God must comfort you, and I doubt not he will do it. Heaven is as near to the children of God in Constantinople as in Hartford; and it is as safe dying here as there. May you, and we, all be ready to welcome the Saviour, whenever he shall come to call us away!

H. G. O. DWIGHT."

EXTRACTS

FROM A LETTER BY THE HUSBAND OF MARY, A FEW DAYS AFTER HER DEATH.

"Oh, my dear precious Father and Mother,—How can I announce to you the fearful calamity which has befallen me, and not only me, but all who have ever known my Mary, my now sainted and forever happy Mary.

* * * * * * * * *

But I must not give vent to my own grief, I must hasten to satisfy your trembling curiosity. My M., your M., is gone. She has fled from this world of pain and sin, and now lies in Jesus' bosom; and her body, the once lovely mansion of the loveliest spirit, sleeps on an eminence that overlooks the city for whose spiritual welfare she laid down her life.

You know it is about six weeks since she began to be ill. Medicine did not succeed in entirely restoring her, though at times it checked her disease. I removed her into town as soon as I could, that she might have constant medical attendance. Under a change of treatment, she seemed to be doing well, when all at once, on Sunday, the

22d, there was a powerful relapse. On Wednesday, her mind began to wander. On Thursday night, she went down very fast. I was constantly by her side. In the morning her limbs were cold. The usual hot applications left them as cold as before—all the heat was concentrated in her breast. But she had her reason, though she could scarcely articulate, or perceive objects around her.

About eleven o'clock, began her agony—and the doctor tells me I have seen all that can be seen in such a moment. But he assures me she neither suffered nor was conscious of any thing. I have reason to believe it, and comfort myself with it. But she expired like the breeze on the ocean, when the ripples beat fainter and fainter on the shore. She breathed slowly, and yet more slowly, and died without a groan, or the slightest motion of a muscle.

Mary's mind had long been preparing for her end. From the first, she believed that she should not recover. She settled all her doubts one by one. On Sunday, before her relapse, she expressed a sweet and perfect confidence in her Saviour, and entrusted all things to him. We had some sweet words together. She said God would take care of me, and wanted to talk about her death. I told her I could not bear it, and that there was no probability of her dying sooner than I. Still she did talk about it. On Monday her mind began to wander. Her fears were roused for a moment, but she checked them at once, and expressed the fullest confidence in Christ, and the firm belief that he would save her.

I have written you something about her derangement. Now I want to say, that from seven o'clock on Friday morning, her mind ceased to wander. She was constantly speaking to herself. All I could distinguish was in strong hope and joyful expectation. I several times made out, 'Oh, how happy!' 'Very happy!' 'How sweet it will be to be there!' I kept whispering in her ear words of encouragement, and as long as she could hear, she seemed to enjoy it much, and responded to it. When I repeated the first stanza of the hymn, 'Jesus, lover of my soul,' there was a strong, bright smile, and she whispered, 'yes,' 'yes,' several times. Soon, however, she could hear nothing. I laid myself before her eyes, and asked if she knew me; she said 'yes,' 'Henry.' But soon she could distinguish us no more. She kept her eyes distinctly fixed toward heaven. Her voice was presently inarticulate, and it was only groans, which soon became strong breathings. For the last time she had spoken of her feelings; she said she felt perfectly well. The agony seemed one in which she had nothing to do. The doctor said he was sure she was unconscious of it. He says also, that all her last forenoon he had seen that her mind was engaged with the world to which she was going.

My dear parents, I am afraid you will think I do not submit to God's will. I do, from the bottom of my heart. I know he does all things right. And how can I murmur when my Mary is so happy. Let us all kiss the hand that smites."

A FEW ADDITIONAL NOTICES FROM A LETTER OF MISS W—N.

CONSTANTINOPLE, *Sept.* 30*th*, 1844.

"You have heard all the sad news ere this—sad for us survivors—most sad for him who has lost the light of his life. God has taken our dear M. to himself, and it is momentarily pleasant to think how happy she is now in the presence of her Saviour, among glorified spirits; but as we are bound down to earth, we feel the loss of one who would have shed sunshine around our path. M. was ever so sprightly, so cheerful, so disposed to make others happy, that all were depending upon her for life and animation during the coming winter. We were only waiting for her to recover, to commence various plans. We had made some arrangements with reference to the children of the mission families; all thinking it important that something should be done to interest and improve them, as they grow up here without the lectures and other varieties which young people have in America. During the day, each were to pursue their several avocations, and at evening were to endeavor to revive, improve, and edify each other. All was depending upon the new comers, as others were too feeble, or too much immersed in cares, to go forward in any new project.

When I came to Constantinople, about the middle of August, Mr. and Mrs. V. L. were down on the sea-coast. I received a note from M., saying that she had not been well for a few days, but wished me to come there as soon as I had seen the lions about C. I spent a week in this way, and then accompanied Mr. V. L. to Makry Keuy. M. appeared well, and stepped about in her usual sprightly way; but informed us that she had that day a return of unfavorable symptoms. She did not rise the next morning, and kept her bed most of every day during the week, and it was not until the end of it, that the disease was checked, when she had become weak, and Mr. V. L. carried her from the bed to the sofa.

On Monday, Sept. 2d, having been there just a week, it became necessary for me to return to Pera. I was thinking whether I should go again to Makry Keuy, when I received a note written by Mary herself, saying they expected to come up to Pera in a few days. On the following Tuesday they came. M. was brought up from the boat in a sedan chair, and laid upon her bed, where I saw her an hour or two afterwards. She appeared much the same as when I left her at Makry Keuy. It was not thought best she should talk much, and thereforê I read to her. She was not disposed for light reading, but seemed pleased with serious subjects. She often said she thought she should not recover from this sickness. She thought over her past life, examined the foundation of her hope of salvation, expressed her fears that she was not as willing to die as she should be—she could not endure to think of her husband, and of her parents in their bereavement. As no new danger was apprehended from her symptoms, I was sorry to hear her talk in this way. She was, however, very cheerful and patient, and during the first week of her return to Pera, talked about any subject that interested me.

She said one day, 'you will see my mother, probably, before I shall. Tell her how much I love her—but *that* you cannot do. Tell her that time and distance do not diminish my interest and affection—and I must thank for her all those friends who so kindly helped in her preparations for leaving home.' She talked over her severe illness at Hartford, and remarked upon the kindness of different individuals to her at the time. How carefully should I have treasured up every word, and how I should have drawn her out upon every subject of interest, instead of deferring them to a time when I thought she would be well, if I had suspected the least danger in her case.

The Tuesday before her death I began to be discouraged about her, and offered to sit up with her during the night, if Mr. V. L. would retire and take some rest. Before leaving in the morning I read to her from the Daily Food, the verse for the day, September 25th, to which she said, 'how beautiful.' She thanked me with her usual warmth for staying with her, and after promising to do so again soon, I left her, never more to see her when she was conscious of my presence. The next night Mrs. Dwight spent there, and she was much the same. The following night Mr. V. L. watched with her himself. She had appeared weaker during the day, and her mind somewhat affected. On Friday morning I did not think of there being any more immediate danger, but at eleven o'clock word came to me that she was dying. I hastily snatched my bonnet, and with Mr. Goodell hurried to her bedside. What a change! She was breathing heavily, her eyes fixed, and she was evidently unconscious. The physician and her husband were at her side; Mr. and Mrs. Dwight near. In a few moments Mr. V. L.'s brother came in, and we all stood speechless, only Mr. Goodell uttered a short prayer commending her spirit to God. We knew the moment of her death only as the physician said to her husband, 'she is gone,' when he fainted and was carried from the room; and Mrs. Dwight and myself were left alone with the lifeless body of our departed sister. Her servant maid, a Greek girl, who had been also present, came in, and we commenced our melancholy office. It was a new and trying scene to me, for I had never seen any thing of the kind. I could not permit my feelings to excuse me— there were no other of the missionary ladies who were well enough to do it, and it must not be left to servants. Little had I thought when I arranged her hair for her day by day, that I was to see it done for the last time so soon, but I forbear. She is gone, and we are left desolate. On Saturday, at two o'clock, the few Christian friends assembled to perform the last sad office. Mr. Goodell conducted the services at the house. Her favorite hymn, 'Jesus, lover of my soul,' was sung. The procession of about thirty gentlemen walked to the grave, and the bier was carried on the shoulders of a number, none of whose names I heard mentioned, excepting Rev. Mr. T., one of the missionaries of the American Episcopal church. The ladies all remained at the house, as it is not the custom for them to go to the grave. I cannot realize the truth that Mary's spirit is in heaven, and her body beneath the ground. It was indeed a sudden stroke to all, and most so I think to her husband. But let us not look down into the narrow house of the body, but up to the blessed mansion where the glorified spirit is chanting the praises of redeeming love."

A BRIEF NOTICE BY MRS. GOODELL.

"Very soon after she came from the country, she requested us to pray that she might have *patience* and *resignation.* She wished us also to repeat to her verses of Scripture, saying, they were so refreshing, and helped to fix her thoughts on God, adding that her mind had become very weak, and that she could not think much. On the morning of the 23d, she requested me to read to her out of her text book, the verse for the day, which I did. In the afternoon I read to her at intervals, passages of Scripture and some hymns, with which she expressed herself much delighted and comforted. Now she is where she needs no such feeble help.

Mrs. Van Lennep looked lovely and pleasant in death, perfectly natural, and with a countenance uncommonly sweet."

A BRIEF EXTRACT FROM A LETTER OF MR. V. L.

February, 1845.

"In thinking over the circumstances of Mary's sickness, I cannot help being struck with the care of her Father in Heaven to prepare her to go home to himself. From the commencement of her indisposition, she had an impression that it would end in her dissolution. At first, she merely hinted the existence of that impression; but she soon stated and repeated it. Her evident object all the day long was to prepare herself for her last change.

Providence kindly provided that we should be placed in a quiet country village, seeing almost no company; so that she could give herself up without any hindrance to a review of all the great features of Christianity, and going to the only foundation of hope to the sinner, might place her feet more firmly than ever on the rock Christ Jesus. I shall never forget the sweet and delightful conversations we had together all the time we were at Makry Keuy. I particularly remember one afternoon, while she was yet in health, we were talking about the blessedness of Heaven, when her emotions became so powerful that she raised her eyes to what was soon to be her own abode, and said, while the tears gushed from them, 'O, it will be sweet to be there.' The character of Christ occupied her mind more than any other topic, and the delightful views contained in 'The Great Teacher,' a book we were then reading, were to her a source of the highest pleasure.

During the last weeks of her life she became very weak, and was unable to bear what required much concentration of thought; but she had a high relish for prayer, and whenever Mr. Goodell called she uniformly asked him to pray. I wish I could remember her many sweet expressions of every Christian emotion; her committing her friends and us all, to the hands of the Redeemer; but her thoughts and the state of her mind so engrossed me, that the words in which she gave utterance to them, have escaped from the memory. Besides, she talked as much with her countenance and gestures as with her lips, and the whole was a clear mirror by which one could gaze into the purest and most angelic soul.*

* The trial of sickness and suffering gave a greater lustre to every excellence in her character, and she is not fully known by those who have not seen her in such circumstances.—Mr. V. L.

* * * * * *

Before losing it forever, I took a last sad look of that sweet countenance which had been the seat of so many emotions, but I deeply felt Mary was not there. On Saturday afternoon, the circle of sympathizing friends met in our large parlor, where Mr. Goodell performed religious services. When the funeral train had started, I took another way in a carriage with Mr. Schauffler, and was at the grave long before they had reached it. I stood by the opening earth ready to receive into its bosom the remnant of my Mary. Oh, how I wished I could lie down in it by her side. At length the mourning train appeared, winding among the solemn trees and the Armenian tombs which border the Protestant grave yard. It slowly ascended the slope, near the summit of which we stood. Mr. Goodell and the Prussian chaplain walked in front. Then came the bier covered with its black cloth, held by some of our brethren. The American ambassador followed. He had requested to carry the cloth, but was told that it would be a sufficient expression of his interest if he walked first after the bier. The Prussian chaplain performed the services at the grave with much feeling, and all that was visible of my sweet Mary disappeared under the earth. * * * * Sleep there until thou rise to a happy resurrection! Sleep! Thy rest is peace, and thy soul is blessed!"

A monument erected by her husband in the Protestant burying ground at Pera covers the spot where her dust reposes. In reference to the place of her burial, Mr. V. L. remarks, "At first I felt disappointed that her remains could not be conveyed to Smyrna, to be buried among the graves of my ancestors, but she sleeps where now I would wish her to sleep, among the people for whose welfare she sacrificed her life. She went to Constantinople at a great personal expense, solely for the sake of the Armenians whom she loved, and in their midst let her sleep among the living and the dead. From her grave you behold the Bosphorus passing under your feet, with its crowded villages on both sides; you also see parts of Constantinople itself. If the spirit ever visits the place of its clay, with what joy will she look around on a people restored to the spiritual worship of God, as I trust they will be before many years have passed."

CHAPTER XIV.

CLOSING REMARKS.

AND now the task is done. It was undertaken by affection, and pursued with a pleasing though melancholy satisfaction, as it furnished the occasion of living over again the dear and tender scenes of days that are past, never to return.

It was the wish of the writer that the preparation of the memoir might have fallen to other and abler hands; but the feelings of the father have not permitted him to look over the papers of his deceased daughter, until the work was nearly ready for the press. Yet this may not prove so serious a loss as was at first apprehended, as it has led to a more copious selection from her writings than might have been made in other circumstances; and thus the subject of the memoir has been, with slight exceptions, her own biographer.

And here the writer might gather up the traits in her character and present them in a connected view, but as this has been done in a sermon appended to the memoir, she will only add a few things which occur to her mind in closing, as contributing to make the portrait more complete.

Every one who has read the preceding pages must have been struck with two things; Mary's love of life and her early preparation to leave it. Her husband, as were others, was constantly impressed with these facts. He says,

"Mary loved life. She loved her friends with a rapturous love. She loved man, of whatever nation, whatever religion, in whatever state." She "desired life, that she might impart to others the blessings which had been so richly bestowed upon her."*

She was also qualified to enjoy life. Of this, no one can doubt who has read her memoir; and yet her friends have a consciousness of the fact, which can never be imparted to others. She looked upon the works of nature as a manifestation of the excellence and glory of their great Creator, and she loved them as the work of her Father's hand. She often spoke of their soothing and elevating influence on the mind, and said of them, that "they were a lovely book to read with the Bible." She loved her work in life; and the people for whose spiritual welfare she had sacrificed so much.† "Hers was a heart whose emotions were powerful, and constantly keeping along with the thousand objects which impressed her."‡

With regard to her being qualified for usefulness, her life speaks for itself, yet the testimony of her husband on this point is too striking to be omitted. He says, "My intercourse with her was a source not only of happiness, but of real, spiritual improvement, and I have grown ten times faster in my Christian character while she has been with me. I blessed God continually for having given her to me."

Her adaptedness to fill with happiness to herself and

* Her own remark.

† An Armenian youth of intelligence and piety, who was in the family of Mr. Dwight at the time Mary was there, said of her, "She loved my people very much. I remember one day she said, (opening her arms) 'if there was only room, I would take them all in;' then she laid her hand upon her heart, as if to say, 'there is room enough here.'"

Her husband says, "I have often been struck with Mary's love for the Armenians. In one of her letters she says, 'when I see these lovely Armenian girls passing through the streets, their dark eyes peeping from under their snowy veils, I long to take them to my arms and teach them a Saviour's love.'"

‡ Mr. V. L.

acceptability to others, the various stations which it was her lot in life to occupy, pass in pleasing retrospect before the mind, yet only a single testimony, and that in reference to the last relation she was called to sustain, shall be quoted: "She was a crown of glory to her husband."*

And yet in the morning of life and in the enjoyment of every thing which could contribute to make life useful and happy, she kept constantly before her mind the day of her death. Indeed, from the time in her tenth year, when she penned the resolution, "Resolved to think often of my dying," the importance of being prepared for a state of purity and blessedness beyond the grave, was never lost sight of. One of her young friends who knew her well, says, "the future world was so much in her thoughts that her early removal to it could have been no great surprise to her, whatever it was to us." The same friend, in speaking of her preparedness for heaven, says, "she let her light so shine, that the world did not wait till after her death to count her among the number of Christ's jewels."

A word or two respecting her religious training might not be out of place here. What that was may be gathered from a chapter in the commencement of this memoir, and also from a few remarks in the sermon before alluded to. In addition it need only be said, that in conducting this part of her education, her parents kept constantly in mind her fallen and ruined state by nature, and the necessity of Divine interposition in order to a recovery from this state. These great and leading truths of Christianity were made the basis of her religious education. They were used as an essential means of giving her a just view of her state as a sinner, and of leading her to Christ as the only Saviour. To the impressions which these truths made upon her mind in her tender years, resulting as they did in her early

* Rev. Mr. Goodell, Constantinople.

piety, is to be traced, all that made her so lovely and useful in life, and prepared her for so early a removal from this to a purer world.

And now may He to whom this beloved child consecrated herself in the morn ng of her days, to whom she was indebted for all that made her what she was, graciously smile upon this humble effort, and condescend to make use of it in the advancement of His own cause, which was dear to the deceased while she lived, and from which it seemed good in His sight so early to withdraw her labors.

LINES BY A FRIEND

TO THE MEMORY OF

MRS. MARY E. VAN LENNEP,

Who died at Constantinople, September 27th, **1844.**

THY grave is with the Moslem dead,
  Far o'er the rolling sea,
Where none of all that loved thee here
  Can go to weep for thee;
Thou who wert to so many hearts
  Dear as the light of day;
Whose sweet voice from our memories
  Can never pass away.

Could earthly love avail to save,
  Or spirit purified,
Or youth and hope and holy faith,
  Thou surely hadst not died.
Thy labor in the vineyard closed
  Long ere the noontide sun;
The dew still glistened on the leaves
  When thy short task was done.

The angel came and called for thee,
  He took thee by the hand,
He led thee to the river's side,
  And showed the shining land;
And thou didst launch thy trembling bark,
  And fearlessly go o'er,
Nor cast one lingering backward glance
  Upon the fading shore,

And glorious was the light that streamed
  Down from the pearly gate;
And glorious were the angel band
  That round thy steps did wait;
And blessed were the harmonies
  That through the air did roll,
The welcome of the host of heaven
  Unto thy blissful soul.

And there thou art in glory shining,
  Such as no eye can see,
And there we think without repining
  That thou shalt ever be:
For though the way is long and dreary
  Up to the hills of light,†
And though our steps are often weary
  With wandering through the night,

We trust in him who was thy Guide
  To lead us all the way,
Till on our souls shall dawn the light
  Of the eternal day.
Sweet are the memories our hearts
  Shall ever keep of thee,
Till in our Father's house at last
  Thy face once more we see.

ON THE DEATH OF MRS. MARY E. VAN LENNEP.

Scarce was the joyance o'er
  That hailed the nuptial rite,
And scarce the tender, parting tear
  Dried in its channels bright,
When o'er the Atlantic surge,
  There came a sound of woe,—
The flower that erst our garden deck'd
  Was in its bloom laid low.

† See page 68 of the Memoir.

Sweet friend—within our souls,
  How fresh each hallowed trace,
Thy meek forgetfulness of self,
  Thy loveliness and grace,
Thy hand the harp that rul'd,
  Thy warbled music sweet,
Thy childhood's early choice to sit
  Low at thy Saviour's feet.

Within the house of God
  There was a marriage train,
A gathered throng, a breathless hush,
  An anthem's thrilling strain,
And thou in snowy robe
  Wert by thy lover's side,
While there a father's voice invok'd
  Heaven's blessing on the bride.

Thy path was o'er the wave,
  To ancient climes afar,
Where turns the pagan's blinded eye,
  From Bethlem's blessed star;
But, soon life's labor o'er,
  There was a peaceful sleep,
Where richly blooms the Moslem rose,
  And dew-eyed myrtles weep.

And now there 's grief for thee,
  Fair inmate of the grave,
Where bright Bosphorus proudly flows,
  And Asia's palm-trees wave,
And deep within *his* soul
  Is anguish unexpressed,
Who held thee for so brief a space,
  A pearl-drop on his breast.

Not in the church-yard green,
  Beneath thy native sky,
Thou by thine infant sister's side,
  Or brother dear might lie,

But with their spirits pure
  Thou join'st a glorious train,
Where ne'er a golden link was broke
  From love's eternal chain.

Sad is thy parent's home,
  And lone their evening fire,
Yet there doth blessed Memory bend
  And holy faith aspire,
As angel comforters
  They point desponding love
To what thou *wert* while here below,
  And what thou *art* above.

L. H. S.

A Father's Memorial of an only Daughter.

A DISCOURSE

DELIVERED IN

THE FIRST CHURCH IN HARTFORD,

SABBATH EVENING, DECEMBER 9th, 1844,

ON THE DEATH OF

MRS. MARY E. VAN LENNEP,

WIFE OF REV. HENRY J. VAN LENNEP,

Missionary to Turkey;

WHO DIED IN CONSTANTINOPLE, SEPTEMBER 27th, 1844

BY JOEL HAWES, D. D.

A SERMON.

He shall enter into peace; they shall rest in their beds, each one walking in his uprightness.—*Isaiah* lvii. 2.
I shall be satisfied when I awake with thy likeness.—*Psalm* xvii. 15.

Besides the general appropriateness of these Scriptures to the occasion on which we are met, there are two special reasons which have led me to the choice of them, as the theme of present discourse.

The dear departed one greatly loved a little manual of devotion, called "Daily Food." She was for years in the habit of reading and meditating on the text selected for the day, as a means of Christian improvement. It was so, that the two verses just read, were the ones for the day on which she died. "He shall enter into peace; they shall rest in their beds, each one walking in his uprightness." "I shall be satisfied when I awake with thy likeness." Sinking under the power of disease, she was probably unable to read or meditate on these Scriptures, on the morning of that day, as she was wont; but just as the sun had passed its meridian, she went, I trust, to realize their full, sweet meaning in the presence of her Saviour. The other reason referred to is this. In the evening before our final parting at Smyrna, on the 10th of last May, I attended a little meeting for conference and prayer, in the family of one of our missionaries. In expectation of the sad farewell on the morrow, my feelings led me to select, as the subject of my remarks, the last of the two verses chosen for my text: "I shall be satisfied when I awake with thy likeness." My dear child was one of the little circle that composed my audience; and it was the last time that she ever listened to the voice of Christian instruction and encouragement from the lips of her father. And I love now to reflect, that my last words were so appropriate to a final interview, and so fitted to help her on through the remainder of her short pilgrimage on earth.

The Scriptures, then, set at the head of this discourse, seem to me to have a peculiar claim to direct our meditations on the present occasion. In speaking from them, I shall endeavor, as far as I can, to lay aside the feelings of a father towards a much loved daughter, and address my audience, just as I would, were I preaching a sermon on the death of any youthful member of my charge. What I may say of the deceased will not be in eulogy, but in praise of that grace which made her what she was, and in thankfulness for that kindness of my Heavenly Father, which comforts my bereaved heart with the blessed hope that he has taken her to himself in glory.

I have wished, also, by falling in with the train of reflection awakened by the death of my daughter in the minds of many, especially of her young acquaintances, more deeply to impress upon them the lessons of this providence, that so, she being dead, might still speak to them who knew and loved her while yet she was with us.

In presenting a brief illustration of the sentiments contained in our text, we may notice,

I. The peaceful death of the righteous. And,

II. The state of blessedness into which they enter on leaving the body.

I. The gospel aside, death is a most gloomy and distressing event. It puts an end to all our enjoyments, purposes, and hopes. It severs us from every thing we hold dear on earth; seals up our senses, stops the warm current of life, and commits our bodies to the cold and silent grave, there to moulder back to corruption and dust. Reason sheds no light on this dark scene; wakes up no hope in the bosom of the departing, and speaks no comfort to the smitten hearts of survivors. It cannot assure us that we shall exist beyond the grave; much less can it tell us in what state we are to exist, or how we may hope to appear, in peace, in the presence of the great Being, whom we cannot but know we have offended by our sins, and who holds our destiny for eternity in his hands. Hence death has been most significantly called the king of terrors; and he fulfills all the dreadful meaning of his name towards such as know not God, and reject the overtures of his grace in Christ.

But life and immortality are brought to light in the gospel. There we are assured by a fullness of evidence that excludes all doubt, that he who made us, has made us for an endless existence, and that, if we are found in him, "who is the resurrection and the life," death hath no sting for us, and the grave no terrors; we go in peace; we rest in our beds; every one that walketh in his uprightness. This is the blessed instruction contained in our text. Let us dwell upon it for a moment.

The peace and rest spoken of are restricted, you perceive, to a particular character; to him that walketh in uprightness. This, in the sense of the Bible, is a peculiar character. It belongs only to true Christians; such as have been born of the Spirit; as love God supremely, and are united to Christ by an affectionate, living faith. No sweetness of natural temper, no amiableness of disposition, no correctness of outward conduct, constitutes, in the sight of God, an upright, or righteous character. These natural traits you may possess in great perfection, and yet your heart be dead to the love of God, and yourself a stranger to all the exercises of true piety. Marvel not, my friends, you must be born again. The youngest, the oldest, the most kind, amiable and moral among you, must experience this great change, or the character of uprightness, to which alone peace and rest in the dying hour are promised, can never be yours; and you can never enter the kingdom of heaven. The Bible throughout is strikingly discriminating on this point. It tells you of peace in your latter end, of rest in your funeral couch, of awaking in the likeness of God, and of being satisfied forever in his presence; and it tells you also to whom these blessings belong, even to such, and only such, as walk in uprightness,—love God, trust in Christ as their Saviour, and serve him in an obedient Christian life. All such are entitled to the blessings indicated in our text. They are pardoned of God, are accepted in Christ, are sealed heirs of heaven; and die when, or how, or where they may, no harm can come to them; death is to them a conquered foe; their Saviour has entered the grave before them, and for them, and all their interests are safe for eternity. In Christ they have a sure foundation of peace as they go down into the dark valley and having his rod and his staff to comfort them, they need fear no evil.

The phrase in our text, he shall enter into peace, is rendered by Bishop Lowth, "he shall go in peace." Thus understood, it denotes the calm and peaceful manner in which the righteous are wont to leave the world. They are not, like the wicked, driven away in their sins; they have hope in their death; their end is peace. Hence it is said in the next clause of the text; "they rest in their beds." The allusion is probably to the grave, which is often represented in the Scriptures as a place of rest. Thus in Job it is said, "There the wicked cease from troubling, and there the weary are at rest." This sentiment is beautifully expressed in the following lines from Watts:

Nor pain, nor grief, nor anxious fear
  Invade thy bounds; no mortal woes,
Can reach the peaceful sleeper here,
  While angels watch the soft repose.

Not that the soul sleeps in the grave, or remains in an unconscious, torpid state, as some have supposed, during the period that intervenes between the death of the body and the general resurrection. The whole current of Scripture is against this gloomy sentiment. We are uniformly taught that to be absent from the body is equivalent to being present with the Lord, and that the souls of the righteous do immediately on leaving their houses of clay, enter into a state of conscious activity and enjoyment. "It is true, a delightful truth, that the bodies of the saved, which at death their souls leave, in order to be with Jesus, do rest in their graves." There, as in peaceful beds, they repose, till awaked by the call of him who summoned Lazarus from his tomb, who shall then make them like his own glorious body, fit tenements of glorified spirits. But the leading idea intended to be conveyed by that part of the text we are now considering is, that the righteous, when they die, go in peace. The fear of death is removed. They are sustained by the hope full of immortality. They are at peace with themselves, at peace with their fellow men, at peace with God; and thus they are prepared to leave the world in peace, and enter into everlasting rest. The grave is to them a place of calm and peaceful repose. No persecution comes there; no trials await them there;

no sin, no sorrow, no evil of any kind. They sleep in Jesus, and are blessed; and in the morning of the resurrection shall come forth to inherit immortal joys in heaven. In this manner, Abraham, Moses, David and the prophets, died. In this manner, Paul and Stephen, and multitudes of the primitive saints died. In this manner great numbers of our own Christian friends have died. And in this manner, thousands of believers in Christ are every hour bursting away from their earthly tabernacles, bidding adieu to earth and time, in peaceful hope of eternal rest in Jesus. We pass to consider,

II. The state of blessedness into which the righteous enter on leaving the body. I shall be satisfied, says the Psalmist, when I awake with thy likeness. This blessed hope is common to all true believers, and they go to realize its fullness immediately on passing into the spiritual world. For though it be admitted, that, in some sense, there is an intermediate state between death and the resurrection, and that *then* a change will take place in the condition of the saved, by which they will be raised still higher in glory and blessedness, that does not prevent their being happy, consciously active and happy, and perfect in the likeness of God their Saviour, the moment they die and leave their bodies. This is plainly the doctrine of the Scriptures. David had no expectation of a long, unconscious sleep in the grave, when he said, I shall behold thy face in righteousness; I shall be satisfied when I awake with thy likeness. Paul, when in a strait betwixt two, wishing to depart, and yet willing to stay, fully believed that if he should die, he would immediately be with Christ. And the penitent malefactor, according to the promise of the Saviour, went, on the very day of his death, to be with him in Paradise. All true believers, then, do at once, on leaving the body, awake in the likeness of God, and are satisfied.

They go to be with Christ where he is; and seeing him as he is, they will be like him. This transformation, this change into the divine likeness will at first be perfect in *kind*, but not in *degree.* All the glorious lineaments of the Saviour's character will be drawn on theirs; and thus arrayed in his likeness, the redeemed will shine forth in all the beauties of holiness. Still there will be progress. As ages roll away, they will continually increase in knowledge, in holiness and in happiness; and so be eternally rising into a nearer, and still nearer resemblance to their divine Lord and Head, and yet be eternally at an infinite remove from his perfection and glory. Then they will be satisfied.

1. In the first place, they will be satisfied with themselves. Here they never were. They carried about with them a body of sin and death. Their temptations, their conflicts, their trials were many; and they groaned, being burdened. But at death they part with imperfection, sin and sorrow forever. They awake in the likeness of their Saviour and are satisfied. Nothing remains in them, or pertains to them to awaken regret, or interrupt enjoyment, or darken hope. Of all that blessed assembly, there is no eye that weeps, no breast that sighs, no tongue that complains, and no heart that does not bear the image, reflect the glory, and rejoice in the presence of God the Saviour. Healed of every disease, freed from every corruption, and breathing the pure air of the celestial regions, every one, on awaking in the divine likeness, will be clothed with immortal youth and vigor, and every grace and every faculty will be ripened into maturity, and brought into a never-ending course of delightful exercise and improvement.

2. Awaking in the likeness of God, the redeemed will be satisfied with the place of their residence. That will be heaven; the world of unclouded light and everlasting blessedness; where all things are as great, as here they

are little; where all things are as substantial, as here they are vain; where all things are as fixed, as here they are transitory. The saved of the Lord, on leaving the body, enter that world as their proper home; it is adorned with infinite magnificence and beauty, a fit residence for angels and glorified spirits in the presence of God and the Lamb. And O, what a change! to be taken from an earthly cottage to the palace of the great King; from the sins and sorrows of earth, to the holiness and joys of heaven; from a frail, diseased, dying body, to the everlasting strength and undecaying vigor of the Paradise of God.

3. They will be satisfied with their society. It will be a society of perfectly holy and benevolent beings; composed of the general assembly and church of the first born in heaven; of the spirits of the just made perfect; of an innumerable company of angels; of Jesus, the Mediator of the new covenant; and of God, the Judge of all. To this society the redeemed are admitted immediately on leaving the world; and they commence an acquaintance with patriarchs and prophets, with apostles and martyrs, and with the most amiable and worthy characters that have ever lived; among them their own dear Christian friends, who have entered before them into glory, and are waiting to welcome them to their everlasting home. Dear friends and relatives, parted here on the shores of time, meet again in heaven, to review together the dealings of God with them in this state of trial, to dwell together in his presence, never more to be separated.

4. They will be satisfied with their employments. These will be of the most pure and exalted kind, perfectly adapted to their immortal natures, and fitted to promote, in the highest degree, their improvement and happiness. Worship and praise will be a part, but not all their occupation. Entering heaven with all their faculties ennobled, and

their hearts glowing with holy love, the redeemed will, doubtless, occupy spheres of extended activity and usefulness, and forever be employed in ways, which will exercise every power, and call forth every benevolent affection in the most perfect manner; all adapted to a state of complete and everlasting blessedness.

5. They will be satisfied with their prospects. These will be equal to their desires; and will eternally be growing brighter and brighter. Here their happiest seasons are usually of short duration, and are always liable to interruption from the anxieties, the cares, the vicissitudes and vanities of this sinful world. But nothing can ever cloud the prospects, or interrupt the joys of the redeemed in glory. Death and sorrow, disease and pain, crying and tears will have fled forever; and they will be able to look forward to interminable ages, and anticipate, not only the continuance, but constant increase of knowledge, holiness and happiness, as long as duration shall last. Their bodies, their minds, their residence, their employments, their society and their fruitions, will form a system of glory and of good, which will know no interruption and no end; which will be refining, brightening and increasing forever. "In thy presence is fullness of joy; and at thy right hand are pleasures forever more."

6. They will be satisfied with all the means which God saw fit to employ to prepare them for, and to bring them to heaven. These often appeared to them, while in this vale of tears, deeply mysterious and painful. But all will be cleared up in the light of eternity; and it will there be seen that the afflictions, disappointments and trials of this life, were all appointed by infinite wisdom and goodness, and were a necessary discipline to wean us from the world and prepare us for heaven. If we, through grace, shall finally be admitted into that world, we shall see, that not

one trial, not one disappointment or affliction was laid upon us here, which was not needful and designed to promote our highest good. What we know not now, we shall know then. We shall remember all the way in which the Lord our God led us in this dark and trying world; and every review of the past will only serve to increase our gratitude and elevate our praises for the goodness and mercy with which our covenant God followed us all the days of our pilgrimage on earth. I add,

7. The redeemed, on awaking in the likeness of God, will be satisfied with every part of the divine counsels and government. This is a world of mysteries. We are a mystery to ourselves; and every thing around us is mysterious. We cannot fathom the purposes of God, nor comprehend the reasons of his conduct; and often his goings are shrouded in darkness, and seem to us planted in the great deep. We see enough indeed in God to inspire confidence and sustain hope; still we see through a glass darkly, and our weak faith is often greatly tried and ready to fail us. It will not be so in heaven. All who enter that happy world will see as they are seen, and know as they are known. The mysteries of providence will then be unfolded. The great plan of Jehovah respecting man will be completed; his redeemed people will all be gathered home to glory; and the reasons of his conduct towards our race will be explained and published to the universe; and in view of all, the ransomed of the Lord will be satisfied. There will be no blemish, no defect in any part of the divine administration. All will appear just as it should be, infinitely wise, benevolent and glorious; and they will thus be prepared to rejoice and be eternally happy in the kingdom and under the government of God.

These, my friends, are great truths. We owe them entirely to the blessed word of our God; and they should awaken in us constant gratitude and praise to him, who inspires us with such hopes in the house of our pilgrimage. What are we, and what our deservings, that we should thus engage the benevolent regards of God our Saviour. Miserable sinners; unworthy of the least blessing that is poured into our cup. And yet we are told of entering into peace; of resting in our beds; of awaking in the likeness of God, and of being satisfied forever with the joys of his presence. God will call and we shall answer him, rise in his image, be made like unto our Head, be where he is, blessed eternally with the visions of his glory. Let us dwell upon the prospect and rejoice in the hope. It will cheer us amid the dark passages of life, make the trials of it light, and fit us for a brighter crown in that kingdom to which we are going.

And how firm a ground for peace and hope have we here, in the prospect of death? What indeed is death to a Christian? The gateway of eternal glory. That passed, he enters into the joy of his Lord, and commences an endless course of improvement, in all that can add dignity and blessedness to an immortal being. A Christian, then, instead of shrinking with fear from the change of death, should look to it with serene and cheerful hope, and when it comes, die, as millions have, in peace and joy, and go to the bosom of his Redeemer and God. The way is not strange, not untried. All the saved, from Abel the first, to the last one that has ascended to glory, have passed that way; and each, as he has mounted upward, in the bright and shining course, has testified to the safety and blessedness of dying in the Lord. This should encourage others who yet linger here on the shores of time, to look upon death with calmness and hope; to welcome its approach as a call from their Redeemer to quit these scenes of mortality, and go to inherit eternal joys in his kingdom.

Dying, to the Christian, is but going home; and who should be unwilling to go home, when that home is heaven, and the society waiting to welcome us there are our own dear friends who have died in the Lord, and the whole glorious company of the redeemed?

Here, too, we find strong consolation in the death of Christian friends. They have gone from us; but they are not lost to themselves, nor to the kingdom of God. They still live; live in all the vigor and activity of their immortal faculties—live in the perfect likeness of Christ, and amid the glories of the heavenly world. And should not this reconcile us to their removal from us by death? Should we sorrow as those that have no hope, now that the great design of all that the Saviour did for them in their redemption, and in calling them by his grace to be his disciples, is consummated in their perfection and everlasting blessedness in heaven? Do we rejoice and give thanks to the God of Providence, when a dear friend of ours, having a dangerous sea to navigate, has made the voyage in safety and attained the desired haven? How much more should we rejoice and give thanks to the God of grace, when our Christian friends have finished the voyage of life; have escaped all the storms and dangers of this boisterous ocean, and are safe in the haven of everlasting rest? We are not indeed forbidden to mourn our loss. Tears were made to be shed; and never is there a fitter occasion for them, than when dear kindred and friends are separated from us by the stroke of death. But we should remember, that if they die as Christians, our loss is their gain, and that while *we* sorrow and weep that we shall see their face no more in the flesh, *they* are rejoicing and singing praise in the kingdom of glory. O, could we look within the veil and see them where Christ is, made like him, dwelling in his presence and beholding his glory, should we wish them to return to us on earth, to conflict again with the temptations and sins, and with the trials and sorrows of this our mortal state? Should we not rather fall down on our knees before God, and thank and praise him for his great grace in fitting for, and taking home to glory those whom we love; and return to these earthly scenes and duties with warmer desires, and more strenuous efforts, that we may be prepared in God's own good time, to go and join our departed friends in heaven, and with them be ever with the Lord?

I trust I feel grateful to God, my friends, that while I open these fountains of consolation to you, I am permitted to drink at them myself in this day of my bereavement and sorrow. God has seen fit to take from me my beloved and only daughter; and I thank him for the precious evidence I have, in her life and in her death, that she has entered into peace, and rests in her Saviour's bosom.

My object in the few brief notices of her, which I may now present, is not to obtrude my sorrows upon your attention, nor to eulogize the virtues of the dear deceased one; but as I have said, to honor the grace of God which made her what she was, and to lead all who hear me, especially her young acquaintances and friends, to prize very highly that religion which she loved, and prepare to go to that heaven where I trust she has gone.

It is a very pleasant remembrance to her parents, that from her earliest years she was a peculiarly affectionate and dutiful child. Her tender mind opened itself in docility and love; and like a fresh flower of spring, shed forth the fragrance of its affections upon all around. To know the desires of her father, or mother, was enough to engage a prompt and cheerful obedience. She was early taught that she was a sinner, and needed the renewing grace of God to fit her for his service and kingdom; and from the time she was eight years of age, she was the subject of more than usually deep religious impressions. She felt that her heart was not right with God; that she needed what every human being, however young, and however amiable, needs, a new heart to be given her by the Holy Spirit.

On entering her tenth year, there was a marked change in her feelings. The scene was one never to be forgotten, either by herself or her parents. It was noticed, that, for some days, her mind was the subject of intense and serious thought. Occasionally the unbidden tear would be seen trembling in the eye, or stealing down the cheek, till one evening, having spent some time in retirement, she was heard singing in a low, sweet voice, when on opening the door of her room, her delightful exclamation was, "O, I am so happy; I have found God; I am so happy; I can pray now." She had knelt, as at other times, with a burdened heart, and under a sense of separation from God, and he had met her and had blessed her. To use her own language; "it seemed like speaking to a dear, kind friend; God seemed near to me; and I felt that he heard me." From that time she gave us every pleasant evidence of being a child of God. Her youthful piety did not, as it often does, pass away like a morning cloud. It was a plant of celestial origin. It was rooted deep in the heart, and it grew and brought forth increasing fruit to God till the end of her life.

From the time she hopefully became a Christian, she had a strong desire to devote herself to Christ in a public profession of religion. But it was thought she was too young. After having patiently waited a year, at the close of a communion season, when she remained at home, she summoned all her powers of argument to reason on the subject with those whom she had ever been accustomed to reverence and obey. She asked, "when our Saviour said, do this in remembrance of me, did he mean to exclude children?" She was told that her father thought her too young to take so important a step. "How old must I be before I obey Christ?" She was answered that twelve was thought to be a proper age to make a profession of religion. "O," she exclaimed, with much emotion, "I shall have to wait a whole year, and I have waited a whole year now." This reasoning of a child seems to me more conclusive now, than it did then, and I should be much more ready to act upon it in admitting young persons to the church.

Soon after she was twelve years of age, her wishes were gratified in being received to the communion. It was with her, a season of great tenderness; and to commemorate the love of her Saviour, at his table, was a privilege which became more and more precious to her as long as she lived. Her Christian course was remarkably uniform and exemplary; and it was pleasant to see how, from time to time, she was growing in grace and in the knowledge of her Lord and Saviour. She felt that her profession of the name of Christ brought with it very tender and solemn obligations, which required of her a peculiar character and deportment; and feeling that she was not her own, but bought with a price, she conscientiously endeavored so to live as to honor the sacred name by which she was called.

Her religion, not a name, or a form, but a living, inward principle of holy love, partook largely of the cheerful and the pleasant. She looked to it as a source of peace and joy and hope. It shed a heavenly light on her mind, sweetened her temper, sanctified her affections, enlarged her views, elevated her aims, and taught her to associate all her purest and best enjoyments, with the love of her Father in heaven, and the delightful anticipation of higher and nobler enjoyments hereafter. She possessed naturally a good mind,—well cultivated, well balanced, active and intelligent; susceptible, in a very high degree, of just impressions from whatever objects engaged her attention; and was characterized also, by a confiding, artless simplicity and affectionateness of character which I have rarely seen surpassed. This was the secret of her influence over the young, in whom she felt so lively an interest, and of the facility with which she won upon the confidence and love of all with whom she associated. She had many friends, but no enemies; and it has been truly said of her, in a letter of sympathy received from an eminent person, who saw her for a little time just before she left this country, "She found a short way to the hearts of every one that knew her."

She had an exquisite relish for the beauties of nature and art; and the interest she felt in these beauties was inexpressibly heightened by the fact, that she looked at them with the eye of a Christian; connected them with the wisdom and goodness of God, and regarded them as pledges of brighter glories to be enjoyed in the heavenly world. Hence, when the shores of Europe and Africa first burst upon her view, she beheld them with the deepest emotion, and wrote in her journal,—"I have been praying that I may look upon all these interesting scenes with the feelings of a Christian; and may all that I see, prepare me for my work in that dear land which comes nearer every hour." And when in 1841, she lay, as was supposed, at the point of death, she said,—"This is a beautiful world, and I love it; all its hills and pleasant prospects, all of it is very beautiful to me. And then, I have many precious friends; O, how precious! and how I love them! And when I think of leaving them, and having no more to do with the scenes here on the earth, never, no, never, till the resurrection morning, then I am sad at the prospect of bidding adieu to them. But when I look on the other side, and think of heaven and of Jesus, and that my Saviour has something for me to do there, then it seems pleasant to me, and I want to go."

I may here remark, in passing, that out of her own family, no human being exerted a greater or more happy influence in the formation of her character than Mary Jane Chester, afterwards Mrs. Hovey. Herself a model of female loveliness, intelligent, affectionate, refined and winning in her manners; a Christian of warm hearted, cheerful piety, disinterested in her aims, and devoted in her duties in an eminent degree, this amiable and excellent young Christian early took a deep interest in my dear Mary; she was for several years her Sabbath school teacher; and I feel grateful to God, that my child, in her tender age, enjoyed the instruction, the prayers and the example of one, who was so well qualified to cherish her piety and to elicit and mature her virtues. From her she received many most valuable suggestions in regard to the daily reading of the Scriptures, the practice of private devotion, self-discipline and the cultivation of personal religion. They were tenderly united in affection here; death separated them for a season; they have met now in the kingdom of light and love, and they will part no more.

The deceased had great tenderness of conscience; a quick perception and a deep feeling of right and duty. While she had a most affectionate regard for the feelings and wishes of others, and instinctively shrunk from giving pain to any human being, she would never yield a hair in sacrifice of duty, or where she thought she might incur the suspicion of wrong. Her religion was a matter of principle; and it led her to study not how far she might go in conforming to the world, without incurring positive guilt; but how she might shun even the appearance of evil, best cultivate her Christian character, and best glorify her

Saviour. If in certain amusements, practiced even in some professedly Christian families, she could not conscientiously unite, it was not because she deemed them positively sinful, but because she thought them of doubtful tendency, leading on to evil, and felt that they might injure her Christian influence. She was right in this; and though some may have thought her too scrupulous on such points, I feel sure it is no matter of regret with her now, that she was so conscientious and exact in her Christian walk while here below

She loved her Bible, and she loved prayer; and it was by an assiduous attention to the Scriptures and the duties of daily devotion, that she cultivated that spirit of cheerful, lively and fruitful piety, which so diffused itself through her whole character and life. She had set times to pray for her friends and for different objects. This habit was early formed, and it was continued, as appears from her journal, till prevented by her last sickness.

In a note to a young friend in this city, dated the 26th of August, the very last perhaps she ever wrote, she says, "O, it is a sweet comfort to pray for our absent friends. In the quiet hours, when the moon looks down upon these silent waters, my thoughts invariably wander to the far away friends, and the yearnings of my spirit to see them, can only be satisfied by lifting up my prayer to Him who can bless them with his own sweet presence." Her affection for her friends was indeed deep and pure, peculiarly disinterested and abiding.

Humble, unsuspecting and guileless in her disposition, she never indulged herself in unkind, ill-natured remarks about others. The law of kindness was on her lips, and she never thought, or suspected evil of others, where she could think of good. She knew the value of time; and she practiced the strictest economy in the use of it. Instant in season and out of season, will apply to her as fully as to any young person I ever knew. Her needle, her book, her pen, or going on some errand of kindness and mercy, filled up all her hours, and thus she was enabled to live much in a short time.

She early engaged in the duties of a Sabbath school teacher; and seldom, it is believed, have those duties been performed in a more exemplary and faithful manner.

She went to them, not as a task, but as a pleasure; and carefully prepared herself for the exercise by prayer, and a diligent study of the lesson. Great was the interest she felt in her pupils, visiting them at their homes, having them visit her, lending them books and writing to them, from time to time, to excite and direct their thoughts on the subject of religion; and many a young person in this house, and many who are not present to hear me, can recollect the tender interest she manifested in their spiritual welfare. May they never forget her instructions and her prayers; and may the impressions made on their minds be ripened into true piety and a bright hope of heaven.

She early felt an interest in the cause of missions; and by a train of providences which I may not detail, it was made plain to her own mind, as it was to her parents, that it was her duty to devote herself personally to this cause. But scarcely had she entered upon the field, which, in connection with her beloved husband, she hoped to occupy in a life of usefulness, ere she was called to fill, I trust, a higher sphere of service in the heavenly state. Though her residence on missionary ground was exceedingly brief, she appears from many testimonies that have come to us from our distant friends, to have made an impression upon all who became acquainted with her, that her heart was wholly in her work, and that she was qualified, had her life been spared, to do much good.* That she was satisfied and happy in the employment she had chosen, is evident from every part of her journals. She appears never to have had any misgivings or regrets on this point. In a letter to a friend in this city, dated on that 26th of August, when, as I suppose, all her correspondence closed,† she says: "It is an unspeakable privilege to be a missionary, and to labor in this land. Much as I long to see your faces, and dear as my home is to me, I would not return to America.

But I hasten to the closing scene. It was expected when she left this country with her husband, that they would be permanently stationed at Smyrna. But many circumstances seemed to require their removal to Constantinople; and I cheerfully concurred in the arrangement, as likely to prove more favorable to her health, and also to open a wider and more promising field of usefulness. I parted with her in May. She was then in excellent health, and continued thus after her removal to Constantinople, till about the middle of August. She then became ill; but her disease was in so mild a form, that for several weeks no apprehension was felt by her friends as to the issue. With herself, however, it was otherwise. "From the very first," as Rev. Mr. Goodell writes, "her own mind was strongly and strangely impressed with the idea of a fatal termination; and was intently occupied with the thoughts of anotherand a better life." "She settled all her doubts one by one, as her husband writes; and on the Sabbath before her relapse, she expressed a sweet and perfect confidence in her Saviour, and entrusted all things to him."

* I love to think of the ardor of zeal and oneness of purpose with which your daughter seemed to be prepared to labor for the Armenians. *She had her heart wholly set on the great work for which she came to these lands.*—Rev. Mr. Dwight, Constantinople.

† Letters of a later date had not reached home when this sermon was written.

Mr. Goodell adds,—"that during the weeks of her indisposition, she scrutinized her heart and life with the greatest possible care and fidelity, we are fully assured. The result was this—that the early dedication of herself to God was not the *ground* of her pardon and acceptance; that her repentance and prayers, and communion seasons, and religious education and religious observances, and active services, were not her Saviour. And may I trust in the bare word of Christ for salvation? said she, in great simplicity of manner. I replied you may. Paul trusted to it, and went to heaven. John trusted to it and to nothing else. And had your life been even more holy than theirs, you would still have found, on examination, that your own righteousness was but filthy rags, that you needed an infinite Saviour, and that you had nothing to hang upon but the bare word of Christ. But this bare word of his is every thing, and whoever hangs upon it shall never be confounded. Blessed salvation this for poor perishing sinners. And this, I have no doubt, was all her salvation, and all her desire. On this rock of ages she appeared to plant both her feet, fearless and secure amidst the raging billows."

Her last message to her parents was a very sweet one. It was two days before her decease. In reply to her husband, who was writing by her side, and asked whether she had any message to send, she said:—"Give my best love, my *very* best love. Tell them I have a great many things to say to them but I cannot now,—*tell them it will be very, very sweet when all the redeemed meet together in heaven.*" Dear child, it *will* be sweet, and there we will hope to meet thee.

On the Sabbath before her death, which took place on Friday, her disease assumed a very alarming aspect, after which her mind occasionally wandered. But on the morning of the day on which she died, her mind became clear and calm, and though unable to converse, so great was her weakness, she yet "whispered words of strong hope and joyful expectation." "Oh, how happy, how sweet it will be to be there." When her husband repeated the first stanza of the hymn, "Jesus, lover of my soul," there was a strong bright smile, and she whispered "yes, yes." Her hearing, her sight, and her strength soon failed her, and she fell asleep, I doubt not in Jesus, and entered into peace. Her grave is in the burying ground of the people to whose spiritual welfare her life was devoted. There, on an eminence overlooking the shores of the Bosphorus, and the city of the moslems, rest her mortal remains till the bright morning of the resurrection dawns, and brings the final, the eternal day of glory and blessedness.

Farewell! dear child, farewell!! Very pleasant wert thou in life, but far pleasanter wilt thou be when we shall meet above. Our separation will be short. Thou wilt not return to me, but I shall go to thee. Thy work is done; thy conflicts over; and what of loveliness was in thee here below is now perfected in heaven. It is well. Let no one ask, why was this waste? The Master had need of her.

"He gave her, he took her, and he will restore her."

His will is done; and the heart that most loved her would not wish it otherwise. Yes, it is well. In our Father's house there are many mansions. And thou, loved child, whose visage, when last we saw thee here, was arrayed in the bloom of health and the smiles of joy, hast put off thine earthly clothing and left these scenes of mortality forever. Thou hast had thy mansion already on two widely remote continents of this world, and now in the new mansion thy Saviour has prepared for thee in heaven, we, in our bereaved affections and fond hopes, place thee, a happy, purified spirit, uniting in the exalted communion and praises of that upper world. Farewell! farewell! for a little time; then may we who now mourn thee, and all thy loved companions and friends, rise to join thee in the mansions of eternal purity and bliss, whither thou hast gone.

"I was one of the many who listened with deep and sympathetic interest to the late discourse of the Rev. Dr. Hawes, upon the death of his daughter. As he presented the picture of her pure and lovely character, the words of Christ were continually present to my heart, 'of such is the kingdom of heaven;' and for many days after, that sermon lingered in my thoughts, and would not leave me, until the following lines had fashioned themselves out of my meditations."—*Religious Herald*, *Dec.* 18*th*, 1844.

A VOICE FROM HEAVEN.

I shine in the light of God,
  His "likeness" stamps my brow,
Through the shadows of death my feet have trod,
  And I reign in glory now;
No breaking heart is here,
  No keen and thrilling pain,
No wasted cheek, where the frequent tear
  Hath rolled and left its stain.

I have found the joy of heaven,
  I am one of the angel-band,
To my head a crown is given,
  And a harp is in my hand:
I have learned the song they sing,
  Whom Jesus hath made free,
And the glorious walls of heaven still ring
  With my new-born melody.

No sin—no grief—no pain,
  Safe in my happy home;
My fears all fled, my doubts all slain,
  My hour of triumph come;
Oh! friends of my mortal years,
  The trusted and the true,
Ye 're walking still in the valley of tears,
  But I wait to welcome you.

Do I forget? Oh! no;
  For Memory's golden chain
Shall bind my heart to the hearts below,
  Till they meet and touch again:
Each link is strong and bright,
  And love's electric flame
Flows freely down, like a river of light,
  To the world from whence I came.

Do you mourn when another star
  Shines out from the glittering sky?
Do you weep when the noise of war,
  And the rage of conflict die?
Then why should your tears roll down,
  And your hearts be sorely riven,
For another gem in the Saviour's crown.
  And another soul in heaven!

L. M. N.

NOTICES

OF THE

MEMOIR OF MRS. MARY E. VAN LENNEP.

THE PUBLISHERS invite the attention of the public to the following notices from distinguished individuals, showing how they appreciate "The Memoirs of Mrs. Van Lennep"—the deep interest which they take in the work, and the estimate which they have formed of its powerful influence for good upon those who may read it. Other testimonials might have been added, but it is enough to say, that in addition to the numerous commendatory notices of the book which have appeared in many of our very respectable public prints and periodicals, the voice of the intelligent and religious community has pronounced it to be one of the best written, most attractive, and useful biographies of modern times; breathing forth a simple, pure and elevated spirit of piety; engaging the admiration and love of Christians of all denominations, and singularly adapted to cherish the same spirit in their own breasts.

From the REV. STEPHEN OLIN, D. D., LL. D., *President of the Wesleyan University, Middletown.*

"Messrs. BELKNAP & HAMERSLEY:

* * * * * * * * * * * This work portrays a character of uncommon excellence and loveliness, in a simple, unexaggerated style, which recommends it to the confidence and good taste of the reader. I greatly overrate the merit of this interesting volume, if it is not destined to operate for good in an extensive sphere. Such examples of early, active, self-sacrificing piety, in graceful combination with the rarest filial, fraternal, and social virtues, should be read and studied in all our Christian families. In the Memoir of Mrs. Van Lennep, we have a Christian character of great strength and intensity, blending the best qualities of an ingenuous, cultivated woman, with those of a devoted disciple of Christ—an enthusiastic lover of nature, of books, of music and

society—an ardent, almost romantic friend—the most affectionate of sisters and of daughters.—Mrs. V. L., through the strength of her Christian principles, and the ardor of her benevolence, became a foreign missionary; and that, in the face of bright worldly prospects, and at an age when most Christian women claim an exemption from all the higher duties of their profession. It is well said by the compiler, that the character here exhibited is the more instructive, because not too high for imitation. It may with justice be added, that few are more worthy of being imitated."

Extract of a Letter to the Rev. H. J. Van Lennep, *from the* Rev. T. H. Gallaudet.

"My heart is so full of the pleasure, and I trust profit, which I have lately received from reading the beautiful Memoir of your dear departed Mary, that I cannot refrain from telling you of it. The book charmed me more than any other work of the kind which I have read for a long, long time.

It surprised me to find in so young a person, whom I thought I knew more of than I now find I did, such symmetry of Christian character, such meekness of wisdom, such elevation of piety, so exquisite a relish for the beautiful and sublime both in nature and in grace, so much practical good sense, such an overflowing of kindly and benevolent feelings, such unostentatious self sacrifice, and then such graphical accuracy and finished taste in description, with a chasteness, simplicity and maturity of style, which we very seldom meet with only in older and experienced writers.

The work I think is destined to do a vast amount of good, both among professors of religion, and those who yet seek the friendship of the world.

May the spirit of truth and grace ever accompany its perusal, and make it the means of adding many new jewels to the Redeemer's crown."

From the Rev. E. N. Kirk, *Boston.*

* * * * * "I am thankful that Mrs. Hawes has drawn up a Memoir, and *such* a Memoir of her daughter. A mother's pride might have been more gratified by a fuller exhibition of her intellectual qualities. But she has chosen well, to show her, as she remarks, in her imitable excellencies. A large circle of young ladies in our congregation are now reading this Memoir with great interest, and as it seems to me, with great benefit. Some appear to be led by it to take higher views of the objects for which life is given, and to see how lovely and how attainable is Christian benevolence."

From the Rev. A. W. McClure, *Editor of the Christian Observatory.*

* * * * "This is one of the few biographies which make the reader feel as if he had a sort of personal knowledge of the

one to whom it relates. It is good to be brought into converse with spirits on whose excellencies death has set his inviolable seal, and made them sacred. This is a good book for all such as are capable of receiving benefit from coming into contact with a mind, in which fine tastes and warm affections were raised to the highest purity and fervor by the hallowed power of grace."

From the Rev. W. B. Sprague, D. D., *Albany.*

"I have read the Memoir of Mrs. V. L., with unmingled pleasure. The character is a remarkable compound of natural loveliness, of intellectual refinement, and of earnest piety. It is certainly sketched with no common skill; and while a mother's love breathes in every page of the book, there is nothing of that weak partiality exhibited, that leads to exaggeration, and awakens distrust. The work is valuable as a record of the workings of a young, accomplished mind, in its preparation for usefulness and for heaven. It is valuable, as presenting to young females an example of excellence that is felt to be attainable—of a character at once free from affectation and eccentricity, and adorned with the more humble and the more active virtues. It is valuable especially as an honorable and fitting tribute to the cause of missions, for which the beloved and lamented counted not her life dear to her. It is a book that cannot be destined to any ephemeral existence. Posterity will place it on the same shelf with Harriet Newell."

From the Rev. H. Humphrey, D. D., *late President of Amherst College.*

"Memoir of Mrs. Mary E. Van Lennep, by her mother. One of the sweetest memorials of youthful piety, and early self consecration to Christ, and the spread of his gospel, that I ever read. I am sure that all who love pure and undefiled religion in its most attractive form, in the artless, and gushing outpourings of a soul, alive to all the beauties of nature, and ravished with the brighter glories beaming down from the 'throne of God and the Lamb,' will feel themselves indebted in no common degree to Mrs. Hawes for the selections which she has given them in this volume from the private journal and correspondence of an only daughter. There is a charm about it which is sure to captivate every young reader who takes up the book, and increasingly to absorb the attention till it is finished. The bereaved mother has with excellent judgment arranged and put the rich materials which her missionary daughter left at her early death, and the Memoir is worthy of a place upon every centre-table in our land."

From Mrs. L. H. Sigourney, *Hartford.*

"In this interesting biography, a monument is reared to the memory of a sainted being, whom to know was to love. To those, in her native place, who were permitted to trace her progress from early infancy, it is gratifying to perceive, that the pen of a mother has been so guided in this delicate delineation, as to swerve neither through tenderness or reserve; and to feel that though all which has been written, is true, yet more might have been added with equal truth, to illustrate her native intellect, refined taste, and earnest piety.

Through this volume she will continue to send forth a voice of melody, to the distant and the unborn. May the good it shall accomplish, aid in consoling the mourners over her early grave, who in their grief might perchance have asked, "why was this waste of the precious ointment,"—had they not seen whose Hand brake the beautiful casket, and believed that with Him, the undying essence was safe forever.

From GEO. W. BETHUNE, D. D., *Philadelphia.*

"This work gives a most admirable picture of intelligent piety and high Christian courage, united to a natural grace and unaffected simplicity. It is not difficult to see in the portions of the book supplied by Mrs. Hawes, whence (under God) this delightful young Christian derived some of her most attractive charms. Happy mother of a glorified child! Thrice happy as the mother of her being, then of her character, and now of her memory."

From the New York Evangelist.

"Memoir of Mrs. Mary E. Van Lennep. One, as I think, of the most interesting Christian biographies that have ever issued from our American press.

It is, in fact, a *bijou*—a gem of the purest qualities. The subject was a lovely young lady—a daughter (the only one that was spared to him) of the Rev. Dr. Hawes, of Hartford. In that very pleasant city she grew up amid its choicest society, receiving all the culture that the best female schools of the place could afford, in addition to the culture of a home of more than common advantages.

The work is admirably arranged. After a brief narrative of a few pages, giving a very interesting account of the early life and conversion of the subject, the reader is made to learn her life, character, and Christian activity, (up to her death in a far distant land) almost wholly from the letters, journals, memoranda, etc., which she wrote.

I have said that this book is a *gem*. It is really such. What elevated and heavenly piety; what an amiable and lovely spirit, breathes through all its pages! What admirable taste and refined sentiment pervades all that she writes! This is a book which ought to be put in the hands of all our dear youth. How it shows to young ladies the true way to find happiness; and proves to a perfect demonstration that the most devoted piety is consistent with the most elevated refinement. It is emphatically a book which ought to be placed in all our female seminaries, and young ladies' boarding schools; for its cheerful and intellectual views of religion are admirably adapted to win the hearts of the inmates of such institutions, for God and his service.

It is just a year since I walked out one very pleasant morning, with the Rev. Mr. Homes, at Pera, near Constantinople, to the Protestant burial ground, which the Turkish government has allowed to be opened, near that of the Armenians. It lies just over the summit of the hill, or ridge of hills rather, up the sloping sides of which, the city of Pera is built. From that spot there is a fine view over the deep ravines and green fields to the north, whilst the village-bordered and beautiful Bosphorus lies, at no great distance to the east. *There* the remains of this lovely Christian rest, in hope of the resurrection of the just. B."

From the New England Puritan.

MRS. MARY E. VAN LENNEP.

On reading her Memoir by her Mother.

BY WILLIAM B. TAPPAN.

I knew her not; a fountain here
Reflects her beauty to my sight;
Its fair proportions mirrored clear,
And beaming with effulgent light.

I see a soul mature and true;
Of taste refined and noble parts,
And earnest love that simply knew
A short sweet way to kindred hearts.

The lineaments are all divine;
The glorious form and starry eyes,
Are such as meet and softly shine
In holy ones that walk the skies.

She loved mankind of every creed:
"Her neighbour" dwelt in every zone;
And life she loved—might she indeed
Bless him with mercies like her own!

"They serve who wait,"—and thus did she,
Whose work, where flames the Eastern sun,
Was planned, commenced, and wrought, while we
Beheld it only as begun.

From dawn to twilight's fading ray
  Some linger on the Master's ground,
Three score and ten their weary day,—
  And such, at last, are "faithful" found.

Oh! not by hours, or full or few,
  Our gracious Lord the toil computes,—
Some, ere exhales the morning dew,
  At morn retire with sheaves and fruits.

And she whose worth is here impearled
  Where skill, maternal, sets the gem—
By labour, brief, has blest the world,
  And early won her diadem.

From the New York Presbyterian.

This is one of the finest, most interesting and valuable works of a most important and excellent class. We have never seen a volume more exactly corresponding with our ideas of what a work of American, Christian female biography should be.

We have never risen from the perusal of any of its pages, without a new admiration of the purity and exaltation of that piety which breathes in every part, and sincere congratulation at the reflection, that the union of Christian principles and enjoyments with the various circumstances, duties and occupations of common American life, is so plainly, justly, affectingly, and therefore, usefully exhibited. Refinement of mind, cultivation of intellect and manners, and habitual devotion to the good of others, are here shown in a thousand interesting but ordinary scenes of daily life, to be the natural and blessed effects of Christian character; and thousands of readers, we trust, especially among the young females of the present day, will have the sense, as well as the principle, to make this invaulable volume occupy the place on their tables and in their hearts, too often and most foolishly, lamentably and criminally occupied by the tale of fiction and romance. We recommend this work most earnestly and unhesitatingly to every parent.

www.ingramcontent.com/pod-product-compliance
Lightning Source LLC
LaVergne TN
LVHW020123110826
845151LV00001B/256

9781425541507